rethinking
reading
comprehension

Solving Problems in the Teaching of Literacy
Cathy Collins Block, *Series Editor*

rethinking
reading
comprehension

edited by
ANNE POLSELLI SWEET
CATHERINE E. SNOW

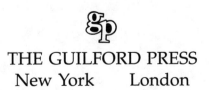

THE GUILFORD PRESS
New York   London

© 2003 The Guilford Press
A Division of Guilford Publications, Inc.
72 Spring Street, New York, NY 10012
www.guilford.com

Printed in the United States of America

This book is printed on acid-free paper.

Last digit is print number: 9 8 7 6 5 4 3 2 1

Library of Congress Cataloging-in-Publication Data
    Rethinking reading comprehension / edited by Anne Polselli Sweet
and Catherine E. Snow.
      p. cm. — (Solving problems in the teaching of literacy)
    Includes bibliographical references and index.
    ISBN 1-57230-892-3 (pbk.) — ISBN 1-57230-893-1 (cloth)
    1. Reading comprehension. I. Sweet, Anne P. II. Snow, Catherine
E. III. Series.
    LB1050.45 .R46 2003
    372.47—dc21
                                        2002155226

No official support or endorsement by the U.S. Department of Education is intended
or should be inferred.

10/25/04

Dedication and Appreciation

This book is dedicated to practitioners—the classroom teachers and other educators for whom this book was written, and whose ceaseless efforts enable our nation's children to learn and grow into lifelong readers. The chapters in this book were contributed by individual members of the RAND Reading Study Group, in some cases along with their chosen co-authors. The editors wish to thank all the members of the RAND Reading Study Group, whose thinking, expertise, and analysis contributed to this book. We also thank the practitioners and researchers in the literacy community whose commentary was invaluable in developing the original report upon which this book is based (*Reading for Understanding* [2002], the report of the RAND Reading Study Group).

About the Editors

ANNE POLSELLI SWEET, who directed the RAND reading study while Scholar-in-Residence at RAND, is with the U.S. Department of Education's research agency, the Institute for Education Sciences, where she focuses on research in reading and K–12 literacy. She oversees national efforts to conduct research, does intramural research on literacy-related issues, and works on interagency research initiatives with the National Science Foundation and the National Institute of Child Health and Human Development. She served as program director in the U.S. Department of Education's Office of Educational Research and Improvement (OERI) and in the National Institute of Education. Preceding her tenure with the U.S. Department, Dr. Sweet was Associate Superintendent for Instruction in Virginia. She taught reading and language arts, elementary through graduate school, and served in various leadership posts in public schooling. Her research interests include cognitive and motivational aspects of reading. Dr. Sweet has edited books, authored book chapters, and written articles for peer-reviewed research journals, most recently the *Journal of Educational Psychology.*

CATHERINE E. SNOW, who chaired the RAND Reading Study Group, is the Henry Lee Shattuck Professor of Education at the Harvard Graduate School of Education. She has coauthored books on language development (e.g., *Pragmatic Development* with Anat Ninio) and on literacy development (e.g., *Unfulfilled Expectations: Home and School Influences on Literacy* with W. Barnes, J. Chandler, I. Goodman, and L. Hemphill) and has published widely on these topics as well as on research and policy issues in second language learning and literacy. For 17 years Dr. Snow was editor of *Applied Psycholinguistics.* She is a cofounder of the Child Language Data Exchange System, a past president of the American Educational Research Association, and a member of the National Academy of Education. She chaired the National Research Council Committee on Preventing Reading Difficulties in Young Children, which produced a report that has been widely adopted as a basis for reforming reading instruction, and is currently pursuing its implications for teacher education and professional development.

Contributors

DONNA E. ALVERMANN is Distinguished Research Professor of Reading Education at the University of Georgia and a member of the RAND Reading Study Group. Formerly a middle grades teacher, Dr. Alvermann's research focuses on youth's multiple literacies in and out of school. From 1992 to 1997 she codirected the National Reading Research Center, funded by the U.S. Department of Education's Office of Educational Research and Improvement. She is coauthor of *Content Reading and Literacy: Succeeding in Today's Diverse Classrooms* and *Popular Culture in the Classroom: Teaching and Researching Critical Media Literacy*, and editor of *Adolescents and Literacies in a Digital World*. Previously she was president of the National Reading Conference (NRC), cochair of the International Reading Association's Commission on Adolescent Literacy, and associate editor of the *Journal of Literacy Research*. Currently, Dr. Alvermann edits *Reading Research Quarterly*. She was elected to the Reading Hall of Fame in 1999, and is the recipient of NRC's Oscar S. Causey Award for Outstanding Contributions to Reading Research.

JANICE A. DOLE is a member of the RAND Reading Study Group. She is currently Associate Professor of Reading Education at the University of Utah. After completing her MA and PhD at the University of Colorado, she held positions at the University of Denver, the Center for the Study of Reading at the University of Illinois at Urbana–Champaign, and Michigan State University. Dr. Dole's research interests include comprehension instruction, conceptual change learning, and, most recently, professional development in reading in K–3 schools. She has published in journals such as the *Review of Educational Research*, *Reading Research Quarterly*, *Journal of Reading* and *The Elementary School Journal*. Her contributions to the field include her participation in several editorial boards of research journals, her work for the National Assessment for Educational Progress, her participation in the Reading Excellence Act and Reading First grants with the U.S. Department of Education, and her reviews of research proposals for the National Institute of Health.

A. JONATHAN EAKLE is a doctoral student in reading education at the University of Georgia. In the 1980s he studied and practiced the visual arts, earning degrees in painting and drawing, and working in photography. In the 1990s he received a graduate degree in middle school education and conducted research in second language and middle school classrooms. Recently, Mr. Eakle has worked on research supported by the Center for the Improvement of Early Reading Achievement. Currently, he is the editorial assistant for *Reading Research Quarterly*; is a research assistant for *Case Technologies to Enhance Literacy Learning*, a 5.6 million dollar educational grant that is funded by the National Science Foundation; and teaches undergraduate preservice teachers at the University of Georgia. In addition, Mr. Eakle is the president of the International Association of Reading Graduate Students. His research interests include multimodal approaches to literacy learning and linguistically and culturally diverse students.

GEORGIA EARNEST GARCÍA, is a member of the RAND Reading Study Group, and is a Full Professor in the Department of Curriculum and Instruction at the University of Illinois at Urbana–Champaign. She teaches courses in reading, bilingual education/ESL instruction, sociolinguistics, and multicultural education. Her research focuses on the literacy development, instruction, and assessment of students from diverse backgrounds, with a major emphasis on bilingual reading. Dr. García has published in the *American Educational Research Journal, Anthropology and Education Quarterly, Review of Research in Education, Reading Research Quarterly*, and *Journal of Literacy Research*. She was named a College of Education Distinguished Scholar and awarded the Faculty Award for Excellence in Graduate Teaching, Advising, and Research. She previously was a senior research scientist at the Center for the Study of Reading. Dr. García was a member of the Board of Directors, National Reading Conference, and currently is a member of the National Literacy Panel on Language Minority Children.

IRENE W. GASKINS is a school administrator and a member of the RAND Reading Study Group. Her EdD is in educational psychology. In 1970, while teaching at the University of Pennsylvania, she founded Benchmark School, a school for struggling readers in grades 1–8. Dr. Gaskins has worked on such significant problems as designing word-identification instruction that works for students who previously made little progress in this area, improving reading performance by increasing students' awareness and control of cognitive styles and other personal factors that affect reading, and designing programs that teach strategies for understanding and learning from texts. From 1988 to 1994 the strategies research at Benchmark was funded by the James S. McDonnell Foundation. Dr. Gaskins has won numerous awards, including International Reading Association's William S. Gray Citation of Merit. Her work has been published in such journals as *The Reading Teacher, Reading Research Quarterly, Journal of Reading Behavior, Language Arts, Elementary School Journal, Remedial and Special Education*, and *Journal of Learning Disabilities*.

ARTHUR C. GRAESSER, a RAND Reading Study Group member, is a Full Professor in the Departments of Psychology and Mathematical Sciences at the University of Memphis. He is currently codirector of the Institute for Intelligent Systems and director of the Center for Applied Psychological Research. Dr. Graesser received his

PhD in psychology from the University of California, San Diego, in 1977. His primary research interests are in discourse processing and cognitive science. More specific interests include text comprehension, reading, tutoring, knowledge representation, question asking and answering, inference generation, conversation, memory, and computational linguistics. Dr. Graesser's reading research focuses on deeper levels of comprehension, such as inference generation, questioning, summarization, rhetorical organization, and pragmatics. He is editor of the journal *Discourse Processes* and is on the editorial boards of the *Journal of Educational Psychology, Journal of Experimental Psychology: LMC, Journal of the Scientific Studies of Reading, Cognition and Instruction, Applied Cognitive Psychology, Cognitive Science*, and *Poetics*. He recently edited the *Handbook of Discourse Processes*.

JOHN T. GUTHRIE is a member of the RAND Reading Study Group. He is Professor of Human Development at the University of Maryland at College Park. He received his PhD in educational psychology from the University of Illinois in 1968. From 1992 to 1997, Dr. Guthrie was codirector of the National Reading Research Center. With teacher collaborators, he developed an engagement model of classroom context, processes of engagement in reading, and reading outcomes. From the model, he developed Concept-Oriented Reading Instruction (CORI) and has conducted quasi-experiments showing that this intervention increases reading comprehension, reading motivation, and science knowledge. Dr. Guthrie's studies are published in peer-reviewed research journals. He has served on several National Research Council committees and National Institute of Child Health and Human Development panels, and was on the expert panel for the Reading Excellence Act, 1999–2000. He is the recipient of a grant from the Interagency Education Research Initiative to investigate how alternative models of instruction, including CORI, influence reading comprehension, motivation, and science knowledge.

MICHAEL L. KAMIL is a member of the RAND Reading Study Group. He is Professor of Education at Stanford University. He is a member of the Psychological Studies in Education and the Learning, Design, and Technology Program. Dr. Kamil's research explores the effects of a variety of technologies on literacy and the acquisition of literacy in both first and second languages. He is a coeditor of the *Handbook of Reading Research*, Volumes I, II, and III, and has been editor of *Reading Research Quarterly* and the *Journal of Reading Behavior*. He is chair of the Planning Committee for the National Assessment of Educational Progress. Dr. Kamil was a member of the National Reading Panel and is currently a member of the National Literacy Panel for Language Minority Youth and Children. His recent work for *Laboratory for Student Success* and *Pacific Resources for Education and Learning* has extended the syntheses of research begun by the National Reading Panel.

HELEN S. KIM is a doctoral candidate at the Stanford University School of Education. Her current research interests include multimedia learning, literacy, and the design of interactive computer technology to support reading and learning. In addition to her research experience at Stanford and the University of California at Berkeley, she has worked with students and teachers to develop activities that support literacy and multimedia learning. Her work has been published in several edited volumes, in the *NRC Yearbook*, and in the third volume of the *Handbook of Reading Research*.

MAX M. LOUWERSE is currently a Visiting Assistant Professor in the Department of Psychology at the University of Memphis and a member of the Institute for Intelligent Systems. Dr. Louwerse received MA degrees in language and literature from the University of Utrecht in The Netherlands and a PhD in linguistics from the University of Edinburgh in Scotland. His interests cover a wide range of topics in interdisciplinary research, including computational linguistics and psycholinguistics. More specifically, his interests include cohesion and coherence relations in monologue and dialogue comprehension and production. Dr. Louwerse has worked on interclausal relationships, discourse markers, question answering systems, mixed-initiative dialog, themes, narrative structure, and various other aspects of discourse processing. He currently is involved in projects on developing coherence measurements in texts, automated question answering systems, automated speech recognition, and automated dialogue management. He recently edited the interdisciplinary volume *Thematics: Interdisciplinary Studies*.

DANIELLE S. McNAMARA is an Associate Professor in the Psychology Department at the University of Memphis. She obtained a BA in linguistics, MS in clinical psychology, and a PhD in cognitive psychology (University of Colorado, 1992). The major thrust of her research concerns the theoretical study of cognition as well as the application of cognition to educational practice. Her National Science Foundation-funded research is directed at providing training to improve text comprehension. This research has sparked the development of an automated reading strategy tutor called iSTART, which teaches learners to self-explain difficult texts. A second focus of her reading research is on text coherence and how that interacts with reader aptitudes. With recent funding from Institute of Education Sciences, Dr. McNamara and her team are designing an automated metric for text coherence (Coh-Metrix). She also studies a variety of phenomena related to comprehension, working memory, pilot communication, expertise, knowledge acquisition, and generation effects. She is a consulting editor for *Discourse Processes, Memory and Cognition*, and *Journal of Experimental Psychology: LMC*.

ANNEMARIE SULLIVAN PALINCSAR is the Jean and Charles Walgreen Jr. Chair of Literacy and a teacher educator at the University of Michigan in the Educational Studies Department. She is a member of the RAND Reading Study Group. Her research has focused on the design of learning environments that support self-regulation in learning activity, especially for children who experience difficulty learning in school. Specifically, her research includes the design and investigation of reciprocal teaching dialogues to enhance reading comprehension; literacy curricula and instruction to engage special education students in using oral, written, and print literacy to accelerate their literacy learning; and the study of how children use literacy in the context of guided inquiry science instruction. Dr. Palincsar served as a member of the National Research Council Committee Council on the Prevention of

Reading Difficulty in Young Children, the National Education Goals Panel, the Schooling Task Force of the MacArthur Pathways Project, and the National Advisory Board to the Children's Television Workshop. She is coeditor of *Cognition and Instruction*.

CATHERINE E. SNOW, see About the Editors.

ANNE POLSELLI SWEET, see About the Editors.

FRANK R. VELLUTINO is a Professor of Psychology at the State University of New York at Albany. He is a member of the RAND Reading Study Group. He currently holds joint faculty appointments in the Department of Psychology (Cognitive Psychology Program), the Department of Educational and Counseling Psychology, and the Program in Linguistics and Cognitive Science of the Department of Anthropology. He is also director of the Child Research and Study Center, a research and student training center. His research has been concerned with the cognitive underpinnings of reading development as well as with the relationship between reading difficulties and various aspects of language and other cognitive functions. His research has generated numerous articles in peer-reviewed journals, in addition to a book and numerous book chapters addressing the causes and correlates of reading difficulties in young children. Dr. Vellutino's most recent research seeks to develop models of early intervention that effectively reduce the number of children who continue to have long-term reading difficulties.

Preface

Noted educator Sterl Artley issued the following plea: "Every teacher a teacher of reading." This book represents a concretization of that plea. But when we join with Artley in aspiring to the goal that every teacher undertake the task of promoting student literacy skills, we, of course, do not mean that every teacher should be teaching students to read words. Rather, we start with the assumption that doing science, history, math, or literature involves specific ways of reading—ways that need to be taught to many students. Furthermore, learning science, history, math, or literature relies inevitably on comprehension of text, and comprehension is itself typically a product of instruction rather than a spontaneous accomplishment.

We have made enormous progress over the last 25 years in understanding how to teach aspects of reading. We know about the role of phonological awareness in cracking the alphabetic code, the value of explicit instruction in sound–letter relationships, and the importance of reading practice in producing fluency. The major thesis of this book, though, is that the fruits of that progress will be lost unless we also attend to issues of comprehension. Comprehension is, after all, the point of reading.

A focus on teaching comprehension is, we argue, a crucial part of literacy instruction during the preschool and primary years and a crucial part of content area instruction thereafter. The chapters of this book provide both warrants for these claims and a summary of the current state of knowledge about how best to teach comprehension across the preschool through secondary years.

This book is designed for teachers and other educational practitioners. It grows out of quite a different kind of effort, though—a report written for the Department of Education's Office of Educational Research and Improvement (OERI) and designed to inform the development of a research agenda for reading. In 1999, Kent McGuire, then assistant secretary for OERI, launched an agenda-setting effort for federal education research, to be focused on math and reading and managed by the RAND Corporation. Two study groups were appointed, each charged with identifying the most pressing needs in its own area. The RAND Reading Study Group (RRSG) formulated an initial draft of a report at a 5-day meeting held in the summer of 2000. The goal was to use that draft to solicit commentary and guidance for the committee in devising its final report. The goal was more than adequately met through a number of mechanisms for dissemination and feedback:

- Seven reading professionals were commissioned to write reviews of the draft.
- The draft report was summarized by members of the RRSG in presentations at numerous professional meetings, and comments and questions were noted for use in revision.
- The draft report was posted to a website, and commentary from the wider public was solicited.

These highly successful efforts garnered a great volume of commentary from scores of different individuals. The RRSG met to consider the critiques and responses carefully, then formulated a plan for revising the report.

During the summer of 2001 the RRSG again met for 5 days and produced a substantially revised report. That report was published early in 2002 as a book entitled *Reading for Understanding: Toward an R&D Program in Reading Comprehension*, and it indeed did serve not only its primary purpose as a source of guidance to the research solicitations, but beyond that provided the impetus for OERI to create a whole new Program of Research on Reading Comprehension (PRRC). Meanwhile, however, the responses from practitioners and teacher educators to presentations about both the original and the revised versions of the report suggested that the RRSG's thinking about reading comprehension might be helpful in confronting issues of instruction and teacher preparation. Thus, we present here a version of *Reading for Understanding* that has been rewritten and supplemented so as to inform practice. The thinking about the process of comprehension and the sources of variation in comprehension success that were articulated in *Reading for Understanding* are recapitulated here in Chapter 1. In addition, members of the RRSG and their collaborators have written additional chapters designed to be of particular value to those grappling with instructional issues. Those chapters focus on the following issues:

- Promoting adolescents' comprehension of subject-matter texts.
- Reading comprehension development and instruction for English-language learners.
- How teachers can approach the issue of variations among learners in the comprehension-focused classroom.
- What readers need to be taught in order to process discourse markers in narrative and expository text.
- Designs for comprehension instruction that have been shown to work.
- How Concept-Oriented Reading Instruction works with middle school students.
- Lessons about comprehension instruction learned at the Benchmark School for struggling readers.
- Instructional technology and its use in the classroom.
- Inservice development focusing on comprehension instruction for teachers.
- The complexities of assessing comprehension.
- A research program for improving reading comprehension.

These issues reflect areas in which members of the RRSG have themselves worked and developed expertise, as well as areas we felt were of the greatest interest to practitioners. We emphasize to our readers, though, that the guidance from research to those faced with providing instruction in reading comprehension is still evolving. Thus, we can here at best summarize the current basis for improvements in practice, while acknowledging that many important questions remain unanswered. We hasten to add that there is some substantial research evidence that we can use to guide instructional practice in reading comprehension. The reader will encounter evidence of this nature in our book. But because there is still so much more we need to learn, we underscore this fact so that practitioners will look forward, along with researchers, to the unfolding of new knowledge that will shape the instructional practices of tomorrow.

Contents

Reading for Comprehension

CATHERINE E. SNOW
ANNE POLSELLI SWEET

DEFINING READING COMPREHENSION

What happens when someone actually comprehends a written paragraph or page? Is the major challenge one of figuring out the words on the page? Or is the major challenge one of constructing a mental representation of the information represented by those words? Major figures in the history of reading research have tended toward one side or the other in answering these questions. Some say that print drives the process, and if the reader can use the print to figure out how to pronounce the words, most of the battle is won. Others say that processing the print is relatively trivial, that constructing meaning after the words have been recognized is the big challenge.

The RAND Reading Study Group (RRSG) comes down squarely in the middle of this debate. We define reading comprehension as the process of simultaneously *extracting* and *constructing* meaning. In other words, we recognize both challenges: figuring out how print represents words and engaging in the translation of print to sound accurately and efficiently (extracting), at the same time formulating a representation of the information being presented, which inevitably requires building new meanings and integrating new with old information (constructing meaning). Thus, we use the words *extracting* and *constructing* to emphasize both the importance and the insufficiency of the text as a determinant of reading comprehension.

Comprehension entails three elements[1]:

1. The *reader* who is doing the comprehending
2. The *text* that is to be comprehended
3. The *activity* in which comprehension is a part

In considering the reader, we include all the capacities, abilities, knowledge, and experiences that a person brings to the act of reading. By text, we mean anything that is read—whether printed or electronic. In considering activity, we include three dimensions: purposes—why readers read; processes—what mental activity they engage in while reading; and consequences—what readers learn or experience as a result of reading.

These three dimensions define a phenomenon that occurs within a larger *sociocultural context* (see Figure 1.1) that both shapes and is shaped by the reader. How students think of themselves—whether as readers or not—is a sociocultural fact. Whether reading is valued or not is similarly a product of sociocultural context. The texts that are available and considered worth reading are socioculturally determined—adolescents value comic books more than adults do; many girls prefer romance novels, whereas boys may prefer informational text; and middle-class adults tend not to think of producing graffitti as a legitimate literacy activity. Similarly, the activities readers engage in with those texts are all influenced by, and in some cases determined by, the sociocultural context—whether the texts are read in isolation or in groups, whether they are memorized and trusted or discussed and disputed, whether books are treated as treasured objects or as objects to be annotated, highlighted, and dog-eared. We will not make good use of research on reading comprehension unless we keep the sociocultural context constantly in mind.

---

[1] It should be noted that we are using terms that others have also used in defining reading comprehension, sometimes in similar and sometimes in slightly different ways. Galda and Beach (2001), for example, define context in a way that is not dissimilar from ours, whereas Spiro and Myers (1984) use context in a way that emphasizes culture less and task or purpose more. Many authors identify much the same list of attributes (purpose, interest, text, knowledge, strategy use, etc.) as we do, but Blachowicz and Ogle (2001), for example, distribute these attributes over the categories of individual and social processes rather than grouping them as we do. Pearson (2001) and Alexander and Jetton (2000) identify reader (learner), text, and context as key dimensions, without including activity as a separate dimension at the same level of analysis. The National Reading Panel report (2000) focuses on text and reader as sources of variability. Gaskins, in analyses with a variety of colleagues (e.g., Gaskins, 1998; Gaskins et al., 1993; Gaskins & Elliot, 1991), has identified comprehension as requiring the reader to take charge of text, task, and context variables, presumably an implicit acknowledgment that text, task, and context are all important in defining reading comprehension and are obstacles to comprehension, and, at the same time the reader is seen as the most central element.

FIGURE 1.1. A heuristic for thinking about reading comprehension.

Figure 1.1 is not meant to suggest that reader, text, and activity are static and independent elements. Reader, text, and activity cannot be considered in isolation. The capabilities of the reader always relate to a particular text. There is no such thing as a "good reader"—though there are, of course, good sixth-grade readers, good readers of young adult fiction, and good readers of science texts. Any good adult reader—like the members of the RRSG—reads some things much better than others. RRSG members are not particularly good readers of texts about solid-state physics. Some of us are poor readers of 17th-century British poetry. Others of us are poor readers of the sports pages, or of *Popular Mechanics*. It is the interaction of reader and text that determines whether reading comprehension will be successful or not.

Readers are also variably successful with different activities. Some of us become easily engaged in escape fiction, and others do not. Some of us learn easily from reading informational text; others need to reread, outline, take notes, and study in order to learn from reading. Some of us automatically note and respond aesthetically to stylistic variation in text, whereas others read primarily for content. Some of us follow recipes after a quick glance, but others have to work hard at using such texts appropriately. The match of activity with reader, again, determines whether the act of reading is successful or not.

In other words, the action in Figure 1.1 occurs not within the three segments of the circle, but at the interfaces between those segments. Some texts lend themselves to certain activities—for example, recipes are meant to be read for immediate application, not typically for aesthetic enjoyment or for long-term learning, whereas sixth-grade history texts are meant to be comprehended in order to generate long-term learning. Historical novels can be read simply for engagement or as a source of information about history—how the text is used often depends on the reader's skills and proclivities.

Reader, text, and activity are also interrelated dynamically, in ways that change across time. It is important to distinguish between what the reader brings to reading and what the reader takes from reading. For example, the reader who picks up a text possesses various cognitive, motivational, linguistic, and nonlinguistic capabilities. Some of these reader characteristics may change during the reading—for example, the reader may learn a few new facts or new vocabulary items or may become more interested in the topic of the text. Some of those changes may even become permanent—so that the reader passes a test on them at the end of the semester or starts the next reading event with increased knowledge and motivation. We know a lot about how specific factors, such as vocabulary knowledge, relate to comprehension success, but there has been little attention to the issue of how such factors may change from prereading to reading to postreading.

The process of comprehension, of course, also has a macrodevelopmental aspect. It changes over time as the reader matures and develops cognitively, as the reader gains increasing experience with more challenging texts, and as the reader benefits from instruction. Among the many factors influencing the macrodevelopment of comprehension, it is instruction, particularly classroom instruction, that is probably the most important for most students.

THE READER

Every classroom teacher knows that some students come to the task of comprehension better prepared than others. Good comprehenders have a wide range of capacities and abilities. These include cognitive capacities such as attention, memory, critical analytic ability, inferencing, and visualization ability. They include motivation, that is, a purpose for reading, an interest in the content being read, and a sense of self-efficacy as a reader. And they include various types of knowledge: vocabulary, domain, and topic knowledge; linguistic and discourse knowledge; and knowledge of specific comprehension strategies. Of course, the specific array of cognitive, motivational, and linguistic capacities and knowledge called on in any act of reading comprehension depends on the texts in use and the specific activity in which the reader is engaged.

Fluency is both an antecedent to and a consequence of comprehension. Some aspects of fluent, expressive reading may depend on a thorough understanding of a text. However, some components of fluency—quick and efficient recognition of words and understanding the grammatical structure of the sentences—appear to be prerequisites for comprehension.

As a reader begins to read and completes whatever activity is at hand, the knowledge and capabilities of the reader change in various ways. For example, a reader may increase domain knowledge during reading. Similarly, vocabulary, linguistic, or discourse knowledge may increase. Fluency can also increase as a function of the additional practice in reading. Motivational factors, such as self-concept or interest in the topic, may change in either a positive or a negative direction during a successful or an unsuccessful reading experience.

Another important source of changes in knowledge and capacities is the instruction that a reader receives. Appropriate instruction will foster both short-term and long-term reading comprehension goals—comprehension of the text under current consideration and comprehension capacities more generally. Thus, even as teachers are focusing their content area instruction on helping students understand a particular passage, they can be helping students learn how to become self-regulated, active, autonomous readers. Effective teachers incorporate both goals into their comprehension instruction. They have a clear understanding of which students need which type of instruction for which texts, and they give students the instruction they need to meet both short-term and long-term comprehension goals.

THE TEXT

The features of a text have a large effect on comprehension. Texts that are badly written or poorly structured are harder to understand. Texts that omit crucial information, or links between bits of information, are also hard to understand. And, of course, texts that draw upon background knowledge unavailable to the reader are hard to understand. Unfortunately, many of the texts students are expected to learn from have these features. Thus, one goal of comprehension instruction must be to help readers learn from even poorly written texts or texts that are challenging for other readers.

While reading, the reader constructs various representations of the text that are important for comprehension. These representations include, for example, the surface code (the exact wording of the text), the text base (idea units representing the meaning), and a representation of the

mental models embedded in the text. Consider, for example, the following text[2]:

> This paper presents an advanced process control system (APCS) for autoclave
> processing of composite materials, currently under development by the Univer-
> sity of Manitoba and the National Research Council Institute for Aerospace
> Research, in collaboration with Bristol Aerospace and Boeing Canada Technol-
> ogy. The goal for the APCS is to develop and implement optimized autoclave
> process cycles that can reduce manufacturing cycle times and product variabil-
> ity, thereby both reducing the costs and improving the quality of advanced
> composite materials. This ambitious goal requires integration of a number of
> leading-edge manufacturing technologies, including process simulation (virtual
> manufacturing), advanced sensing technologies, and adaptive process control
> and optimization. Herein we present the framework for the APCS, describing
> its key components and modes of operation. An example of some results from
> early "off-line" optimization trials is also presented. Preliminary results are en-
> couraging, suggesting the promise of the APCS concept, although significant
> challenges are also apparent, particularly in the areas of sensing technologies
> and in meeting the requirements for application of such a system to an indus-
> trial manufacturing environment.

The careful reader will, at the end of reading this text, perhaps be able to
remember some of the relatively novel lexical items from the surface code
(e.g., *advanced process control system, optimized autoclave process cycles,
process simulation [virtual manufacturing], advanced sensing technologies,
and adaptive process control and optimization*), will have developed a general sense of the text base (an APCS for autoclaving processed materials is
being developed collaboratively, cutting-edge techniques are being used,
getting it done will be challenging but will reduce costs and improve quality, some of the needed technology may not yet be fully developed), and will
have understood something about the mental models or presupposed understandings embedded in the text (improving the consistency and quality
of autoclaved composite materials is a worthy goal, reducing costs is a worthy goal, collaboration is often necessary to achieve complex technological
aims, accomplishing something in the laboratory is not equivalent to demonstrating its feasibility in a factory, and so on). Of course, it would greatly
help in reading this text if one knew a lot about autoclaving, optimization
processes, manufacturing composite materials, and so on. Nonetheless,
even the relatively unskilled reader develops representations of the text at a
number of different levels.

---

[2] This text is an abstract of an article entitled "Design and Development of an Advanced Pro-
cess Control System for Autoclave Processing of Composite Materials," written by A.
Johnston, N. Mrad, R. Cole, and L. P. Hendrickson (*Journal of the Canadian Aeronautics and
Space Institute*, 2001).

The proliferation of computers and electronic text means that we must include electronic text and multimedia documents, in addition to conventional print, in our thinking about text. Electronic text can present particular challenges to comprehension, such as dealing with the nonlinear nature of hypertext. It also has the potential to support a reader's comprehension of complex texts, for example, through hyperlinks to definitions or translations of difficult words or to paraphrasing of complex sentences. As electronic text is increasingly incorporated into instruction and into student use, we need to consider how comprehending it differs from comprehending linear text.

Texts can be difficult or easy, depending on factors inherent in the text, on the relationship between the text and the knowledge and abilities of the reader, and on the activities in which the reader is engaged. For example, the content presented in the text has a critical bearing on reading comprehension—most of us found the APCS text cited earlier hard to comprehend because we lacked relevant domain knowledge. In addition to content, the vocabulary load of the text and its linguistic structure, discourse style, and genre also interact with the reader's knowledge. The APCS text was an abstract—a particular genre with its own rules, which both writers and readers have to learn. When too many text factors are poorly matched to a reader's knowledge and experience, the text may be too difficult for optimal comprehension to occur. This is when instruction toward the immediate goal of understanding the text is needed, without forgetting the long-term goal of promoting students' comprehension abilities more generally.

Further, various activities are better suited to some texts than to others. For example, electronic texts that are the product of Internet searches typically have to be scanned for relevance and for reliability, whereas assigned texts are meant to be studied more deeply.

Teaching reading comprehension has become harder as all students are expected to read more text and more complex texts. Schools can no longer track students so that only those with highly developed reading skills take the more reading-intensive courses. All students now need to read high-level texts with comprehension to pass high-stakes exams and to make themselves employable. Thus, we must use all the resources available in the research literature to support content area teachers in their teaching of comprehension.

THE ACTIVITY

Reading does not occur in a vacuum. It is done for a purpose, to achieve some end. *Activity* refers to this dimension of reading. A reading activity involves one or more purposes, some operations to process the text at hand,

and the consequences of performing the activity. Before reading, a reader has a purpose, which can be either externally imposed (e.g., completing a class assignment) or internally generated (wanting to program a VCR). The purpose is influenced by a cluster of motivational variables, including interest and prior knowledge. The initial purpose can, of course, change as the reader reads. That is, a reader may encounter information that raises new questions and sends him or her off in a new direction. When the purpose is imposed, as in instruction, the reader may accept the purpose and complete the activity; for example, if the assignment is "read a paragraph in order to write a summary," the compliant student will accept that purpose and engage in reading operations designed to address it. If readers do not fully understand or accept the mandated purpose, incomplete comprehension is a likely result. For example, if students fail to see the relevance of an assignment, they may not read purposively, thus compromising their comprehension of the text.

While reading, the good reader processes the text with a particular purpose in mind. Processing the text involves decoding, certainly, but also higher-level linguistic and semantic processing and monitoring. Each process is more or less important in different types of reading. Skimming (getting only the gist of a text) requires a different array of processes than studying (reading text with the intent of retaining the information for a period of time).

Finally, the consequences of reading are part of the activity. Some reading activities lead to an increase in the reader's *knowledge*. For example, someone who picks up the historical novel *Andersonville* simply hoping for an enjoyable book may learn quite a bit about the U.S. Civil War while reading. An American history major reading an assigned text about the Civil War may find herself enjoying the text even though her major purpose was to learn from it. A second possible consequence of reading activities is finding out how to do something. These *application* consequences are often related to the goal of the reader. Repairing a bicycle and preparing bouillabaisse from a recipe are examples of applications. As with knowledge consequences, application consequences may or may not be related to the original purposes. Finally, other reading activities have *engagement* as their primary consequence. Reading the latest Tom Clancy novel may keep the reader involved while on vacation at the beach. We are not suggesting, however, that engagement occurs only with fiction. Good comprehenders can be engaged in many different types of text.

Knowledge, application, and engagement can be viewed as direct consequences of the reading activity. Activities may also have other, longer-term consequences. Any knowledge (or application) acquired during reading for enjoyment also becomes part of the knowledge that a reader brings to the next reading experience. Learning new vocabulary, acquiring incidental knowledge about Civil War battles or bouillabaisse ingredients, or discovering a new interest may all be consequences of reading with comprehension.

THE CONTEXT

An important set of reading activities occurs in the context of instruction. Understanding how the reader's purposes and operations are shaped by instruction, and how short- and long-term consequences are influenced by instruction, is crucial in any attempt to improve instruction.

When we think about the context of learning to read, we think mostly of classrooms. Of course, children bring to their classrooms vastly varying capacities and understandings about reading, which have, in turn, been developed as a consequence of their experiences in their homes and neighborhoods.

Classrooms and schools themselves reflect the neighborhood context and the economic disparities of the larger society. The differences in instruction and in the availability of texts, computers, and other instructional resources between schools serving low-income neighborhoods and those serving middle-income neighborhoods are well documented. If children from less economically advantaged families are to achieve as well as children from richer families, their schools and instructional experiences need to be even better than those available to their more privileged agemates.

Sociocultural theories of learning and literacy describe how children acquire literacy through social interactions with peers and adults. According to Vygotsky (1978), with the guidance and support of an expert, children are able to perform tasks that are slightly beyond their own independent knowledge and capability. As they become more knowledgeable and experienced with a task, support can be withdrawn without affecting the children's performance. From a sociocultural perspective, both the process (the way the instruction is delivered) and the content (the focus of instruction) are of major importance. Much research has shown that both process and content are likely to vary as a function of economic and cultural factors—with children from poor families more likely to be in classrooms with impoverished content and to be receiving instruction that is largely teacher directed (Tharp & Gallimore, 1988).

The effects of contextual factors, including economic resources, class membership, ethnicity, neighborhood, and school culture, can be seen in oral language practices, in students' self-concepts, in the types of literacy activities in which individuals engage, in instructional history, and, of course, in the likelihood of successful outcomes. The classroom learning environment (e.g., organizational grouping, inclusion of technology, and availability of materials) is an important aspect of the context that can affect the development of comprehension abilities.

CONCLUSION

The RAND Reading Study Group used the definition of reading comprehension offered in this chapter to facilitate its deliberations while developing a proposed research agenda for reading comprehension, which was published in its report, *Reading for Understanding* (2002). This report served as a foundation for a dialogue between the U.S. Department of Education and other agencies that fund education research and development, as well as researchers and practitioners in the field of the study of reading. The RRSG's thinking was informed by a vision of proficient readers—readers capable of acquiring new knowledge and understandings, applying information from text appropriately, and being engaged and reflective while reading. This vision led the study group to define reading comprehension as the process of simultaneously extracting and constructing meaning through interaction and involvement with written language. In brief, understanding comprehension requires these elements: the reader, the text, and the activity, or purpose for reading. These elements define a phenomenon—reading comprehension—that occurs within a larger sociocultural context that shapes and is shaped by the reader. The broader context infuses each of the three elements. The chapters that follow use this definition and conceptualization of reading comprehension as a starting point for discussions of what we know about how to improve comprehension instruction.

REFERENCES

Alexander, P. A., & Jetton, T. (2000). Learning from text: A multidimensional and developmental perspective. In M. L. Kamil, P. B. Mosenthal, P. D. Pearson, & R. Barr (Eds.), *Handbook of reading research: Volume III* (pp. 285–310). Mahwah, NJ: Erlbaum.

Blachowicz, C., & Ogle, D. (2001). *Reading comprehension: Strategies for independent learners.* New York: Guilford Press.

Galda, L., & Beach, R. (2001). Response to literature as a cultural activity. *Reading Research Quarterly, 36,* 64–73.

Gaskins, I. W. (1998). There's more to teaching at-risk and delayed readers than good reading instruction. *The Reading Teacher, 51,* 534–547.

Gaskins, I. W., Anderson, R. C., Pressley, M., Cunicelli, E. A., & Satlow, E. (1993). Six teachers' dialogue during cognitive process instruction. *The Elementary School Journal, 93,* 277–304.

Gaskins, I. W., & Elliot, T. T. (1991). *Implementing cognitive strategy instruction across the school: The Benchmark manual for teachers.* Cambridge, MA: Brookline Books.

National Reading Panel (NRP). (2000). *Teaching children to read: An evidence-based assessment of the scientific research literature on reading and its implications for reading instruction.* Washington, DC: National Institute of Child Health and Human Development.

Pearson, P. D. (2001). Life in the radical middle: A personal apology for a balanced view of reading. In R. Flippo (Ed.), *Reading researchers in search of common ground* (pp. 78–83). Newark, DE: International Reading Association.

Spiro, R., & Myers, A. (1984). Individual differences and underlying cognitive processes in reading. In P. Pearson, R. Barr, M. Kamil, & P. Mosenthal (Eds.), *Handbook of reading research* (pp. 471–501). New York: Longman.

Tharp, R. G., & Gallimore, R. (1988). *Rousing minds to life: Teaching, learning, and schooling in social context.* Cambridge: Cambridge university Press.

Vygotsky, L. (1978). *Mind in society: The development of higher psychological processes.* Cambridge, MA: Harvard University Press.

2

Comprehension Instruction

Adolescents and Their Multiple Literacies

DONNA E. ALVERMANN
A. JONATHAN EAKLE

The normative view of adolescents—as "not-yet" adults and thus less competent and less knowledgeable than their elders—is not our view. Instead, we like to think of adolescents as knowing things that have to do with their particular life experiences and the particular spaces they occupy in a fast-changing world. This situated perspective on youth culture recognizes that school literacy, though important, is but one among multiple literacies that these young people use daily. As they are quite adept at multitasking, it is not uncommon for adolescents at the middle and high school level to use their knowledge of print, online maneuvering, media, and visual literacies simultaneously. If this seems unlikely, picture a teen seated at her computer searching the Internet for information she can use in writing a report that is due in history class tomorrow as she engages in instant-messaging friends about a favorite recording artist's latest CD, the lyrics of which appear in another open window on her screen.

Granted, there are problems with this picture, not the least of which is the issue of access to new technologies, sometimes referred to as a *digital divide* that leads to inequity in opportunities for youth living at or just above the poverty level. There are also questions concerning student focus and the quality of homework completed under such conditions. Though important and deserving of attention, these concerns are beyond the scope of this chapter; however, the reality of young people's flexibility in using multiple literacies is central to it. Our goal is to use the concept of multiple literacies as a lens through which to explore research on adolescents' reading comprehension and its implications for the classroom. The basis for the implications we draw is the RAND Reading Study Group's (2002) synthesis of research on the requisite knowledge, skill, and disposition to read that adolescents need if they are to comprehend their subject-matter texts and succeed academically. First among the chapter's six sections is a brief overview of the history of adolescent literacy as a field of study, which we see as necessary background information for interpreting the significance of reading comprehension instruction in subject-matter classes. The next four sections summarize what is known from the research on reading comprehension about (1) teaching adolescents to read critically, (2) planning appropriate instruction for English-language learners, (3) working with readers who struggle, and (4) motivating adolescents to want to read. A final section summarizes the implications of this research for adolescent literacy instruction and points to areas needing further investigation.

BRIEF OVERVIEW OF THE HISTORY
OF ADOLESCENT LITERACY AS A FIELD OF STUDY

Adolescent literacy is a concept with a history. As a specialty area within literacy education, its roots can be traced to the early part of the 20th century, and more specifically to the work of William S. Gray, a psychologist at the University of Chicago (Moore, Readence, & Rickelman, 1983). Beginning with Gray's (1919) research on studying in relation to reading subject-matter texts, a long line of reading educators worked to build awareness of the need to teach students at the secondary and college levels how to comprehend the content of their subject-matter textbooks. For example, in 1970, Harold Herber published the first textbook devoted exclusively to content area reading instruction at the high school level. In his text Herber introduced a method for teaching reading *not* taught separately by a reading specialist in a pull-out program, but as an integrated process that content area classroom teachers could use in guiding students' comprehension of their texts.

More recently, the term *content area reading* has given way to *adolescent literacy*. Although there is still a focus on the instructional methods and strategies used in secondary classrooms to help students comprehend their assigned readings in subject-matter materials, changing demographics and digital technologies are causing the field to largely redefine itself (Alvermann, Hinchman, Moore, Phelps, & Waff, 1998). Part of that redefinition involves recognizing the multiple literacies young people use in their everyday lives as members of the so-called Net Generation. In a nutshell, adolescent literacy instruction, although encompassing the psychological perspectives on reading and studying introduced a century ago and reemphasized during the cognitive revolution of the 1980s, is today more broadly concerned with the sociocultural issues that embed such instruction.

TEACHING STUDENTS TO READ CRITICALLY

Why do the words "What does the text say?" roll so easily off our tongues? Is there a teacher who hasn't asked that question of a student at least once? We know we have uttered those words on more than one occasion, even though we are well aware that researchers working in the area of reading comprehension have shown repeatedly that meaning does not exist *in* text. It is the readers who actively construct meaning using both their world knowledge (e.g., everyday experiences) and their domain knowledge (e.g., how biology differs from history in structure) to interpret print and nonprint texts. Yet a lingering tendency to locate meaning in the text leads us to ask the inevitable at times.

Constructing meaning requires readers to set purposes for what they read and to actively monitor whether or not those purposes are being met. This implies a strategic effort on the reader's part, and that is where teachers come in. Evidence from both quantitative and qualitative research shows that teaching students strategies for self-questioning, graphically depicting the relationships between and among texts, identifying various text structures, and summarizing important information all lead to improved comprehension (National Reading Panel, 2000). Moreover, evidence from both quantitative and qualitative research indicates vocabulary instruction and its associated strategies for developing word meaning can facilitate students' comprehension, but exactly how that facilitation takes place is unknown at present (Harmon, 1998; National Reading Panel, 2000).

Although teaching students in the middle and high school grades to be strategic in their approach to reading is essential to their academic growth, it is not sufficient for developing their ability to read texts critically. Comprehension is only the first step toward developing a critical awareness of all kinds of texts. It is often said that comprehending is equivalent to constructing a text's meaning, whereas reading critically is focused on figuring out how a text comes to have a particular meaning. Taught to read critically, students will be able to analyze how writers, illustrators, and others involved represent people and their ideas—in short, how individuals who create texts make those texts work (Alvermann, 2001). This is not a trivial matter, especially given that new technologies are fundamentally and irreversibly affecting how ideas are represented in texts and communicated. As the RAND Reading Study Group (2002) pointed out, we cannot assume that the comprehension skills necessary for reading linear text will transfer to reading hypertext, hypermedia, or any number of other new text forms.

Also on the table for discussion is the perceived need to develop adolescents' critical awareness of how all texts (print, visual, digital) position them as readers and viewers, not for the purpose of having them search for the villains or heroes in their texts, nor for the oppressors or emancipators among us, but, rather, as Morgan (1997) puts it, for considering how doing away with these simplistic categories may lead to "a different view of how people may act, provisionally, at a particular time and within particular conditions" (p. 26). For teachers, the implications of this perspective may translate instructionally into helping adolescents analyze the credibility of selected websites or evaluate the potential for hypermedia to create opportunities for manipulating information in ways that are unavailable to readers and writers of print media.

In a similar vein, teachers who are concerned that their students' lack of know-how in critically evaluating websites will lead to an unquestioning acceptance of content while completing online homework assignments, may consider teaching them strategies for questioning the authority of a site and its links. Still other strategies essential to efficient online searches are those that help students monitor their navigation of various text nodes and links with the least amount of disorientation and distraction possible (RAND Reading Study Group, 2002).

PLANNING APPROPRIATE INSTRUCTION FOR ENGLISH-LANGUAGE LEARNERS

> En un lugar de la Mancha, de cuyo nombre no quiero acordarme, no ha mucho tiempo que vivía un hidalgo de los de lanza en astillero, adarga antigua, rocín flaco y galgo corredor . . . los ratos que estaba ocioso, que eran los más del año, se daba a leer libros de caballerías, con tanta afición y gusto, que olvidó casi de todo punto el ejercicio de la caza y aun la administración de su hacienda. Y llegó a tanto su curiosidad y desatino en esto, que vendió muchas hanegas de tierra de sembradura para comprar libros de caballerías en que leer, y así, llevó a su casa todos cuantos pudo haber dellos. . . . (Cervantes, 1605/2001)

While reading this passage, you may have experienced some of the challenges faced by adolescent English-language learners and their teachers in the United States. To others of you who are Spanish-speaking readers, this text may be readily recognized as the opening lines of Cervantes' classic *Don Quijote* (Quixote); in fact, the lines may be impressed so greatly on your memories that the words can be recited verbatim, as a U.S.-born adolescent might deliver the opening phrases of the Gettysburg Address.

To less proficient "readers" of Cervantes' lines, the text may appear as simply a series of marks, some more familiar than others. If these readers are proficient decoders of English-only orthography, with some explicit instruction in the phonetic variations and similarities between the English and Spanish sound-to-symbol systems, they may be taught to articulate the words. Nonetheless, with this knowledge alone there will be little, if any, comprehension of Cervantes' message.

Beyond decoding the sounds of words, an approach to teaching this Spanish-language content to an English-only reader might be to concentrate on the meaning of key vocabulary words found in the text, for we know that vocabulary is a predictor of reading comprehension (RAND Reading Study Group, 2002). Learning that reading (from "leer"—to read) "libros de caballerías" (books of knightly deeds) led the Quijote to give up possessions and to forget about practical matters, is essential to the meaning of the opening passage. Indeed, we have evidence that learning the surface features of a text, the word-by-word critical vocabulary as well as its syntactic structures (how sentences are segmented into phrases), will have a positive influence on reading comprehension. Yet this is not enough for the most thorough comprehension of *Don Quijote*.

Putting vocabulary knowledge aside for a moment, the "sententious terseness" to which the humor of Cervantes' classic owes its greatness is its use of the Spanish language, and, at best, a translation will only palely imitate the text's qualities (Ormsby, 1885/2001). This distinction reflects what Rosenblatt (1978) has described as the differences between efferent and aesthetic reading. Briefly, efferent reading is what takes place when the text is used to extract information that can be used for outward and future goals, whereas aesthetic reading entails that which occurs during the reading event, a transaction that involves an intensity, feeling, and tension. Often, in aesthetic reading, the relation of word sounds is central to understanding the text message. Although approaching Cervantes from the perspective of a word-by-word translation can lead to retrieving some main ideas from his writing, the richness of the language, the cultural underpinnings, and, arguably, the deeper purposes of the text are lost.

Keeping these features in mind, consider the many factors at work in the adolescent English-language learner, some of which can be related to group differences, others to variations between individuals. The relationship between word knowledge and conceptual knowledge is unpredictable among English-language learners, and thus it is critical to examine the contributions and interactions of these two types of knowledge when planning instruction for these students (RAND Reading Study Group, 2002).

If, for instance, a recent adolescent immigrant has previously learned some of the conceptual nuances of Mexican history, such as how European ideology was introduced to the Aztecs in the 16th century, it might be easier for him to relate this background knowledge to the somewhat similar treatment of other Native Americans described in U.S. history textbooks. Building on background experiences or "funds of knowledge" (Gonzalez & Moll, 1995), this student may need only to attend to some unknown English vocabulary and text structure to reach a critical understanding of the textbook content.

Unfortunately, some students learning the mainstream language who have broad conceptual understandings may nonetheless be labeled "disabled" because they have not achieved proficiency in the school language. Moreover, schools may so label students or reduce the quality of instruction, based on biases toward linguistic differences or on other factors such as class, nationality, or race. Because a primary influence in becoming an academically successful reader is an adolescent's perception of the self as competent (RAND Reading Study Group, 2002), such labeling can be devastating, contributing to greater retention and dropout rates for linguistic-minority students than for mainstream students. Thus, when English-language learners are experiencing difficulties in reading comprehension, rather than focusing on their difficulties with the English language; respecting their heritage and past experiences and providing them with clear goals and strategies is likely to have a much more positive effect on their reading achievement.

Some research has addressed how bilingual adolescents may learn surface-level vocabulary while building and capitalizing on their first-language knowledge (RAND Reading Study Group, 2002). Promising directions for instructional practice have focused attention on teaching cross-linguistic transfer strategies in order to promote second-language learning. These strategies include the use of cognate relationships (the meaning and/or spelling similarities of words across languages), code mixing (substituting words from the first language within a sentence), code switching (switching languages between sentences), and translating. For example, knowledge of the cognate *langue* (French), *lenguaje* (Spanish), or *linguagem* (Portuguese) may help unlock the meaning of the English word *language*. However, when preparing instruction for linguistically diverse classrooms, it must be considered that cognate approaches may work well for some languages but not for others.

Although there are few studies that specifically address content area learning and cognitive reading strategies for English-language learners, there are indications that modifying and extending what we know about these strategies from teaching first-language students may be valuable. In support of this notion, researchers have reported the benefits of cognitive reading instruction for bilingual middle school students. For example, Jimenez (1997) used culturally relevant materials to teach low-literacy second-language students not only mainstream reading strategies (e.g., inferencing and asking questions) but also cross-linguistic approaches that increased their reading motivation. In another study, Garcia (1998) found that English-language-learning students not only used cognates, but also used other bilingual reading strategies, such as code switching, that suggested enhanced comprehension. These areas of cross-linguistic research have strengthened ideas that support the use of first languages for learning English in classrooms. Furthermore, indications are that using multiple languages promotes social, analytic, and divergent thinking skills.

Moving from the part (words) and back to a broader text, we close this section as we began: with the Quijote. For many readers, the lingering and most vivid image of Don Quijote is that of a gangly man on a broken-down steed, jousting with windmills, structures that he mistakenly thought were giants. But this is an incomplete picture. Rather, we offer another image of him as the journeyer, who, as the pages of Cervantes' narrative progress, becomes the knight who recognizes qualities others cannot see.

Too often English-language learners are categorized as struggling and disabled when they, like Don Quijote, are confronted with the revolving windmills of public school education. To help them move along successfully in their reading, multiple avenues for growth should be made available, such as new interactive communication technologies that utilize their home languages, cognitive strategy instruction, and opportunities to use their first languages and cultural experiences to build upon and learn new subject area content.

WORKING WITH READERS WHO STRUGGLE

Like so many terms in the reading field, the *struggling reader* is a contested label. A cursory analysis of the research literature reveals that *struggling* is used to refer to youth with clinically diagnosed reading disabilities as well as to those who are English-language learners, "at risk," low achieving, unmotivated, disenchanted, or generally unsuccessful in school literacy tasks. A smorgasbord of descriptors, these labels tell little or nothing about the possible sociocultural construction of such readers. For example, according to anthropologists McDermott and Varenne (1995), it is society at large that produces the conditions necessary for some individuals to succeed, others to struggle, and still others to fail outright.

In applying this premise to education, one could interpret it to mean that the condition known as traditional school culture is *making* struggling readers out of some youth, especially those who have turned their backs on a version of reading and writing commonly referred to as school literacy. In an effort to raise the bar by implementing high standards—a noteworthy goal by most people's reasoning—schools may be promoting certain normative ways of reading texts that are disabling some of the very students they are trying to help. The practice of constructing certain types of readers as "normal" and others as "struggling" is even more problematic when one considers that some normative ways of reading are losing their usefulness, and perhaps to some extent their validity, in a world increasingly defined by the Internet, hypermedia, instant messaging, and wearable computers (Lankshear & Knobel, 2002).

The changing and multiple literacies these new media and interactive communication technologies evoke can be used to support an extended view of both reading and the so-called struggling reader. For instance, one might think of students who have difficulty comprehending their assigned subject area texts as being on a continuum from low need to high need in the instructional support they will require to succeed in today's culturally and linguistically diverse classrooms. All readers, even proficient ones, can find themselves at the high-need end of the continuum from time to time, depending on how challenging a text is to them (e.g., if it is poorly written, conceptually dense, or filled with unfamiliar words and syntactical structures). Likewise, what a reader is asked to do with the information presented in a text (e.g., recall it, analyze it in relation to other information presented in other texts, critically evaluate it, or apply it in a new situation) can have an impact on where that reader is on the need continuum. Fortunately for teachers who are on the front line and responsible for meeting the varying needs of all their students, there are research-backed ideas for working effectively with readers who have difficulties with particular texts.

One such idea is to explicitly teach the strategies these students will need to comprehend their assigned materials. According to the research synthesized by the RAND Reading Study Group (2002):

> Explicit instruction provides a clear explanation of the criterion task, encourages students to pay attention, activates prior knowledge, breaks the task into small steps, provides sufficient practice at every step, and incorporates teacher feedback. It is particularly important for the teacher to model the comprehension strategies being taught. Careful and slow fading of the scaffolding is important. (p. 33)

Adolescents with a history of reading difficulties often present particular challenges to their teachers. Because they read so infrequently, these youth typically have not acquired the requisite background knowledge and specialized vocabulary needed for comprehending most subject-matter texts. Content area teachers understandably become frustrated when this occurs and sometimes resort to what Finn (1999) calls a "domesticating education." That is, they expect less of these high-need students in exchange for the students' goodwill and reasonable effort in completing content area assignments that require less, if any, reading. Over time, however, distinctions in who is eligible for what kind of education may create a classroom culture that fails to please both teachers and students. And, in some instances, students who are aware of the distinctions in the quality of education offered them may speak out, as in the case of a young woman who was overheard telling a roomful of teachers in a West Coast high school:

> "We know we aren't very well educated. We know there are things we should know by now that we don't. But we're not stupid; most of us are really smart. You just need to show us, break it down for us, work with us and expect us to do it." (in Schoenbach, Greenleaf, Cziko, & Hurwitz, 1999, p. 10)

Interestingly, there is research that speaks to this young woman's request for help. For example, there is ample evidence that instructional scaffolding—a method for showing students *how* to read a history, chemistry, literature, health, or some other content area text by the teacher's modeling and breaking down the task of comprehending into manageable parts—is especially effective when used with students who struggle with reading. Teachers who preview texts and teach key vocabulary prior to expecting students to read a particular text are known to assist in the comprehension process, as are those who involve students in activating relevant background knowledge in preparation for reading. However, when students' background knowledge is based on inaccurate assumptions, as is frequently the case in math and science classes, teachers must assist students in directly questioning those assumptions so as to bring about new understanding. Finally, research has shown that students who struggle to comprehend narrative texts benefit from being shown how authors structure those texts to make them more memorable, and from being taught to organize information graphically (National Reading Panel, 2000; RAND Reading Study Group, 2002).

In sum, there is much that research has to offer in helping teachers assist students in reading their subject-matter texts. What has yet to be discussed in this chapter on adolescent literacy, however, is students' disposition or motivation to engage with the texts they are expected to read. A willingness on the part of adolescents to become engaged in school-related tasks is vital to the entire teaching–learning process.

MOTIVATING ADOLESCENTS TO WANT TO READ

It is our view that readers not only need to develop cognitive skills to become motivated lifetime literacy learners, but are also affected by the contexts in which they practice literacy, by the purposes that motivate them to read, by their self-efficacy as readers, and by their interest in the content of the reading material. It is this dynamic mixture of qualities that we find in the engaged reader (Baker, Afflerbach, & Reinking, 1996). If students are unmotivated to read because of contextual factors, have no meaningful reason to do so, or are not interested in the content, then reading skill or strategy instruction alone will not engage them. However, common sense suggests that if engagement can occur, content can then be taught and achievement will increase (RAND Reading Study Group, 2002).

The schoolhouse gold standard of learning is engagement in academic content. Engagement is an absorption in the material being read and may be described as a "flow" event (Csikszentmihalyi, 1990), one of being absorbed by the reading experience. Most often this type of reading engagement signals enjoyment of the material and intrinsic interest in a particular topic. It can also be stimulated by the purpose of gaining additional understanding beyond that previously acquired, extending the prior knowledge base of the reader. Intrinsically motivated reading in its purest sense occurs because of the pleasure derived from the activity.

We also recognize that literacy engagement can take place while students prepare for or participate in class lessons, yet this engagement most often occurs for different reasons than that of intrinsically motivated reading. Reading textbook content in classrooms is more often than not regulated by outside variables, or extrinsically, by a need to meet performance standards or values imposed by others. Meeting standards can take the form of earning good grades, pleasing a parent or teacher, or gaining others' acknowledgment and praise. In this same vein, adolescents can be motivated by future external goals, such as achieving admission into a university. Interestingly, where pleasure ends and where external goals begin is a difficult matter to determine, leading some motivational theorists to conclude that the boundaries between the intrinsic and extrinsic are at best blurry (Vallerand, 2000).

Critics of extrinsic motivators have described these practices as being behaviorist and manipulative, operating for short-term gains such as test scores rather than toward the longer-range and more important goal of developing students' intrinsic interest in literacy learning. In recent years experimental evidence has supported their claims and bolstered the criticisms often mounted against extrinsically motivating reading programs. Nonetheless, at least in the short run, these approaches may achieve reading engagement as students work toward promised rewards. What may be adversely affected in the long term, however, are their general attitudes toward reading.

Other literacy experts have noted that there are occasions when the use of either intrinsic or extrinsic motivators is desirable to achieve different goals. For example, it has been suggested that to teach lower-level literacy skills such as word identification, rewards may be necessary, whereas higher-order thinking processes are best learned under intrinsically motivated instructional circumstances (Sweet & Guthrie, 1996). We believe that the latter is certainly the more desirable goal in teaching most adolescent learners at most times. However, we recognize that for students in high-need categories, resorting to extrinsic measures temporarily may be in order. Clearly, a balance should be struck between these approaches, taking into consideration the disposition of the students and the goals a teacher wishes to achieve.

Unfortunately, there is evidence that many classroom practices—specifically, reading textbooks and completing teacher-directed classroom reading assignments—are the least favorite and motivating reading activities for adolescents. When faced with these materials and circumstances, students have reported boredom and difficulties in comprehending. These attitudes discourage adolescents from reading beyond what is merely required for completing an assignment, and, regrettably, students who do little independent reading in various and diverse texts will have difficulty with school learning (RAND Reading Study Group, 2002).

Taking these factors into consideration, it may seem reasonable to offer adolescents a wide scope of free-choice reading material to increase their fluency, comprehension, and motivation to read. Based on surveys of middle school readers, classroom material might therefore include magazines, adventure books, mysteries, and scary stories (Ivey & Broaddus, 2001). Nevertheless, it is unclear as to whether practices such as providing free reading time in schools, using high-interest material, improve reading (National Reading Panel, 2000). This is a topic that deserves additional research.

We do know that interest can be stimulated and student attitudes can be modified by teachers by setting varied and perhaps individualized purposes prior to students' reading activities. For instance, having students approach a relevant problem, such as global warming, by assuming the perspective of a nuclear chemist may be engaging for some students, and studying the problem as a conservationist may be stimulating for others. In this case, varied scenarios in which students can become involved in real-world problems that they may face in later years is likely to be more engaging than simply reading about molecules reacting in the upper atmosphere. Structured student choice, using authentic approaches such as these, not only fosters comprehension (RAND Reading Study Group, 2002) but also allows adolescents to develop critical future vision.

As mentioned earlier in this chapter, these situational aspects of literacy have led to reconceptualizations of content area reading: student-centered pedagogies that take into account not only curricular goals, but also the content material and literacy practices that are particularly relevant to adolescents. This perspective supports conclusions that interest in the topic being read has a positive influence on comprehension (Schiefele, 1992). We also have evidence that students with high interest in a particular area often are able to surpass their typical reading levels, whereas students with little interest in a subject typically display lower comprehension of that material, regardless of whether the text is considered developmentally appropriate for the reader (Snow, Chapter 11 in this book). Therefore, it is critical for schools and researchers to consider the varied interests of adolescents and how what they might choose to read can help them become lifelong readers and learners.

Motivating adolescent readers by offering them multiple pathways to comprehending school content does not imply easier reading. In fact, allowing them to assist in making decisions about how and from what materials they learn may be one of the greatest challenges for them as well as for teachers. It is a challenge, nevertheless, that leads to self-initiating actions on the part of the reader and cultivates effective comprehenders.

IMPLICATIONS FOR CLASSROOM INSTRUCTION

Current research on reading comprehension is clearly supportive of teaching adolescents to be strategic in interacting with texts of all kinds and within subject-matter classes where "strategies are taught in the service of interpreting text, not as ends in and of themselves" (RAND Reading Study Group, 2002, p. 46). This approach, sometimes called the "content determines process" approach, is not a new idea (see Herber, 1970). Briefly, it refers to the fact that implicit within the content of subject-matter texts, which teachers expect students to read, lie the reading processes (or skills and strategies) students need to comprehend the material. The point in giving content prominence over skills and strategies is to emphasize that we do not equate instruction in content area reading with teaching reading as a separate, or pull-out, subject. Isolated comprehension instruction is neither effective nor facilitative in developing students' independence in reading and responding to content materials.

This is particularly true for adolescents who struggle to read in subject area classrooms. They deserve instruction that is developmentally, culturally, and linguistically responsive to their needs. To be effective, such instruction must be explicit, it must be embedded in the regular curriculum, and it must take into account struggling readers' abilities to read, write, and communicate orally as strengths, not as deficits.

The research also suggests that it is important to be mindful of when it is inappropriate to enlist explicit instruction as an approach to teaching students strategies for reading their texts. For example, students at the low-need end of the continuum for a particular task have been shown to benefit less from explicit instruction than those at the high-need end. That is, for some students, explicit or direct instruction has been shown to be superfluous. Explicit instruction is also viewed as ineffective when the goal is to help students transfer the strategies they are taught in one context to another context. Although explicit instruction typically generates an immediate application of a particular strategy, there is no guarantee that students will use it long term or in a new situation (RAND Reading Study Group, 2002).

There is clear research support for teaching all students to be strategic readers, but what is not so clear is why strategic reading leads to improved comprehension. Noting that this is a question that merits further investigation, members of the RAND Reading Study Group (2002) hypothesized that improvement may occur "not because of the specific strategies being taught but because students have been actively interacting with the texts . . . [which] triggers the use of strategies that inactive learners possess but do not normally use" (p. 33). This hypothesis seems to have implications for teachers in that it suggests the need for participatory approaches—not a transmission approach—to teaching and learning. Participatory approaches actively engage students in their own learning (individually and in small groups); they situate the learner, not the teacher, at the center of the classroom. Another distinguishing feature of these approaches is the role of the text in students' learning. In transmission classrooms, texts (like teachers) are viewed as dispensers of knowledge, whereas in participatory classrooms, students use texts as *tools* for learning and constructing new knowledge. The latter approach helps to ensure that texts are not treated as repositories of information to be memorized and then all too quickly forgotten (Wade & Moje, 2000).

Although adolescents' everyday literacy practices are changing at an unprecedented pace as a result of their interest in the Internet—in fact, according to a recent survey, if students could have access to only one medium, they would choose the Internet over the television, telephone, and radio (Knowledge Networks, 2002)—school literacy tasks look pretty much the same. Textbooks predominate, with the content of such texts being rarely questioned by either students or teachers. This unquestioning approach to comprehending is especially problematic when one considers the vast number of textual messages adolescents are exposed to on the Internet.

We believe this situation suggests the need to teach students to read with a critical eye toward how writers and illustrators represent people and their ideas—in short, how individuals who create texts make those texts work. It also suggests a need for teachers to show students how all texts, including their textbooks, routinely promote or silence particular views.

The implications of the research on motivating youth so that they not only *can* read but also *choose* to read are quite clear. We know that certain types of instructional practices, such as setting multiple and individualized purposes for reading, can encourage some students to read, but we are less confident in our understanding of the long-term effects of goal-oriented, extrinsic reward practices. However, those who read for enjoyment or are motivated for similar intrinsic reasons may have an edge academically and later in life. Even so, there are reports that school reading materials and reading activities may be less than engaging and that students have clear preferences in what and how they want to read. Given this research, teachers might consider using trade books or Internet resources to supplement content area textbooks. It seems that to best engage students in curricular content, alternatives and/or supplements to content area textbooks merit further consideration in both research and classroom practice, especially as reading practices are rapidly changing, partly as a result of the new technologies and their visual characteristics. In addition, we believe that attending to the social aspects of reading, such as using strategies that involve collaborative reading groups, cultivate curiosity, and increase self-efficacy, should be a part of instructional planning.

We know that social engagement between adolescents during reading activities allows for exchanges that can lead not only to broader conceptual knowledge as well as understandings of how they approach their readings differently (RAND Reading Study Group, 2002). For example, some students may be skilled in eliciting meaning from text graphics, whereas others may be proficient at searching for and organizing main ideas across various texts or disciplines. The sharing of these different strategies between peers may not only be motivating and engaging, allowing students to showcase skills not always recognized in a particular content area, but may also offer fellow students multiple and diverse pathways for comprehending topics in content area texts. Perhaps most important, literacy activities such as these develop students' abilities to work together collaboratively in their classrooms and in the future.

Although implications from the research on comprehension instruction for adolescents provide guidance in the areas just discussed, there are other areas we know less about, which are in need of further investigation before firm recommendations can be made. These are considered next.

Certainly, the multiple literacies that adolescents already have at their disposal, plus those they will acquire, give us indications of the practices that need to be researched in schools. These literacies also suggest the need for research on the literacy skills that young adults will need in order to compete successfully in a digital world. Instructing students who have not learned to be critical users of the new media and information communication technologies may be one of the most practical ways of engaging them in subject matter content. Up-to-the-minute web-based resources that display information such as breaking news, stock quotes, weather reports, and sport scores can be fertile ground for motivating students to engage in authentic literacy tasks. Research on how digital information is shared between students may be another window into how adolescents negotiate their needs and desires. It is this type of research and its concomitant implications for instruction that hold promise for demonstrating the ways in which genuine uses of multiple literacies can be motivating to students.

Equally important, we argue, is what future research will have to say about teaching comprehension in culturally and linguistically relevant ways, especially given the growing numbers of students in the United States who do not speak English as their first language. In most respects, current research on English-language learners is in its infancy and has been often distracted by politics and other external pressures. We know from research on mainstream monolingual populations that opportunities for discussion, questioning, and critical thinking lead to increased knowledge of content and to comprehension in general (RAND Reading Study Group, 2002). Less clear is how access to two or more languages can contribute to overall academic achievement, not only for those learning English, but also for students in multilingual classrooms who speak the majority language.

In addition, there is much to learn about what level of second-language oral proficiency is necessary for students to best benefit from English-language content area instruction. The high performance of many immigrant students, schooled earlier in their mother tongue, in science and mathematics suggests the benefits of transferring what they already know to new academic content. It seems reasonable that the same achievement may be realized in other content areas that rely more on oral language if students are likewise given opportunities to use their background languages and experiences. Considering these potentials, some of the most pressing research needs are for studies addressing how quality instruction that combines both first and second languages might lead to learning subject-matter content.

Other areas that merit study include tools and materials that may offer support to classroom teachers with little or no second-language training or experience. This is especially relevant, given the dramatically increasing numbers of non-English-speaking immigrants in U.S. classrooms and the few multilingual teachers available to teach them. These areas also include the use of computer-assisted multilingual software, although thus far experimental evidence involving computer-assisted instruction is inconclusive or nonexistent (National Reading Panel, 2000; RAND Reading Study Group, 2002). In addition, the effects of pictorial and graphic aids, multimedia, and online learning on English-language learners', as well as other adolescents', content area reading comprehension show promise. Much research into the effects of such instructional support is needed.

Finally, clarification regarding the efficacy of using multimedia and interactive communication technologies for content learning, or computer programs for comprehension development, especially among so-called struggling readers, may provide teachers with a better sense of how to integrate school literacy with other forms of literacy that adolescents use successfully outside of school. Although there is little empirical research to date that applies specifically to media literacy instruction at the middle and high school level (National Reading Panel, 2000), the evidence that does exist suggests the efficacy of literacy instruction that integrates print and visual texts, including hypermedia, hypertext, the Internet, and interactive CD-ROMS (Kamil, Intrator, & Kim, 2000; Leu, 2000). What teachers can take from this research is an understanding that multimedia texts offer students both visual and verbal information simultaneously, which, according to a dual code theory of information processing, means that there are two memory traces instead of one. Theoretically, this should make multimedia texts more memorable (Sadoski & Pavio, 2001). In practice, classroom instruction that considers multiple approaches to literacy learning promises greater access not only to content information, but also to meaningful and engaging learning experiences for linguistically and culturally diverse students.

REFERENCES

Alvermann, D. E. (2001). Reading adolescents' reading identities: Looking back to see ahead. *Journal of Adolescent & Adult Literacies, 44*, 676–690.

Alvermann, D. E., Hinchman, K. A., Moore, D. W., Phelps, S. F., & Waff, D. R. (Eds.). (1998). *Reconceptualizing the literacies in adolescents' lives.* Mahwah, NJ: Erlbaum.

Baker, L., Afflerbach, P., & Reinking, D. (1996). *Developing engaged readers in school and home communities.* Mahwah, NJ: Erlbaum.

Cervantes Saaverdra, Miguel de. (2001). *El ingenioso hidalgo Don Quijote de la Mancha.* [online]. Retrieved June 27, 2002, from Biblioteca Virtual Miguel de Cervantes, *http://cervantesvirtual.com/FichaObra.html?Ref=4441&portal=40.*

Csikszentmihalyi, M. (1990). *Flow: The psychology of optimal experience.* New York: Harper & Row.

Finn, P. J. (1999). *Literacy with an attitude: Educating working-class children in their own self-interest.* Albany, NY: State University of New York Press.

García, G. E. (1998). Mexican-American bilingual students' metacognitive reading strategies: What's transferred, unique, problematic? In D. J. Leu & C. Kinzer (Eds.), *The forty-seventh yearbook of the National Yearbook Conference Yearbook* (pp. 253–263). Chicago: National Reading Conference.

Gonzalez, N., & Moll, L. C. (1995). Funds of knowledge for teaching in Latino households. *Urban Education, 29,* 443–471.

Gray, W. S. (1919). The relation between studying and reading. In *Proceedings of the fifty-seventh annual meeting of the National Education Association* (pp. 580–586). Washington, DC: National Education Association.

Harmon, J. M. (1998). Constructing word meanings: Strategies and perceptions of four middle school learners. *Journal of Literacy Research, 30,* 561–599.

Herber, H. L. (1970). *Teaching reading in content areas.* Englewood Cliffs, NJ: Prentice-Hall.

Ivey, G., & Broaddus, K. (2001). "Just plain reading": A survey of what makes kids want to read in middle school classrooms. *Reading Research Quarterly, 34,* 224–343.

Jimenez, R. T. (1997). The strategic literacy abilities and potentials of five Latina/o readers in middle school. *Reading Research Quarterly, 34,* 224–343.

Kamil, M. L., Intrator, S. M., & Kim, H. S. (2000). The effects of other technologies on literacy and literacy learning. In M. L. Kamil, P. B. Mosenthal, P. D. Pearson, & R. Barr (Eds.), *Handbook of reading research* (Vol. 3, pp. 771–788). Mahwah, NJ: Erlbaum.

Knowledge Networks. (2002). More kids say the Internet is the medium they can't live without. [Downloaded July 20, 2002], available: *http://www.knowledgenetworks.com.*

Lankshear, C., & Knobel, M. (2002). Do we have your attention? New literacies, digital technologies, and the education of adolescents. In D. E. Alvermann (Ed.), *Adolescents and literacies in a digital world* (pp. 19–39). New York: Peter Lang.

Leu, D. J., Jr. (2000). Literacy and technology: Deictic consequences for literacy education in an information age. In M. L. Kamil, P. B. Mosenthal, P. D. Pearson, & R. Barr (Eds.), *Handbook of reading research* (Vol. 3, pp. 743–770). Mahwah, NJ: Erlbaum.

McDermott, R., & Varenne, H. (1995). Culture *as* disability. *Anthropology and Education Quarterly, 26,* 324–348.

Moore, D. W., Readence, J. E., & Rickelman, R. J. (1983). An historical exploration of content area reading instruction. *Reading Research Quarterly, 8,* 419–438.

Morgan, W. (1997). *Critical literacy in the classroom.* New York: Routledge.

National Reading Panel. (2000). *Report of the National Reading Panel.* Washington, DC: National Institute of Child Health and Human Development.

Ormsby, J. (Trans.). (2001). Translator's note to *Don Quixote* [online]. Retrieved June 25, 2002, from Texas A & M University, The Cervantes Project website: *http://www.csdl.tamu.edu/cervantes/english/ctxt/DQ_Ormsby/.*

RAND Reading Study Group. (2002). *Reading for understanding: Toward an R&D program in reading comprehension.* Santa Monica, CA: Science and Technology Policy Institute, RAND Education.

Rosenblatt, L. M. (1978). *The reader, the text, the poem. The transactional theory of the literary work.* Carbondale, IL: Southern Illinois University Press.

Sadoski, M., & Pavio, A. (2001). *Imagery and text: A dual code theory of reading and writing.* Mahwah, NJ: Erlbaum.

Schiefele, U. (1992). Topic interest and levels of text comprehension. In K.A. Renninger, S. Hidi, & A. Krapp (Eds.), *The role of interest in learning and development* (pp. 151–182). Hillsdale, NJ: Erlbaum.

Schoenbach, R., Greenleaf, C., Cziko, C., & Hurwitz, L. (1999). *Reading for understanding.* San Francisco: Jossey-Bass.

Sweet, A. P., & Guthrie, J. T. (1996). How children's motivations relate to literacy development and instruction. *Reading Teacher, 49,* 660–662.

Vallerand, R. J. (2000). Deci and Ryan's self-determination theory: A view from the hierarchical model of intrinsic and extrinsic motivation. *Psychological Inquiry, 11,* 312–318.

Wade, S. E., & Moje, E. B. (2000). The role of text in classroom learning. In M. L. Kamil, P. B. Mosenthal, P. D. Pearson, & R. Barr (Eds.), *Handbook of reading research* (Vol. 3, pp. 609–627). Mahwah, NJ: Erlbaum.

3

The Reading Comprehension Development and Instruction of English-Language Learners

GEORGIA EARNEST GARCÍA

Alejandro Goméz is 10 years old and in the fourth grade. He was born in El Salvador, speaks Spanish as his native (home) language, and immigrated to the United States with his family when he was 5 years old. Alejandro was enrolled in an early-exit bilingual education program from kindergarten through third grade, in which he received initial literacy instruction in Spanish along with English-as-a-second-language (ESL) instruction. By second grade Alejandro was receiving at least 50% of his classroom instruction in English, and by third grade 70% of his instruction was in English. At the end of third grade he was exited from the bilingual education program and placed in an all-English classroom. Although Alejandro still is not performing at grade level in English, he is orally proficient in English. He speaks Spanish at home, but rarely speaks it at school.

Tuan Bien is 10 years old, Vietnamese American, and in the fourth grade. He was born in the United States. In first, second, and third grade Tuan received 60 minutes of pull-out ESL instruction a day, in which oral English was emphasized, and spent the rest of the school day in all-English classrooms. During first and second grade he also received occasional help from Vietnamese tutors. Tuan no longer receives ESL instruction or tutoring in Vietnamese. He sounds fairly proficient in English, but is not performing at grade level in English. His parents report that he has lost much of his Vietnamese, making it difficult for them to communicate with him.

María Jiménez is 10 years old and in the fourth grade. She is Mexican American, born in the United States and speaks Spanish as her native language. She has been in a maintenance bilingual education program, in which she has received literacy instruction in Spanish along with ESL instruction, since first grade. Although María received a high percentage of instruction in Spanish in the first and second grades, in the fourth grade she is receiving 40% of her classroom instruction in Spanish and 60% of her classroom instruction in English. She will continue to receive these percentages of instruction in the two languages through elementary school. She currently is orally proficient and literate in both Spanish and English and is developing a high level of academic competence in English. She will be placed in all-English classrooms in middle school and high school.

Current estimates indicate that about 22% of school-age children in the United States live in homes in which a language other than English is spoken (Anstrom, 1996; Crawford, 1997). Spanish speakers are the largest language group, representing two-thirds of the second-language population. Some of the other language groups include speakers of Arabic, Cantonese, Hmong, Korean, Mandarin, Polish, Russian, and Vietnamese.

Although large numbers of second-language learners of English, currently known as English-language learners, do not receive any bilingual education or ESL instruction, federal law requires school personnel to address the second-language needs of English-language learners through appropriate instruction (Crawford, 1997). Like Alejandro Goméz and María Jiménez, some English-language learners at the elementary level are enrolled in bilingual education programs in which they receive instruction in their native language along with ESL instruction. Like Tuan Bien, others are enrolled in different types of ESL programs or placed in all-English classrooms with native English speakers. English-language learners at the middle school and high school levels may receive ESL instruction and/or native-language assistance from a bilingual aide or tutor or a bilingual teacher in a resource classroom. Many of them are taught in all-English classrooms.

A problem that confronts educational personnel who work with English-language learners in the United States is that research on the development and instruction of reading comprehension for school-age English-language learners is relatively limited (García, 2000). We know much more about the development and instruction of reading comprehension for monolingual (one-language) native English speakers than about such development and instruction for English-language learners. Moreover, as the opening vignettes imply, analyzing the reading comprehension performance of English-language learners is a complex endeavor because of the multiple program, instructional, language, cultural, and affective factors that may intersect and affect their English reading development.

In an attempt to guide U.S. educational personnel who work with school-age English-language learners from a range of language backgrounds and in a variety of instructional settings, this chapter draws from

U.S. and international research to highlight important findings and to raise instructional implications and questions. The chapter is divided into two sections. In the first section, the reading comprehension development of English-language learners is briefly compared with that of monolingual English speakers. Factors that uniquely characterize the reading comprehension development of English-language learners are emphasized. In the second section, instructional research related to the reading comprehension development of English-language learners in grades 3–12 is reviewed. Then, based on the research reviewed and the questions and instructional implications raised, the chapter concludes by listing several recommendations for improving the reading comprehension development and instruction of English-language learners.

THE READING COMPREHENSION DEVELOPMENT OF ENGLISH-LANGUAGE LEARNERS

Although English-language learners appear to use many of the same general reading processes or strategies as monolingual native English speakers to decode and comprehend English text, there are some key differences. In terms of similarities, both groups of students appear to make use of graphophonic (sound–symbol), lexical (vocabulary), semantic (meaning), syntactic (language structure), and background and textual knowledge (schemata) to decode and comprehend English text (Bernhardt, 2000; García & Bauer, in press). Jiménez, García, and Pearson (1996) reported that Spanish-speaking English-language learners and monolingual native English speakers in grades 6 and 7 who were strong readers in English also used similar types of cognitive strategies (e.g., questioning, rereading, and visualizing) to comprehend English text.

In terms of differences, several researchers have pointed out that because English-language learners are not native speakers of English and members of the dominant culture of the United States, they often encounter more unfamiliar English words and fewer familiar topics while reading in English than monolingual English speakers (García, 1991; Jimenez et al., 1996). In fact, García considered unfamiliar English vocabulary to be the major linguistic factor that adversely affected Spanish-speaking fifth and sixth graders' English reading test performance as compared with that of their native-English-speaking classmates. The Spanish-speaking students performed as well as the native-English-speakers on topics for which they had appropriate prior knowledge, but performed less well on those topics for which they did not have the appropriate prior knowledge. When differences in prior knowledge were statistically controlled, the two groups of students did not vary in their ability to successfully answer textually explicit and text-based inferential questions. In contrast, the Spanish-speaking students did significantly worse on the scriptally implicit questions, or questions that required them to use background knowledge. As compared with the low- and average-performing native-English-speakers, the low- and average-performing Spanish speakers did not know when they were supposed to rely on background knowledge to answer some of the test questions and instead attempted to answer them through a literal interpretation of the text.

The relationship between English-language learners' syntactic knowledge of English and their text comprehension is rather complex and may intersect with their vocabulary knowledge, background knowledge, and second-language oral proficiency. Based on a study in the Netherlands, Droop and Verhoeven (1998) reported that when Moroccan and Turkish students read culturally familiar expository passages in Dutch, they outperformed the Dutch students on passages that were linguistically simple and performed the same as the Dutch students on passages that were linguistically complex. In a review of adolescent and adult second-language literacy studies, Bernhardt (2000) noted that the syntactic complexity of a text did not always predict second-language readers' text comprehension.

Several researchers have found that English-language learners sometimes use strategies unique to their bilingual status to aid in their English reading (García, 1998; Jiménez et al., 1996). Four factors that may uniquely characterize the English reading comprehension of English-language learners are their native-language literacy development, use of cross-linguistic transfer strategies, oral English proficiency and second-language status, and bilingual status, or ability to use the native language to think about and respond to English text.

Native-Language Literacy

A number of researchers have reported that English-language learners already literate in their native language have an advantage over those students who must acquire literacy for the first time in English (Collier & Thomas, 1989; Crawford, 1997). Theoretically, when students are given an opportunity to develop literacy in a language that they already speak, they can avoid the cognitive confusion that may occur when they have to acquire literacy, for the first time, in a language that they do not speak or are in the process of acquiring. As these students acquire English, they can also continue to use their native language to learn about themselves and the world around them, thus avoiding delays in academic knowledge.

Another argument for supporting native-language literacy development for linguistic minorities in the United States is that it helps to bolster students' self-esteem, shows respect for their home language and culture, and can result in improved parent–school communication (Cummins, 1989; García, 2000). Given the historically low literacy performance of English-language learners in the United States, regardless of the program of instruction (Crawford, 1997), affective and motivational factors that may promote students' literacy development and academic achievement clearly must be taken into account when their reading comprehension development is considered.

Cummins's threshold and interdependence hypotheses (1981, 1989) are usually cited in support of native-language literacy development. Cummins claimed that students could transfer knowledge and strategies acquired in one language to a second language as long as they had developed cognitive proficiency in the first language and had been adequately exposed to the second language.

Collier and Thomas (1989) provide some evidence for the advantage of native-language literacy. They tracked the progress of immigrant children from advantaged families who entered U.S. schools at different ages. They found that students who entered U.S. schools at the ages of 8 and 9 and who had been schooled in their home countries for 2 to 3 years could approach grade level on standardized tests in English after 5–7 years of schooling in the United States. In comparison, students who entered U.S. schools at the ages of 5 and 6 needed 7–10 years of schooling in the United States before they could approach grade level. Collier and Thomas explained that the 8- and 9-year-olds were already literate in the native language, whereas the 5- and 6-year-olds were not.

According to Collier and Thomas (1989), immigrant students who entered U.S. schools at the middle school and high school levels also had difficulty in attaining grade-level performance even though they were literate in the native language. They explained that the cognitive demands of academic work in English at the middle school and high school levels were too high for many of these students to perform at grade level in less than 4–6 years of instruction in English. Their finding illustrates Cummins's (1981, 1989) argument that English-language learners can often develop basic interpersonal skills in 2–3 years of instruction in English, but need more time to develop the type of cognitive academic proficiency necessary to fully comprehend and learn from English text.

Cross-Linguistic Transfer

One reason that native-language literacy seems to help facilitate the English reading development and comprehension of English-language learners is cross-linguistic transfer, or bilingual students' ability to transfer knowledge and strategies acquired in one language to a second language. Theoretically, the ability to use what is already known in reading one language to approach another should mean that bilingual readers do not have to start over when they approach reading in another language. For example, there is some evidence that young English-language learners who have developed phonological awareness in their native language can transfer this awareness to reading in English, their second language, without formal instruction (Durgunoğlu, Nagy, & Hancin-Bhatt, 1993). Goldman and her colleagues (Goldman, Reyes, & Varnhagen, 1984) also found that Spanish-speaking fourth graders were able to transfer their knowledge of fables from their Spanish reading to their English reading without any formal instruction.

Unfortunately, cross-linguistic transfer does not seem to be automatic in all bilingual students. Jiménez et al. (1996) reported that sixth- and seventh-grade English-language learners who were not successful English readers thought that they had to keep their reading in Spanish and English separate or they would be confused. These students had a bottom-up view of reading that emphasized decoding and accurate English pronunciation. In contrast, the successful English-language learners had a unitary view of reading across Spanish and English that focused on comprehension, as illustrated in the following quote by Alberto, one of the students in the study:

> "There aren't really any differences [between reading in English and Spanish], I mean they're both based on the same thing, how you understand it, how you read it, and how you take it and how you evaluate it and all that." (Jiménez et al., 1996, p. 10.)

Several of the successful English readers used knowledge acquired while reading in one language to make hypotheses and inferences while reading in the other language. In addition, they reported that they knew that they could use similar types of high-level metacognitive (e.g., evaluating) and cognitive strategies (e.g., questioning, rereading) to monitor and repair comprehension in the two languages. Although both the successful and less successful English readers encountered unfamiliar English vocabulary, the successful English readers employed a multistrategic approach to figure out the vocabulary meanings (by using context, invoking prior knowledge, restating, and making inferences), which also led to enhanced comprehension, whereas the less successful readers did not. Jiménez et al. (1996) wondered to what extent the differences in the less-successful and successful bilingual readers' views of reading in the two languages and their approaches to reading were due to the type of instruction the students had received.

García (1998) warned that we should examine the types of strategies that students transfer before we automatically equate cross-linguistic transfer with positive features of bilingual reading. In a qualitative think-aloud study of fourth graders who had scored high on a Spanish reading test, she reported that three of the four students varied their use of cognitive strategies while reading in English or Spanish according to the difficulty and genre of the text (expository versus narrative). Because they used similar types of strategies by genre across the two languages, she viewed her findings as indicative of cross-linguistic transfer. However, one of the four students used low-level strategies (e.g., restating, decoding, and inaccurate inferencing) across both languages, regardless of genre or text difficulty.

Several researchers have questioned whether bilingual students' ability to use some cross-linguistic strategies to comprehend text might be developmental or if their use of strategies could be improved through explicit instruction (García, 1998; Nagy et al., 1993). For example, one strategy that Spanish-speaking students can use to figure out unknown English vocabulary is cognate knowledge. Cognates are words in two languages that have ancestral roots and that are similar in form and meaning (e.g., *climate* and *clima* are cognates in English and Spanish). Nagy et al. (1993) reported that after they controlled for Spanish-speaking fourth-, fifth-, and sixth-graders' English vocabulary knowledge, the students' knowledge of specific Spanish cognates and recognition of the cognate relationships significantly predicted their comprehension of unknown English cognates while reading in English, indicating that the students had made use of Spanish cognates to figure out the unfamiliar English words. However, the fourth graders made significantly less use of cognates as compared with the fifth and sixth graders, and all of the students underutilized their knowledge of Spanish cognate vocabulary.

Oral English Proficiency and Second-Language Status

How much oral English is necessary before English-language learners can optimally benefit from literacy instruction in English is a question that still is being investigated (García, 2000). In a review of the literature on bilingual reading, García noted that findings for young bilingual students (kindergarten through grade 2) from several languages and from a number of international settings showed that measures of native-language reading were much stronger predictors of their second-language reading than measures of their second-language oral proficiency. In contrast, measures of second-language oral proficiency were stronger predictors of older bilingual students' (grades 3–6) performance on second-language reading measures than their performance on reading measures in the native language. It may be that there is a much better match between the types of information assessed on the oral proficiency and reading measures for older students (e.g., vocabulary, syntax, decontextualized language) than there is for younger students.

Regardless of these findings, students' level of oral English proficiency certainly affects their English reading comprehension development and has implications for their English reading instruction. For example, an assumption that characterizes beginning reading instruction for monolingual English speakers is that the words that they are learning to decode are already in their oral vocabulary. Once they decode a word, they should recognize it, which helps them to understand the relationship between decoding and meaning. In contrast, because of their second-language status, English-language learners often do not know the meanings of all of the words they can decode in English (García & Bauer, in press). To prevent creating a situation in which English-language learners become excellent decoders but have difficulty with comprehension, teachers should help students decode words they already know in English as well as teach them the meanings of new English words as they decode them.

Both beginning and advanced English-language learners may make mistakes while orally reading in English because of differences in pronunciation between the native language and English (García, 2002 May). It is often not easy to determine whether the student is merely mispronouncing a word, having difficulty decoding it, or does not recognize the meaning of the word. In the following example from García's ongoing work (2002 May), Marta, a Spanish-speaking fourth grader who was reading above grade level in Spanish and English, reports in a think-aloud that she can understand some words in English that she has difficulty decoding: "The atmosphere of Venus is another sci, science, sickness, significant. I know that word but I can't say it. I can't pronounce it."

Fluent oral reading in English is viewed as a characteristic of excellent beginning reading for native-English speakers, but because of the pronunciation problems that English-language learners sometimes experience, we do not know whether this type of fluency is also a necessary condition for them. If students are able to read fluently in their native language, then their fluency in English may automatically improve as they become more English proficient.

In contrast, Jiménez (1997) reported that middle school Spanish-speaking students who had received reading instruction only in English and who were considered poor readers did improve their English reading when their English reading instruction emphasized the oral and rapid rereading of culturally familiar text until they read more fluently. Understanding the source of the oral reading errors that English-language learners make while reading in English may help teachers to determine whether these students need help with fluency.

Bilingual Status

Several researchers have reported that English-language learners who speak or who are in the process of acquiring two languages can sometimes use strategies unique to their bilingual status to reveal or enhance their comprehension (García, 1991, 1998; Jiménez et al., 1996). For example, bilingual students sometimes code mix (use words from one language while speaking or writing in the other), code switch (alternate languages at sentence boundaries), and use one language to explain or figure out what they have read in another (García, 1998; Jiménez et al., 1996). In the following example from García's ongoing work (2002 May), Marisa, a fourth-grade Spanish-speaking student, shows how she sometimes uses Spanish to think about the text that she is reading in English. She also demonstrates that she can use code mixing to figure out the meaning of the English word "blanket" (code mixing is underlined):

> *Text*: These clouds are a part of the planet's blanket of air, its atmosphere.
> *Marisa*: Las nubes eran una parte especial del planeta, cobija, blanket, cobija de aire, de atmosphere. [The clouds were a special part of the planet, blanket, blanket, blanket of air, of atmosphere.]

García (1998) also found that when fourth-grade Spanish-speaking students successfully used paraphrased translating (put what they read in one language into their own words in the other language) in text think-alouds, they actually demonstrated that they had understood the text. A number of researchers have noted that bilingual students often provide more evidence of English text comprehension when they are allowed to use their native language to discuss or write about what they have read in English (García, 1991, 1998; Goldman et al., 1984; Jiménez et al., 1996).

INSTRUCTIONAL RESEARCH ON THE READING COMPREHENSION OF ENGLISH-LANGUAGE LEARNERS

Although increasing numbers of educational researchers have begun to explore how to improve the English reading comprehension of school-age English-language learners, much more needs to be investigated. In this section, the type of reading comprehension instruction that English-language learners often receive is described first. Next, instructional practices and innovations that have focused specifically on improving aspects of English-language learners' reading comprehension are discussed. Finally, how English-language learners fare in different types of bilingual education and ESL programs is reviewed.

Description of Instruction

It is difficult to know how well English-language learners would do in school if they were given high-quality literacy instruction, because such instruction occurs so infrequently. Several researchers have reported that the type of reading instruction that English-language learners receive at the elementary school level, regardless of the language of instruction or instructional program, tends to be passive, teacher directed, whole class, and oriented toward low-level skills (García, 2000; Moss & Puma, 1995; Padrón, 1994). Padrón conducted a comparison of the type of reading instruction offered to fifth and sixth graders in 15 schools in an urban school district. She found that the type of instruction that the Hispanic students received (50% of whom were English-language learners) at 8 of the schools did not differ from that received by students from diverse populations at the other 7 schools. The students basically were taught in whole-class settings and did not spend very much time reading, because their reading instruction consisted primarily of watching or listening to their teachers read.

One reason that so many English-language learners may not receive high-quality reading instruction is that many of them are enrolled in underfunded districts and often have teachers who are not certified (Moss & Puma, 1995). In an evaluation of Title I services for English-language learners in grades 1 and 3, Moss and Puma reported that more than 50% of the students who were supposed to be taught literacy in Spanish had teachers who were not proficient in Spanish.

Instructional Practices and Innovations

Several researchers have tested or evaluated the efficacy of instructional reading practices in English derived from instructional reading research with monolingual native-English speakers. Others have adapted programs that were originally developed for native-English speakers. A few have developed instructional programs/practices specifically for English-language learners.

For example, literature-based practices in English seem to work when they have been specifically adapted for English-language learners (Brock, McVee, Shojgreen-Downer, & Dueñas, 1998; Elley, 1991) or when they are based on what is known about bilingual learners (Moll, Sáez, & Dworin, 2001). Elley (1991) reported findings from two experiments in the South Pacific and Southeast Asia with 8- and 10-year-olds who were already literate in their native language but in the first year of English transition or instruction. He found that students who received ESL instruction that provided them with comprehensible instruction and reading instruction based on the influx of a large number of high-interest storybooks in English, termed a book flood, along with independent book choice and silent reading, significantly outperformed two other groups of students on academic measures in English. The other students received either structured reading in English along with systematic oral ESL instruction or controlled English reading along with audiolingual ESL instruction.

Brock and her colleagues (Brock et al., 1998) used a case study of a third-grade beginning English-language learner from Mexico to point out the difficulties that the student encountered in making sense of a monolingual English-speaking teacher's Book Club instruction in English. In the Book Club approach, the teacher modeled comprehension strategies and had the students complete written comprehension activities related to the book read (e.g., make predictions, create a character map), do personal and critical writing in response to book-related prompts, and participate in small- and whole-group discussions about the book. Although the student had support from other Spanish speakers in the class, most of her written work consisted of either literal interpretations of the book or summaries that listed story events. The authors concluded that the student did not seem to understand the teacher's instructional purpose and therefore did not benefit from the instruction as anticipated.

In contrast to the findings of Brock et al. (1998), Moll and his colleagues (Moll et al., 2001) presented a case study of a third-grade English-language learner who did appear to benefit from literature-based practices that focused on themes, learning centers, and active or inquiry-based learning. In this instance, the teacher created an instructional setting in which she and the students used both Spanish, the girl's native language, and English to mediate learning and to complete literacy tasks.

Other researchers have found that English-language learners seem to benefit from instruction that focuses on metacognitive and cognitive strategies. For example, Padrón (1992) found that third-, fourth-, and fifth-grade Spanish speakers reported using more sophisticated reading strategies and fewer weaker strategies while reading in English after receiving either reciprocal teaching or question-answer-relationship instruction for a month (30 minutes twice a week). Muñiz-Swicegood (1994) provided third-grade Spanish-speaking students in the United States with metacognitive strategy instruction in Spanish on how to use self-generating questions (90 minutes of daily instruction for 6 weeks). She found that the students' standardized test scores in both Spanish and English increased, suggesting that students had applied what they had learned in Spanish reading to their English reading without cognitive strategy instruction in English.

Slavin and his colleagues have adapted Success for All, a multifaceted elementary school reform effort, for English-language learners enrolled in ESL instruction and for Spanish-speaking students enrolled in transitional bilingual education settings, naming the latter Éxito Para Todos (Slavin & Madden, 1999). Adaptations that have commonly occurred in the ESL settings include providing ESL manuals and ESL training for all the teachers at the school, as well as assigning ESL teachers to serve as reading teachers and tutors. In Éxito Para Todos, Spanish-speaking bilingual education teachers are the reading instructors and tutors for the Spanish literacy instruction. For the most part, the third-grade scores for English-language learners enrolled in the ESL or bilingual versions of Success for All, as compared with those of matched students in control groups in the same district, were significantly higher on the English and/or Spanish version of the Woodcock Passage Comprehension subtest. In fourth and fifth grades, the ESL students in Success for All continued to outperform the control students on the Woodcock Passage Comprehenson subtest, with all of them performing at or above grade level. Unfortunately, we do not know how these students would perform on other reading comprehension measures. As Slavin and Madden (1999) point out, qualitative analysis, along with componential analysis, would also help us to understand more about the increase in student performance. For example, it would be helpful to know whether the ESL students' increase in performance was because of their teachers' ESL training and use of ESL techniques or because of specific aspects of the Success for All program.

Saunders and Goldenberg (1999) describe an instructional literacy program they developed specifically for Spanish-speaking students in grades K–5 who are enrolled in a transitional bilingual education program in grades K–3. A unique feature of their program is the continued ESL support that is provided to students in the fourth and fifth grades who are no longer enrolled in the transitional bilingual education program. Although specific components of the elementary literacy program vary according to grade level, a constant throughout the program is the study of literature through the Experience–Text–Relationship (ETR) approach (Mason & Au, 1986). In this approach, the teacher helps students to make connections between an assigned text, one or more themes, and students' personal experiences. At the fourth- and fifth-grade levels, Saunders and Goldenberg's literacy program includes nine components: reading comprehension strategy instruction; teacher read-alouds; writing projects; assigned independent reading; weekly dictation exercises; lessons on writing conventions; pleasure reading; literature logs, in which students write in response to prompts about a book being studied; and instructional conversations, in which students, in small groups guided by the teacher, reflect on and analyze the book being studied, its theme, and their personal reactions to the book.

Saunders and Goldenberg (1999) were particularly interested in evaluating the impact of the literature logs and instructional conversations on students' English reading comprehension. In an experiment with fourth and fifth graders in the transitional classes, they compared the pre- and post-story comprehension of four groups of students who were randomly assigned to participate in four types of instruction over a period of 10–15 days: literature logs, instructional conversations, combined literature logs and instructional conversations, and a control group. On the factual and interpretive questions, the students in the instructional conversation group and in the combined literature log and instructional conversation group significantly outperformed the other two groups, with the latter group doing slightly better than the former group. However, when the students' understanding of a story's theme was assessed through essay writing, then the students' performance varied according to their English proficiency. The fluent English speakers in all three groups outperformed the control group, and the limited-English-proficient students in the combined literature log and instructional conversation group outperformed the limited-English-proficient students in the other three groups.

Jiménez (1997) conducted a formative experiment with five low-literacy seventh-grade Latina/o students who were receiving reading instruction in English that combined fluency and strategy instruction with the use of culturally relevant text. Drawing on what he had learned from his previous work (Jiménez et al., 1996) and based on observations of the students' reading instruction and performance, he developed eight cognitive strategy lessons, which he taught the students over a 2-week period. In addition to working on students' reading fluency and word recognition skills in English, he taught the students how to figure out unknown vocabulary, ask questions, make inferences, search for cognates, and use knowledge acquired in one language to approach the other. One of his goals was to get the students to talk about and reflect on what they were reading. He found that using culturally relevant text and encouraging the students to discuss the text in both languages resulted in more extended discourse, increased engagement, and improved inferences.

Although vocabulary is a major challenge for English-language learners, only a few researchers have investigated how to improve students' reading vocabulary. Klingner and Vaughn (2000) investigated how well a fifth-grade classroom of 37 students (35 of whom were Spanish-English bilingual but of varying English proficiency) and their classroom teacher were able to use Collaborative Strategic Reading to improve their science reading vocabulary. Collaborative Strategic Reading is a social-interaction instructional approach that integrates cooperative learning with reading comprehension strategy instruction and involves teacher modeling, role-playing, and think-alouds, as well as peer assistance to improve students' use of four comprehension strategies and construction of knowledge while reading English text. The four comprehension strategies include how to preview text, identify difficult concepts and words in a passage as well as figure out repair strategies, restate the most important idea in a section or paragraph, and summarize what was learned as well as generate teacher-like test questions. Students' knowledge of English reading vocabulary was assessed on the same researcher-made pre- and posttest, which asked students to write definitions for words included in the two science chapters they read. Over the 1-month period during which the students participated in Collaborative Strategic Reading, analysis of their small-group interactions demonstrated that they predominantly focused on figuring out unknown English vocabulary. Although the paired t-tests showed vocabulary gains for all of the students, the limited-English-proficient students did not make as many gains as the other students. The authors concluded that these students might not have known enough English to have been able to participate at the level needed and might have benefited from smaller groups and more teacher attention.

In a second study, Neuman and Koskinen (1992) compared how well four groups of seventh- and eighth-grade bilingual students gained scientific reading vocabulary in English as a result of incidental exposure. The students were assigned to one of four groups: to watch a captioned science television show, watch the same television show but without captions, read science material that was presented in the show, or read the material in a science textbook (the control group). They found that students who saw the captioned television show outperformed the other three groups on word knowledge measures. On degree of word learning measures, the students in the captioned television group outperformed the two reading groups but did not always outperform the group that simply watched the television show. Overall, the authors concluded that viewing captioned television helped to enhance the students' incidental vocabulary acquisition by providing them with comprehensible input. However, as in Klingner and Vaughn's (2000) finding, those students who were the most proficient in English had the highest vocabulary scores. Neuman and Koskinen questioned whether there might be a level of English proficiency that students needed before they could optimally benefit from television viewing with or without the captions.

Content-based ESL instruction—the learning of English through the use of ESL techniques to shelter (support) students' learning of a content domain such as science or social studies—is a much heralded approach for instructing English-language learners, especially for those in middle school and high school. Although not all content-based ESL approaches focus on Chamot and O'Malley's (1996) Cognitive Academic Language Learning Approach (CALLA), many of them draw on the rationale provided by Chamot and O'Malley for content-based ESL instruction. According to these authors, it makes more sense to teach students ESL relevant to a content domain because language is involved in all learning. The use of ESL techniques to teach content enables ESL students to acquire not only the domain knowledge but also the necessary vocabulary and linguistic structures relevant to the domain. In the process, they learn how to negotiate meaning in an authentic setting, thereby improving their English. The specific approach that Chamot and O'Malley propose for intermediate and advanced English-language learners at the upper primary, middle school, and high school levels explicitly teaches students how to use three types of strategies—metacognitive, cognitive, and social strategies (e.g., requesting clarifications)—to comprehend a specific content domain: mathematics, social sciences, science, or literature.

Although CALLA appears promising, it has rarely been evaluated with students at the appropriate grade and English proficiency levels. Waxman and his colleagues (Waxman, Walker de Felix, Martínez, Knight, & Padrón, 1994) compared how well third-, fourth-, and fifth-grade English-language learners performed on a standardized reading test in English after they gave training to the students' teachers in one of the following: CALLA, how to use time effectively, a combined focus on CALLA and the effective use of time. They found that students in the combined group did worst and those in the effective-use-of-time group did best, although students in the CALLA group also outperformed students in the combined group and a control group that did not receive any specialized ESL instruction. They thought that they might have tried to cover too many topics in the CALLA teacher training session, and that it might not have been appropriate to provide the English-language learners with CALLA instruction without a native-language literacy base. They also did not test how well students who were taught with CALLA performed in a particular content area.

Features of Effective Bilingual Education and ESL Programs

Based on a longitudinal evaluation of ESL and bilingual education programs, Thomas and Collier (1996) identified the type of instruction that English-language learners received who had reached grade level in English after 4–5 years of schooling and who had generally continued their progress in academic classes at the high school level. Their instruction was characterized by "cognitively complex academic instruction" in the native language for as long as possible (e.g., 40% of instruction in grades 4–6) and in English; active, inquiry-based learning in both languages; an additive bilingual environment, in which bilingualism was viewed positively; and a transformative school climate, in which relations between minority and majority students were balanced so that a safe and positive school climate was provided for all learners (p. 1).

Thomas and Collier (1996) also identified the two types of programs that most often exemplified these features: two-way bilingual education (sometimes called dual immersion) and maintenance bilingual education (sometimes called late-exit bilingual education), the type of program in which María Jiménez (in the third of the opening vignettes) was enrolled. In two-way bilingual education programs, English-language learners from the same language group (often Spanish) and native-English speakers are enrolled in the same classrooms throughout elementary school. Students receive instruction in the native language and English, with second-language techniques being used to shelter instruction for each of the languages. Two-way bilingual education programs vary in the amount of literacy instruction initially provided in the native language. For example, in first grade, some programs provide 90% of instruction in the native language and 10% of instruction in English, eventually reaching a 50–50 split at about third or fourth grade, whereas others provide 50% of instruction in both languages from the outset.

Thomas and Collier (1996) reported that students who entered U.S. schools at the secondary level had the best opportunity for success when they received content-based ESL instruction. Characteristics of effective instruction included emphases on higher-order thinking skills, students' prior knowledge, cooperative groups, respect for students' native languages and cultures, inquiry and discovery-based learning, and multiple assessments.

CONCLUSIONS: INSTRUCTIONAL RECOMMENDATIONS

Although there still is much more we need to know about improving the reading comprehension of English-language learners, several instructional recommendations may be drawn from a consideration of the research reviewed. The following list of recommendations is ordered so that those applicable to all three settings (native language, ESL, and all-English) are presented first, followed by recommendations specific to the native language and ESL/all-English settings.

• We need to see how well English-language learners would do if they were given high-quality reading comprehension instruction in all three settings, along with extensive opportunities to read and use narrative and informational text for pleasure, to further their knowledge, and to pursue specific academic domains.

• Teachers need to open up their instruction (e.g., through individual conferences or tutorials, monitoring of small groups, use of think-alouds, and/or instructional conversations) so that they know how English-language learners approach and interpret text. They need to know whether students are effective at integrating background knowledge with textual knowledge, making appropriate inferences, figuring out unknown vocabulary, and monitoring and repairing their comprehension.

• Several researchers have reported that small-group work and inquiry-based learning provide English-language learners with the support and encouragement they need to actively engage in their own construction and interpretation of text and knowledge. These techniques appear to work best when students are given structured and purposeful opportunities to discuss and share how they are extracting and constructing meaning from text. Placing students from varied language proficiency levels in the same groups may be helpful.

• To offset the tendency of some English-language learners to over-rely on bottom-up processes (e.g., decoding and literal interpretation of the text), English-language learners should be given ample opportunities to read and discuss text for which they have the appropriate prior knowledge and text for which they do not. Teachers may have to model and guide students in using an interactive approach, in which English-language learners are shown how to use both top-down and bottom-up strategies, while reading familiar and unfamiliar text.

• Explicit strategy instruction (such as reciprocal teaching, question–answer relationships, self-generating questions, figuring out unknown vocabulary) that involves teacher and student modeling, along with guided and independent practice at the group and individual levels seems promising.

• Explicit instruction on differences in language and rhetorical conventions that characterize the native language and English may be beneficial.

• It is important to remember that English-language learners, regardless of the instructional setting, have been exposed to two languages and two cultures across the media (television), home, community, and school. Acknowledging their bilingualism and biculturalism by allowing them to use both languages to make sense of text and to discuss their reactions to English text in their native language, or through code mixing and code switching, often leads to increased engagement and enhanced demonstration of comprehension. Encouraging the students to make use of information they have learned in one setting to comprehend text in another also may help them to develop a unified view of reading across their languages.

• Coordinating instruction across native language, ESL, and all-English settings is very important. When new ideas, strategies, or activities are presented first in the native language, it should be much easier for teachers in the other settings to expand and build on the information gained. Instead of having to learn new concepts or strategies in English, students should be able to acquire and apply English labels for concepts or strategies already learned in the native language setting.

• Thematic instruction across the various settings is recommended because it enables students to encounter the same vocabulary and background knowledge in multiple contexts, increasing their opportunity to acquire reading vocabulary and allowing them to make more appropriate predictions and inferences.

• One reason that English-language learners who are enrolled in maintenance or dual-language programs may do better academically than students in the other programs is that the former students are provided with considerably more time to interact with academically challenging texts in the native language at higher grade levels. Therefore, it seems important to provide English-language learners in bilingual education programs with high-quality comprehension instruction and opportunities to read and use narrative and informational texts that are academically challenging in the native language.

• It is quite likely that if students know that they can transfer comprehension strategies from one language to the other, they will be able to transfer metacognitive and cognitive strategies that they have acquired while reading in their native language to their English reading. Several researchers recommend that teachers in the native language setting provide students with explicit strategy instruction and show them how to transfer information and strategies from one language to the other. At the fourth- or third-grade level, explicit instruction on how to use cognates in languages that have a common history with English (such as Spanish) should be helpful.

• When students are not very proficient in English, providing them with English literacy instruction through the use of ESL techniques should help to make their instruction more comprehensible (e.g., speaking slowly, clearly enunciating, using gestures, and providing students with multiple ways to understand what is being said or read through hands-on experiences and by accompanying oral language with illustrations, videos, dramatizations, and print).

• In assessing English-language learners' oral reading, it is important to separate their oral reading performance in English from their reading comprehension. If students skip over words or do not pronounce them correctly, assessing whether they understand the words may help to determine whether they are having difficulty reading.

• Because unknown English vocabulary is a major challenge faced by English-language learners, helping them to increase their knowledge of English reading vocabulary should aid their comprehension.

Finally, in working with English-language learners, it is important to remember that low reading test scores in English may be due to the students' limited English proficiency and not to any real literacy or cognitive processing difficulties. The instructional needs of English-language learners may be quite different from those of native-English speakers who are poor readers or who have serious reading difficulties. The progress of English-language learners may vary according to their native-language literacy and cognitive development; their opportunities to acquire not just oral, but also academic, competency in English; and the type of reading instruction they have received. When teachers shape and modify their reading comprehension instruction based on what is currently known about the reading development and instruction of English-language learners, they usually discover that working with English-language learners is very rewarding.

REFERENCES

Anstrom, K. (1996). Defining the limited-English-proficient population. *Directions in Language and Education, 1*(9) (summer). Washington, DC: National Clearinghouse for Bilingual Education.

Bernhardt, E. B. (2000). Second-language reading as a case study of reading scholarship in the 20th century. In M. L. Kamil, P. B. Mosenthal, P. D. Pearson, & R. Barr (Eds.), *Handbook of reading research* (Vol. 3, pp. 791–811). Mahwah, NJ: Erlbaum.

Brock, C. H., McVee, M. B., Shojgreen-Downer, A. M., & Dueñas, L. F. (1998). No habla íngles: Exploring a bilingual child's literacy learning opportunities in a predominantly English-speaking classroom. *Bilingual Research Journal, 22*(2, 3, & 4), 175–200.

Chamot, A. U., & O'Malley, M. (1996). The cognitive academic language learning approach: A model for linguistically diverse classrooms. *Elementary School Journal, 96* (3), 259–274.

Collier, V. P., & Thomas, W. P. (1989). How quickly can immigrants become proficient in school English? *Journal of Educational Issues of Language Minority Students, 16*, 187–212.

Crawford, J. (1997). *Best evidence: Research foundations of the Bilingual Education Act.* Washington, DC: National Clearinghouse for Bilingual Education.

Cummins, J. (1981). The role of primary language development in promoting educational success for language minority students. In California Sate Department of Education (Ed.), *Schooling and language minority students: A theoretical framework.* Los Angeles: Evaluation, Dissemination and Assessment Center, California State University.

Cummins, J. (1989). *Empowering minority students.* Sacramento, CA: California Association for Bilingual Education.

Droop, M., & Verhoeven, L. (1998). Background knowledge, linguistic complexity, and second-language reading comprehension. *Journal of Literacy Research, 30*, 253–271.

Durgunoğlu, A., Nagy, W. E., & Hancin-Bhatt, B. J. (1993). Cross-language transfer of phonological awareness. *Journal of Educational Psychology, 85*, 453–465.

Elley, W. B. (1991). Acquiring literacy in a second language: The effect of book-based programs. *Language Learning, 41*, 373–411.

García, G. E. (1991). Factors influencing the English reading test performance of Spanish-speaking Hispanic children. *Reading Research Quarterly, 26*, 371–392.

García, G. E. (1998). Mexican-American bilingual students' metacognitive reading strategies: What's transferred, unique, problematic? *National Reading Conference Yearbook, 47,* 253–263.

García, G. E. (2000). Bilingual children's reading. In M. L. Kamil, P. B. Mosenthal, P. D. Pearson, & R. Barr (Eds.), *Handbook of reading research* (Vol. 3, pp. 813–834). Mahwah, NJ: Erlbaum.

García, G. E. (2002, May). *Issues surrounding cross-linguistic transfer in bilingual students' reading: A study of Mexican-American fourth graders.* Featured speech presented at the Research Conference, International Reading Association, San Francisco, CA.

García, G. E., & Bauer, E. B (in press). The selection and use of English text with English language learners. In J. Hoffman & D. Schallert (Eds.), *Texts in primary classrooms.* Mahwah, NJ: Erlbaum.

Goldman, S. R., Reyes, M., & Varnhagen, C. K. (1984). Understanding fables in first and second languages. *NABE Journal, 8,* 835–866.

Jiménez, R. T. (1997). The strategic reading abilities and potential of five low-literacy Latina/o readers in middle school. *Reading Research Quarterly, 32,* 224–243.

Jiménez, R. T., García, G. E., & Pearson, P. D. (1996). The reading strategies of bilingual Latina/o students who are successful English readers: Opportunities and obstacles. *Reading Research Quarterly, 31,* 90–112.

Klingner, J. K., & Vaughn, S. (2000). The helping behaviors of fifth graders while using collaborative strategic reading during ESL content classes. *TESOL Quarterly, 34*(1), 69–98.

Mason, J. M., & Au, K. H. (1986). *Reading instruction for today.* Glenview, IL: Scott Foresman.

Moll, L. C., Sáez, R., & Dworin, J. (2001). Exploring biliteracy: Two student case examples of writing as social practice. *Elementary School Journal, 101*(4), 435–449.

Moss, M., & Puma, M. (1995). *Prospects: The congressionally mandated study of educational growth and opportunity: First year report on language minority and limited English proficient students.* Washington, DC: U.S. Department of Education.

Muñiz-Swicegood, M. (1994). The effects of metacognitive reading strategy training on the reading performance and fluent reading analysis strategies of third grade bilingual students. *Bilingual Research Journal, 18,* 83–97.

Nagy, W. E., García, G. E., Durgunoğlu, A., & Hancin, B. (1993). Spanish-English bilingual children's use and recognition of cognates in English reading. *Journal of Reading Behavior, 25*(3), 241–259.

Neuman, S. B., & Koskinen, P. (1992). Captioned television as comprehensible input: Effects of incidental word learning from context for language minority students. *Reading Research Quarterly, 16,* 35–52.

Padrón, Y. (1992). The effect of strategy instruction on bilingual students' cognitive strategy use in reading. *Bilingual Research Journal, 16,* 35-52.

Padrón, Y. (1994). Comparing reading instruction in Hispanic/limited English-proficient schools and other inner-city schools. *Bilingual Research Journal, 18,* 49–66.

Saunders, W. M., & Goldenberg, C. (1999). Effects of instructional conversations and literature logs on limited- and fluent-English proficient students' story comprehension and thematic understanding. *Elementary School Journal, 99*(4), 277–301.

Slavin, R. E., & Madden, N. (1999). Effects of bilingual and English as a second language adaptations of Success for All on the reading achievement of students acquiring English. *Journal of Education for Students Placed At Risk, 4*(4), 393–416.

Thomas, W. P., & Collier, V. (1996). Language-minority student achievement and program effectiveness. *NABE News*, 33–35.

Waxman, H. C., Walker de Felix, J., Martínez, A., Knight, S. L., & Padrón, Y. (1994). Effects of implementing classroom instructional models on English-language learners' cognitive and affective outcomes. *Bilingual Research Journal, 18*(3 & 4), 1–22.

USEFUL WEBSITES

www.ncela.gwu.edu   National Clearinghouse for English Language Acquisition and Language Instruction Educational Programs
www.cal.org   Center for Applied Linguistics
www.tesol.edu   Teaching English as a Second Language

4

Individual Differences as Sources of Variability in Reading Comprehension in Elementary School Children

FRANK R. VELLUTINO

Reading comprehension may be simply defined as the ability to obtain meaning from written text for some purpose. It is a complex process that depends on adequate development of two component processes: word recognition and language comprehension. Word recognition is the process whereby the individual visually recognizes a particular array of letters as a familiar word and retrieves the name and meaning of that word from memory. Language comprehension is the process whereby the individual is able to understand and relate the meanings of words and sentences encountered in spoken and written text, and combine them in ways that allow understanding of the broader concepts and ideas represented by those words and sentences.

Individual differences in knowledge, skills, and abilities that underlie word recognition and language comprehension, along with individual differences in dispositions such as the reader's motivation, goals, and purposes, are all important sources of variability in reading comprehension. Such factors interact in complicated ways, both with each other and with the text the reader engages, as determinants of comprehension. They are also influenced by related factors such as home and family background, educational history, peer influences, classroom culture, and socioeconomic status, as well as cultural and subcultural factors. These multiple and interacting influences ultimately define inter-and intra-individual differences in a person's ability to acquire skill in reading—that is, strengths and weaknesses that differentiate individuals as well as strengths and weaknesses within the same individual, any or all of which may be usefully considered in educational and remedial planning.

In this chapter, I discuss the individual differences in knowledge, skills, and abilities underlying word recognition and language comprehension processes as determinants of variability in reading comprehension in elementary school readers. I first discuss variables that may be sources of interindividual differences in the acquisition of fluency in word recognition and, thereafter, discuss variables that may be sources of interindividual differences in language comprehension. I then discuss interindividual differences that contribute to variability in acquiring reading competencies and close with some practical suggestions as to how teachers can use the knowledge we have gained about the sources of variability in reading comprehension to develop effective instructional programs.

INTERINDIVIDUAL DIFFERENCES IN SKILLS AND ABILITIES UNDERLYING WORD RECOGNITION

In order to comprehend written text, a child must be able to identify the words contained in the text with enough fluency (accuracy and speed) to allow processing of word and sentence meanings within the short amount of time this information is available in memory. In fact, we know from research done over the past two decades or so that fluency in word recognition is a prerequisite for adequate reading comprehension. We also know that language comprehension processes and higher-level cognitive processes affecting language comprehension (e.g., application of world knowledge or domain-specific knowledge, reasoning, etc.) do not become fully operative in text comprehension until the child has acquired such fluency (Adams, 1990; Hoover & Gough, 1990; Perfetti, 1985; Stanovich, 1991; Sticht & James, 1984; Vellutino, Scanlon, Small, & Tanzman, 1991). This is because the meanings of the words and sentences that contribute to the broader meanings contained in written text can be held in memory for no more than a few seconds to a few minutes. As a consequence, a child whose word recognition skills are inaccurate and/or labored will lose or have limited access to meaningful ideas in the text, and comprehension will suffer. Consider, for example, the following excerpt from a story about a boy named Jeff who owned a black dog named Sam:

> Jeff had a black dog.
> The dog's name was Sam.
> Sam liked to play with Jeff's hat.
> One day Sam saw a big fat cat.
> Jeff said, "Sam can catch that cat."
> Sam tried to catch the cat, but it got away.

The research to date has shown that a child who has difficulty identifying key words such as "dog," "cat," "play," "saw," or "catch" will, no doubt, have difficulty identifying the central characters and/or central theme of this segment of the story. And even if the same child manages, with considerable effort, to identify all or most of the words in this excerpt, the time taken to do so will likely impede his or her ability to combine information about the actions and events contained in this segment of the story with information about the actions and events contained in previous segments, given natural memory constraints. As a result, comprehension of the story as a whole will be less than perfect.

Finally, we know that children who have poor word recognition skills tend to perform less well than children who have good word recognition skills on measures of reading comprehension (Perfetti, 1985; Stanovich, 1991; Vellutino et al., 1996; Vellutino & Scanlon, 2002). And because long-standing reading difficulties inevitably lead to deficiencies in higher-level comprehension skills and content knowledge, which, themselves, depend on reading proficiency (Stanovich, 1986; Vellutino, Scanlon, & Spearing, 1995), comprehension problems will be compounded in children who have difficulty acquiring fluency in word recognition.

It seems reasonable to conclude from these findings that reader differences in the acquisition of fluent word recognition skills are the primary and most common source of variability in reading comprehension in elementary school children. This conclusion is given additional support by research showing that tests evaluating word recognition and related skills such as spelling and letter–sound decoding predict performance on reading comprehension tests more reliably in beginning readers than in more advanced readers (Hoover & Gough, 1990; Vellutino et al., 1991). In contrast, tests evaluating language comprehension skills such as vocabulary and syntactic knowledge predict performance on reading comprehension tests more reliably in advanced readers than in beginning readers. A similar pattern of results has been observed in comparisons of skilled and less-skilled adult readers (Sticht & James, 1984).

Components of Word Recognition

Print Awareness and Print Concepts

There are several types of knowledge beginning readers must acquire in order to learn to read. First, they must have a firm grasp of the nature and purpose of print, along with a reasonably good understanding of the unique properties of the orthography (writing system) they are learning about—what are often called print awareness and print concepts (Clay, 1985; Morris, 1993). For example, in order to learn to read written English, children must come to understand that printed words are symbols for words in spoken language; that a series of printed words, together, represent thoughts and ideas in spoken language; that printed words are separated by spaces; that printed words are sequenced from left to right; that they are composed of letters; that letters have names that identify them and that they represent individual speech sounds (phonemes) in spoken language. Print awareness and knowledge of print concepts are the foundation of reading acquisition. Because of rich home-literacy experiences that provide them with extensive contact with print and many opportunities to acquire print awareness and print concepts, many children enter school well equipped to profit from beginning reading instruction. Some have already begun to learn to read. These children have a decided advantage in learning to read over children who have not come from rich home-literacy backgrounds, and they are better equipped to profit from beginning reading instruction than are less advantaged children.

Alphabetic Knowledge

A second type of knowledge beginning readers must acquire in order to learn to read is knowledge about how the alphabet works. Written English, like all alphabetic writing systems, contains many words that look alike because some of their letters are the same (e.g., *pot/top*; *was/saw*; *cat*, *rat*, *fat*). This creates an extraordinary strain on visual memory. As a result, novice readers cannot rely exclusively on what has come to be called the "logographic" approach to word identification, whereby whole words are associated, through rote memory, with their names and meanings and treated as though they were logos or picture symbols (Ehri, 1991; Frith, 1985). They must also discriminate between letters of the alphabet and learn to use individual letter sounds and the sounds associated with redundant clusters of letters (e.g., *ch*, *sh*, *est*, *ight*, *tion*, *ing*) to aid word identification (Ehri, 1991). In more technical language, novice readers must eventually acquire phonological decoding skills and mastery of the alphabetic code in order to become fluent readers. These skills are important, not only to help children acquire an increasingly large corpus of words they can identify on sight, but also to help them identify words that they cannot identify on sight. Developing readers encounter many words in written text they cannot identify, and they are not always able to rely on context clues to help them make reasonable guesses as to their identity. If they do not have the phonological decoding skills needed to identify such words, comprehension will be impaired. The probability of encountering many unfamiliar words is especially high in the case of informational texts containing new concepts and a large number of technical words. Obviously, the child who has good phonological decoding skills has a better chance of navigating through, comprehending, and learning from such texts than the child who has limited phonological decoding skills. In fact, there is now abundant research evidence that children who have great difficulty acquiring alphabetic knowledge generally have less adequate word recognition and comprehension skills than children who have little difficulty acquiring alphabetic knowledge (Snow, Burns, & Griffith, 1998; Vellutino, 1987; Vellutino et al., 1996).

Spelling

A third important ingredient in learning to read is knowledge of word spellings. Aside from its obvious importance to a child's becoming fully literate, increasing proficiency in spelling has a positive effect on the acquisition of word recognition skills. This is because spelling requires more fine-grained analysis of the structural properties of spoken and printed words; so positive experience in spelling will improve accuracy in word recognition and vice versa (Templeton & Morris, 2000). For example, it is largely through their initial attempts at spelling (often called "invented spelling") that novice readers begin to learn about the alphabetic principle (Ehri, 1991; Frith, 1985; Henderson, 1990). Moreover, practice in correctly spelling irregularly spelled words that are not easily decoded using letter–sound rules (*said, their, were, of, is*) helps in learning to identify them on sight. Positive experience in spelling also helps the child learn about recurrent patterns within and between syllables that govern the way given words are pronounced (e.g., silent-*e* rule in *tape* vs. *tap*; doubling rule in *pillow* vs. *pilot*).

Finally, positive experience in spelling helps the child learn about regularities within families of words related by their meanings (e.g., *bomb, bombard, bombardier*). Such experience improves vocabulary knowledge as well as skill in word recognition. Thus, it is not surprising to find that poor readers are inevitably poor spellers. Conversely, good spellers tend to be good readers, although good readers do not necessarily become good spellers (Frith, 1980).

Whole Word Identification

Whole word identification (often called sight word identification) entails rote association of a word's name and meaning with its printed counterpart. Practice in whole word identification, both apart from and during text reading, is important for acquiring fluency in text reading. It is also important (along with spelling) for learning to identify irregularly spelled words, such as *the, said, their, were, of,* and *is,* that cannot be easily identified using a phonological decoding strategy. Moreover, because many of these words are noncontent "parts of speech" (e.g., *the, was, and*) that have a pivotal rather than a referential role in language (i.e., they help in relating content words such as *dog, name,* and *Sam* in "The dog's name was Sam"), they appear in print more frequently than content words. It follows that children who have many opportunities to encounter noncontent words in print, and have enough reading ability to profit from such opportunities, will learn to identify them faster and more accurately than children who have fewer opportunities to encounter them in print and limited reading ability. Conversely, practice in identifying noncontent and/or irregularly spelled words out of context will improve children's ability to read them in context.

Cognitive Abilities Underlying Word Recognition Skills

Phonological Awareness

The beginning reader's ability to acquire phonological decoding, spelling, and word recognition skills is, itself, partly dependent on several related skills, abilities, and types of knowledge. One is the ability to acquire phonological awareness. Phonological awareness may be defined as the child's conceptual grasp and explicit awareness that spoken words consist of segments such as syllables and individual speech sounds (phonemes). Reading researchers generally agree that the child who understands this concept, who becomes sensitive to the similarities and differences in spoken words (e.g., through rhyme and alliteration) and acquires the ability to segment and manipulate their sound components (e.g., "say *fat* without the beginning sound"; "say *fat* backwards," etc.), is better able to learn letter–sound relationships and acquire reasonably good phonological decoding skills than the child who has not acquired phonological awareness and has limited ability to segment and manipulate speech sounds. Some even believe that phonological awareness is a prerequisite to understanding how the alphabet works and ultimate mastery of the alphabetic code (Liberman, 1983). Although this may or may not be true, there is good evidence that phonological awareness, letter–sound decoding, spelling, and word recognition are reciprocally related reading subskills, such that positive experience and growth in one facilitates positive experience and growth in another (Perfetti, Beck, Bell, & Hughes, 1987).

For example, the child who understands that the word *cat* has three individual phonemes (/c/ /a/ /t/) and can segment and manipulate them is in a better position to understand the logic behind using letters of the alphabet to represent these phonemes to help identify and spell *cat* and other words that can be identified using a letter–sound decoding strategy. Conversely, positive experience in using phoneme segmentation to help identify and spell *cat* and other words, such as *fat, hat, can,* and *catch,* will help to strengthen phoneme segmentation and phonological awareness skills, which, in turn, will increase the child's facility in letter–sound decoding.

That phonological awareness facilitates the acquisition of phonological decoding and other word-level skills is supported by a large body of research documenting that most children who have difficulty learning to read have deficient phoneme awareness and phonological decoding skills (Adams, 1990; Blachman, 2000; Liberman, 1983; Snow et al., 1998; Vellutino, 1987; Vellutino et al., 1996). Even more impressive is convergent evidence from intervention studies showing that training and remediation to facilitate phonological awareness and the acquisition of phonological decoding skills significantly improve word recognition skills and reading proficiency in general (Adams, 1990; Blachman, 2000; Bradley & Bryant, 1983; Snow et al., 1998; Torgesen, 2000; Vellutino & Scanlon, 1987; Vellutino et al., 1996).

Orthographic Awareness

Another important type of knowledge in becoming a skilled reader is orthographic awareness. Orthographic awareness refers to a person's sensitivity to the regularities and redundancies characteristic of words in an orthography (writing system) derived from an alphabet. It is a by-product of extensive and positive experience with families of words containing pronounceable clusters of letters that appear with some frequency in different word contexts (*at* in *cat, fat,* and *rat; ight* in *light* and *fight*) and is reciprocally related to phonological awareness, letter–sound decoding, and spelling (Adams, 1990; Ehri, 1991; Henderson, 1990; Templeton & Morris, 2000). The child who becomes aware of redundant letter clusters in the writing system (often called "spelling patterns" or "phonograms"), and learns to capitalize on their pronounceable properties, is better equipped to acquire functional decoding, word identification, and spelling skills than the child who does not become aware of such redundant units. For example, when confronted with the unfamiliar word *that* in the sentence "Sam can catch that cat," the child who has become sensitive to redundant spelling patterns would be more inclined than the child who has not become sensitive to such patterns to notice that the unfamiliar word contains two familiar units—*th* and *at*—(from familiar words such as *the*, *them*, *cat*, and *fat*) and then blend these units together to decode "that." Positive experience in using this and similar strategies to help identify unfamiliar words increases the former child's sensitivity to redundant spelling patterns and strengthens orthographic awareness, whereas negative experience in using these strategies decreases the probability that the latter child would become sensitive to redundant spelling patterns and acquire orthographic awareness.

Vocabulary Knowledge

It seems reasonable to assume that children will find it easier to learn to read words that are in their speaking vocabularies than to learn to read words that are not in their speaking vocabularies. If so, then it may be expected that children who have reasonably good vocabulary knowledge will acquire word recognition skills more readily than children who have poor vocabulary knowledge. There is, in fact, a good deal of evidence that deficient vocabulary and oral language skills can lead to difficulty in the acquisition of word recognition and related phonological skills, especially in disadvantaged and bilingual children (Snow, Barnes, Chandler, Goodman, & Hemphill, 1991). For example, the words used in the story about Jeff and his dog, Sam, mentioned earlier, would probably be in the speaking vocabularies of most children whose native language is English, but this may not be true of many children who are just learning to speak English. Such children will likely have difficulty learning to read many of the words in this story, especially the more abstract words such as *was*, *with*, and *the*. In fact, such words are more difficult to learn to read than concrete words such as *dog*, *cat*, and *play* even for native-English-speaking children. Thus, individual differences in vocabulary knowledge may well be a source of individual differences in word recognition, at least in some children.

Basic Cognitive Abilities

Three rather basic cognitive abilities that also contribute to individual differences in word recognition are phonological memory, visual memory, and visual–verbal learning ability. Phonological memory can be defined as short- and long-term memory for units of language—phonemes, syllables, and groups of syllables, such as phrases and sentences or even random strings of words or nonsense words. Phonological memory is distinguished from verbal memory, which is more narrowly defined as short- and long-term memory for meaningful units of language. Phonological memory is important in acquiring vocabulary knowledge, in learning the names of printed words, in analyzing and segmenting spoken words, in holding spoken and written text in memory during listening and reading, and in acquiring language-based skills in general (Baddely & Logie, 1999; Gathercole & Baddely, 1989). Visual memory is the ability to store and retrieve visual images of things. It is important in learning to recognize the unique spellings of printed words. Visual–verbal learning ability is the ability to associate visual and verbal information—for example, the visual and spoken counterparts of printed words such as *dog*, *cat*, and *Jeff* or the names and sounds of the letters in these words. It depends not only on adequate linguistic and visual abilities, but also on the ability to establish strong connections in memory between the visual and verbal counterparts of printed words.

There is a great deal of evidence that individual differences in reading-related abilities that depend, in part, on phonological memory (e.g., phonological awareness, name learning, name retrieval, etc.) are strongly correlated with individual differences in the acquisition of word recognition and letter–sound decoding skills, as are individual differences in visual–verbal learning ability (e.g., Vellutino, 1987; Vellutino et al., 1991, 1996). These skills reliably distinguish between good and poor readers as well. For example, many poor readers have weak phonological skills, as reflected in poor performance relative to normal readers, in nonsense word learning and verbal memory tasks, as well as in phonological awareness, and phonological decoding tasks. Such weaknesses are believed to contribute to the difficulty these children have in learning the names of printed words or in learning the names and sounds of their letters. Individual differences in visual memory are also correlated with individual differences in word recognition and letter–sound decoding skills, but less strongly than the phonological and visual–verbal learning skills just mentioned. Moreover, visual memory tasks do not reliably distinguish between good and poor readers (Vellutino, 1987; Vellutino et al., 1991, 1996). Such results suggest that reading is essentially a language-based skill that can tolerate a wide range of individual differences in visual memory.

General Intelligence

One cognitive ability that does not appear to be an especially influential determinant of the ability to learn to read, contrary to popular belief, is general intelligence. There is now abundant evidence that measures of intelligence are not highly correlated with performance on measures of word recognition and related skills such as phonological decoding (see Vellutino, Scanlon, & Lyon, 2000, for a recent review of this research). Such evidence suggests that language-based abilities, especially phonological abilities, are more important determinants of individual differences in print decoding than are higher-level intellectual abilities.

Fluency in Word Recognition

As I indicated earlier, reading comprehension is critically dependent on the reader's fluency in identifying printed words, as reflected in the reader's accuracy and speed in identifying the words in a passage as well as in his or her ability to read smoothly with appropriate expression. Fluent reading depends heavily on a great deal of practice in reading, spelling, and writing. It also depends on reading and re-reading material at an appropriate level of difficulty (Hiebert & Martin, 2001). Thus, children who have many opportunities to read, spell, and write given words and a good deal of practice and positive experiences in doing so, both during and apart from text reading, will represent those words in memory more strongly and come to identify them with greater speed and accuracy, than will children who have few opportunities to read, spell, and write those same words and less practice and positive experiences in doing so (Ehri, 1991; Perfetti, 1985; Stanovich, 1991). Similarly, children who encounter given words in text pitched at their instructional levels, where words can be identified with 85 to 90% accuracy, will navigate through and comprehend the text better, and therefore come to remember the words better, than children who encounter the same words in text that is too difficult for them. Many children have adequate phonological decoding skills but less than optimal fluency in word recognition; as a result, their comprehension is less than optimal.

INTERINDIVIDUAL DIFFERENCES
IN SKILLS AND ABILITIES
UNDERLYING LANGUAGE COMPREHENSION

A second major source of variability in reading comprehension is interindividual differences in factors that directly or indirectly influence language comprehension. Such factors include (1) language and language-based knowledge and competencies, including vocabulary knowledge, comprehension of syntax, awareness of language structures, and verbal memory, (2) discourse knowledge, (3) world knowledge and domain-specific knowledge, (4) nonlinguistic abilities and processes—in particular, attention, visual imagery, and higher-level intellectual skills such as inference, reasoning, and critical analysis, (5) cognitive and metacognitive strategy development, and (6) engagement and motivation. These factors are discussed in the following sections.

Language and Language-Based Knowledge and Competencies

Language and language-based knowledge and competencies are, perhaps, the most fundamental source of variability in language and reading comprehension in children who have acquired enough facility in word recognition to comprehend in written language what they would normally comprehend in spoken language. To comprehend spoken and written language, readers must have sufficient knowledge of the meanings of individual words that appear in text they are likely to encounter. They must also have sufficient knowledge of grammar and syntax. Such knowledge includes implicit (or explicit) acquaintance with parts of speech (e.g., nouns, verbs, adverbs, adjectives, etc.) and the different roles they are assigned in language processing; age/grade understanding of the different roles assigned root words, prefixes, and suffixes (e.g., *un* in *unhappy*; *s* in *cats*); and age/grade ability to comprehend different types of syntactic structures (e.g., active vs. passive sentences, conjoined sentences, embedded and relative clauses, etc.).

Language and reading comprehension also depend on metalinguistic awareness, that is, awareness of language structures, including syntactic awareness and pragmatic awareness. Syntactic awareness refers to the child's sensitivity to grammatical form in terms of errors that violate conventional usage in spoken and written language (e.g., "Mom brung the dog to the vet"). Such sensitivity reflects implicit knowledge of spoken language conventions. Pragmatic awareness refers to the child's sensitivity to the various ways language is used for purposes of communication, as reflected in his or her awareness of conventions in using language in social situations. Such conventions include the need to understand the speaker's (or writer's) intent in initiating a dialogue; turn taking during the dialogue; changes in intonation, volume, and intensity in speech to convey different types of meaning (signaled in print by punctuation marks); awareness of the need to register and relate ideas in a spoken (or written) dialogue (e.g., the need to pay attention to the speaker), and so forth. Syntactic awareness is important for monitoring comprehension in terms of word recognition errors that produce ungrammatical and/or meaningless sentences. Pragmatic awareness is important for comprehending and keeping track of the ideas exchanged during a dialogue in listening and reading and for understanding the goals and purposes of the dialogue.

Language and reading comprehension also depend on verbal memory. Verbal memory is the ability to retrieve meaningful units of language stored in short-term memory, working memory, and long-term memory. Short-term memory is a storage system that holds information in verbatim form for about 30 seconds and supports the processing of words in sentences or clauses (e.g., "Jeff had a black dog") long enough to access their meanings. Working memory is a storage system that holds information in more abstract form for a few minutes and allows a person to combine facts and ideas obtained from one segment of text with facts and ideas obtained from later segments—for example, combining earlier and later descriptions of events involving Jeff and his black dog, Sam, in the interest of comprehending the story being told about these characters. Long-term memory is a storage system of unlimited capacity that holds all acquired knowledge, including language-based information. Language processing in short-term and working memory depends, in part, on phonological memory—that is, verbatim memory for units of language. It also depends on the person's ability to retrieve relevant verbal information from long-term memory and relate such information to verbal information taken in while attempting to comprehend spoken or written text.

The degree to which these linguistic competencies develop in an individual child (or adult) quite likely accounts, in part, for individual differences in the development of skill in language and reading comprehension. Support for this possibility is provided by research showing that tests evaluating vocabulary knowledge, comprehension of syntax, awareness of language structures, and verbal memory (1) tend to differentiate good and poor comprehenders, (2) reliably predict performance on language and reading comprehension tests, and (3) are reasonably good predictors of literacy acquisition in developing readers (Hoover & Gough, 1990; Just & Carpenter, 1992; Perfetti, 1985; Snow et al., 1991; Sticht & James, 1984; Tunmer, Herriman, & Nesdale, 1988; Vellutino et al., 1991).

Discourse Knowledge

Discourse knowledge is knowledge about the unique properties of different types of text. It includes knowledge about the structural and organizational characteristics of narrative versus expository and informational texts and knowledge about the differences between them. The child who has had extensive experience with narrative text (stories) comes to understand that the writer's central purpose is to entertain the reader and that such text typically has a central theme or story line, a beginning section introducing that theme, a middle section in which that theme is expanded and developed (often called plot development), central and subordinate characters that implement the theme, and an ending section in which the theme is brought to some interesting conclusion. In contrast, the child who has had extensive experience with expository and informational text comes to understand that the writer's central purpose is to convey information about a particular topic of interest (in science, social studies, current events, etc.) and that the content of such text is typically organized hierarchically and sequentially, often with headings and subheadings, and entails discussion that provides factual information about the topic.

Knowledge about the structural characteristics of different types of text helps the child to organize and process the text in ways that facilitate comprehension. For example, after reading, "Jeff had a black dog"—the topic sentence in the excerpt from the story about a boy and his dog exemplified earlier—the child who has some acquaintance with narrative discourse, by virtue of having read (or heard) many stories, will expect to be presented with an episode having Jeff's dog as the central character and will be focused on the dog rather than Jeff in reading the rest of the section. Similarly, on reading "Sam tried to catch the cat, but it got away," the same child will expect to read text explaining why Sam did not catch the cat he chased, and perhaps even some discussion about such things as how Jeff and Sam felt about Sam's failure to catch the cat, what the cat's reactions were, and like motifs. Such expectations help organize the events in a story and focus the reader's attention in ways that aid comprehension of the text and memory for the principal characters and events portrayed in the text.

For a contrasting example, consider the following excerpt from informational text providing factual descriptions of how given types of fish prepare nests in which to lay eggs:

> Fish lay eggs in different kinds of places. Some lay their eggs in mud. Others lay their eggs on stones or underwater roots. Still others lay their eggs on top of the water. (Stone & Burton, 1960)

Upon reading this paragraph, the child who has had extensive experience reading (or hearing) informational text will expect to read (or hear) a more detailed description of one or more of the different ways given types of fish create nests for laying their eggs. However, the same child would probably not expect to find that a fish assigned a human-like persona would be the central character in a story about a fish laying eggs. In other words, the experienced and able reader will organize and attend to informational text in ways that are quite different from the ways he or she organizes and attends to narrative text, and will bring different types of background knowledge into play in processing each type of text. The less experienced and less able reader may not adequately distinguish between the structural and functional properties of these two genres of text and, as a result, may organize and attend to each type of text less efficiently and less profitably than the more experienced and more able reader.

Research documenting that knowledge of linguistic discourse is an important source of individual differences in reading comprehension has a long history (Duke & Kays, 1998; Mandler & Johnson, 1977; Stein & Trabasso, 1981; van Ostendoorp & Goldman, 1999). The evidence indicates that good comprehenders tend to have a better appreciation of different types of discourse structure than do poor comprehenders and, as a result, are better able than poor comprehenders to navigate through and profit from different types of texts.

World Knowledge and Domain-Specific Knowledge

Two other types of knowledge that are highly influential determinants of language and reading comprehension are world knowledge and domain-specific knowledge. World knowledge is knowledge about events and activities that occur in everyday life involving real people and real things that exist in real time and real places. In addition to autobiographical knowledge about events and activities that occur in the child's daily life (e.g., scripted knowledge such as dinner and bedtime routines, school-related routines, holiday routines, etc.), world knowledge includes knowledge about events, activities, persons, places, and things that are not part of the child's daily life, but that the child may have learned about through either direct experience (e.g., family vacations, field trips, etc.) or vicarious experience (e.g., reading or listening to stories, television, etc.). Domain-specific knowledge is knowledge that is unique to a given content area (e.g., science, social studies, sports, entertainment, etc.). Knowledge of both types is stored in complex mental structures called "schemata" (Anderson & Pearson, 1984). Such schemata aid children's comprehension by helping them to draw inferences about and interpret concepts encountered in texts that are related to knowledge they have already acquired. Thus, children who have acquired a great deal of world knowledge and/or domain-specific knowledge, and well-elaborated schemata representing both types of knowledge, are better equipped to comprehend and profit from text drawing upon such knowledge than children who have acquired less world knowledge or domain-specific knowledge.

Consider, for example, the excerpt from the text describing the different ways fish build nests mentioned earlier. The child who is a budding naturalist, who likes to fish and learn about fish, and has had considerable exposure to real-life situations and/or texts describing fish and other animal behaviors and habitats, will have much greater background knowledge to bring to the task of reading and comprehending this text than will the child who has had little exposure to such situations and texts. Thus, the former child will be better able to learn from this and like texts than the latter child (see Ericsson & Kintsch, 1995, for an informative review of relevant research).

Nonlinguistic Cognitive Abilities

Attention

As indicated earlier, variability in language and reading comprehension can also be influenced by individual differences in non-linguistic cognitive abilities. The ability to maintain controlled and focused attention is one such ability. Most teachers would agree that deficiencies in maintaining controlled and focused attention negatively affect reading comprehension and learning to read in general, and there is some evidence that reading difficulties in some children are partly caused by attention deficits of neuro-developmental origin (Shaywitz, Fletcher, & Shaywitz, 1995). However, attention problems directly affecting language and reading comprehension can also be caused by other factors, such as limited vocabulary, limited background knowledge, poor word recognition skills, limited interest in the text, and/or less than optimal motivation for reading (or listening). These are not mutually exclusive sources of attention problems in language and reading comprehension, and it is important to distinguish between them.

Visual Imagery

Language processing in reading (and listening) may also be influenced by individual differences in the ability to store and retrieve visual images. The use of visual imagery as an aid to verbal memory, vocabulary acquisition, and verbal learning in general has been studied extensively in both children and adults. The evidence suggests that individuals can and often do make effective use of visual imagery to help them remember linguistic information that has a high degree of concrete, referential meaning (Levin, 1993; Paivio, 1986; Vellutino et al., 1995). There is also research showing that differences in visualization ability may be an important source of individual differences in using pictorial material and illustrations to aid reading comprehension (Gyselinck & Tardieu, 1999). Thus, individual differences in visual imagery may well contribute to individual differences in reading comprehension, notwithstanding the contribution they make to the acquisition of word-level skills in learning to read and spell.

General Intelligence

Finally, there is widespread agreement that individual differences in intellectual skills such as reasoning, critical analysis, and the ability to make logical inferences are also important sources of individual differences in language and reading comprehension. Consider, for example, the following comprehension question that a teacher might ask a child about the story featuring Jeff and his dog, Sam: "What do you think Sam might have been doing when he saw the big fat cat?" A plausible inference in answering this question would be that Sam was playing with Jeff's hat. This inference is justified by the sentence in the text stating that Sam liked to play with Jeff's hat, which appeared just before the sentence indicating that Sam became aware of the cat he proceeded to chase. It seems safe to assume that the intellectually able child would be more likely to make this inference than would the less intellectually able child. Research findings support this assumption, in that measures of intelligence tend to be strongly correlated with measures of reading and language comprehension and generally distinguish between good and poor comprehenders. Such findings are in contrast to research demonstrating that measures of intelligence are not highly correlated with measures of word recognition and other word-level skills and do not reliably distinguish between children who have difficulty acquiring these skills and those who do not have such difficulty (see Vellutino et al., 2000, for a review).

Cognitive and Metacognitive Strategies

Cognitive and metacognitive strategies are consciously controlled mechanisms the proficient reader uses to improve his or her ability to understand and profit from text. Cognitive strategies are consciously controlled mechanisms the reader uses to organize and interpret the text. They include such devices as inference, reasoning, and critical analysis, use of prior knowledge to raise questions about and interpret the content of the text, use of linguistic context and other meaning-based mechanisms (e.g., pictorial clues) to aid word identification and comprehension, and so forth. Metacognitive strategies are mechanisms that emanate from the reader's awareness of the cognitive demands of the text, the goals and purposes that will be accomplished in reading given texts, and the need to generate a variety of cognitive strategies in accomplishing these objectives. Metacognitive strategies include accepting responsibility for and analyzing one's own learning, monitoring comprehension to ensure understanding, actively generating learning strategies such as note taking, reading, reciting, and rereading to facilitate memory for concepts that are difficult to remember, shifting strategies in accord with the difficulty level of the text, and like mechanisms.

The use of cognitive and metacognitive strategies to aid reading comprehension also has a long history, and there is considerable research evidence that good comprehenders tend to use such strategies more often and more effectively than poor comprehenders (e.g., Palincsar & Brown, 1984; Pearson & Fielding, 1991; Pressley, 2000). This research also suggests that cognitive and metacognitive strategies can be effectively taught and can improve comprehension.

Engagement and Motivation

That engaged and intrinsically motivated children will become more proficient readers than less engaged and less intrinsically motivated readers is a
truism that generalizes across advantaged and disadvantaged populations.
There is, in fact, abundant research evidence to support this truism (e.g.,
Guthrie, Wigfield, & Von Secker, 2000; Snow et al., 1991; Sweet, Guthrie,
& Ng, 1998). Motivated and engaged readers are also purposeful and goal-
directed readers, and the same evidence supports the generalization that
purposeful and goal-directed readers become better comprehenders and acquire more knowledge than less purposeful and less goal-directed readers.
However, a child's motivation to engage in reading as an academic enterprise and to sustain his or her efforts in the interest of becoming a proficient reader seems to be dependent on the child's success in learning to
read. This success, in turn, seems to be dependent on such factors as the
child's initial preparedness and the continuing support for reading in terms
of home background, enrichment, and endorsement; reading-related cognitive abilities that set constraints on reading achievement; and the quality of
reading instruction to which the child is exposed, especially during the initial periods of reading development.

INTRA-INDIVIDUAL DIFFERENCES
IN ELEMENTARY SCHOOL READERS

Intra-individual differences that contribute to variability in acquiring reading competencies—that is, individual patterns of strengths and weaknesses—
can be observed during each phase of reading development. Such differences are manifested in uneven development of important skills and
subskills that underlie proficient reading. For example, during the beginning phases of reading development, when children are acquiring basic
word recognition, phonological decoding, and text processing skills, it is
not uncommon to find significant imbalance in the acquisition of one or
another of these skills in a given child, to the detriment of that child's progress in becoming a proficient and independent reader who is motivated to
read (Scanlon & Vellutino, 1996; Vellutino & Scanlon, 2002). This type of
imbalance, in most cases, is a by-product of such important influences as
home literacy experiences, the child's instructional program, and/or the
particular way in which the child conceptualizes reading. Thus, one child
may have a strong and growing inventory of sight words and strong text-
processing skills (e.g., comprehension monitoring, use of context, knowledge of discourse, etc.), but little or no ability to use phonological decoding

skills to help identify unfamiliar words encountered in text. Another child may have strong phonological decoding skills, but a limited inventory of sight words and weak text-processing skills, and, as a result, is destined to become a letter-by-letter, word-by-word reader, with less than optimal ability to comprehend what he or she reads. Still another child may have a strong inventory of sight words and strong phonological decoding skills, but weak text processing skills, as manifested in a limited sense of discourse structure, a limited sense of the pragmatic relations embedded in the text, little or no tendency to monitor understanding, and little or no use of semantic, syntactic, or pictorial clues to aid word identification and text comprehension. Such a child is also destined to become a word-by-word reader, with less than optimal ability to comprehend what he or she reads.

Of course, intra-individual differences in capabilities other than word recognition and rudimentary text processing skills may also set limits on a child's growth in reading or may affect, in some appreciable way, the child's ability to acquire knowledge in areas that depend on reading. For example, despite adequate development of word recognition and phonological decoding skills, the child with limited vocabulary knowledge and/or limited world knowledge will have difficulty comprehending texts that presuppose such knowledge. Similarly, given the important role of extensive and diverse reading in acquiring vocabulary knowledge, in encountering and representing the more abstract and more complex syntactic structures, and in acquiring a broad-based knowledge of discourse structure (Olson, 1994), the child who does little independent reading, and who is not motivated to read extensively and diversely, will be ill equipped to engage and profit from the broad array of expository and technical texts encountered in school learning, even if he or she has no basic intellectual deficits or basic deficits in reading or oral language development. Further, the child who has not acquired the cognitive and metacognitive strategies and study skills necessary to use reading as an instrument of learning will undoubtedly profit less from reading in a given domain than the child who has acquired these skills, along with the disposition and tenacity to use them, even if the two children have comparable reading, oral language, and intellectual skills (Palinscsar & Brown, 1984; Pearson & Fielding, 1991; Pressley, 2000). Moreover, the child who is not motivated to acquire knowledge in a given domain, or to engage the school curriculum and school learning at large, will not acquire much knowledge in any given domain and will not profit much from school learning in general.

On the positive side, the tenacious and inquisitive child with basically strong intellectual skills, a high degree of intrinsic motivation to become a good student, strong study skills, and a positive and goal-directed attitude toward reading and school learning, may acquire a level of proficiency in reading and writing that would allow him or her to become a good student, despite inherent limitations in reading-related cognitive abilities that make it difficult for that child to acquire the full range of literacy skills. Thus, it should be clear that the challenge for researchers and practitioners alike is to acquire the means for assessing these intra-individual differences. It will also be necessary to develop instructional techniques and formats for helping the child correct or compensate for weaknesses while utilizing strengths and high-interest domains as the springboard for acquiring proficiency in reading and becoming an engaged, motivated, and successful student in the later grades.

IMPLICATIONS OF THE RESEARCH FOR INSTRUCTION

The different sources of variability in reading comprehension discussed here have clear-cut implications for both classroom and remedial instruction. Given the overwhelming amount of evidence that proficient word recognition skills are a prerequisite to proficient reading comprehension, it seems that fostering the development of fluent word recognition skills should be the first major objective in beginning reading (or remedial) instruction. However, once a child has acquired enough facility in word recognition to become a reasonably independent reader and learner, the focus in instruction should shift to higher-level language comprehension and text-processing skills. The following recommendations are made in the interest of helping the teacher accomplish these objectives.

Teach Print Concepts If Necessary

As indicated earlier, print awareness and knowledge of print concepts are the foundation of literacy acquisition. Thus, teachers of novice readers and/or struggling readers should make certain that the children have a firm grasp of the nature and purpose of print, focusing on the structural properties of written English (words are composed of letters that have names and sound values, they have spaces between them, etc.), as well as their functional properties (printed words represent spoken words, they are sequenced from left to right, etc.). Reading with the children is, of course, the method of choice for teaching print concepts (Clay, 1985; Morris, 1993). However, this enterprise should be interactive and should allow children ample opportunity to ask questions and respond to pointed questions designed to assess their understanding of print concepts. Moreover, it is important to keep in mind that many children enter school quite well versed in the nature and purpose of print, so print concepts instruction should be provided only for those children who need it.

Teach Phonological Decoding Skills

Once it has been established that the children have a firm grasp of print concepts, it is critically important to teach them phonological decoding skills. We have learned a great about the teaching of phonological decoding skills over the past decade or so, and there are certain components of phonological skills instruction that most believe to be vital (Stahl, Duffy-Hester, & Dougherty Stahl, 1998). At the initial stages of such instruction, it is important to ensure that children are able to discriminate between letters of the alphabet, because those who cannot do so will have difficulty learning letter–sound relationships (Adams, 1990) and acquiring word recognition skills. Multiple-choice recognition and letter naming are complementary ways to teach letter discrimination (Vellutino & Scanlon, 2002). When the children learn to recognize and identify given letters, they should be taught the sounds associated with those letters, beginning with the most common consonant sounds; this instruction should be followed by selective teaching of the most common vowel sounds. The primary objective of initial phonics instruction is to provide children with a corpus of consonant and vowel sounds that can be used to help them learn about how the alphabet works. The remaining consonant and vowel sounds can be taught after the children have had some experience in alphabetic coding and begin to understand the alphabetic principle.

However, initial phonics instruction should proceed hand in hand with activities to facilitate phonological awareness, because acquiring this skill facilitates a conceptual grasp of how the alphabet works (and vice versa). The initial stage of phonological awareness instruction typically involves sensitizing children to similarities and differences in spoken words (e.g., through rhyme and alliteration). This is most effectively done through shared and interactive reading. Once the children have acquired such sensitivity, they can move on to activities that provide them with practice in segmenting words into syllables (*hot* and *dog* in *hotdog*) and, thereafter, activities that provide them with practice in identifying and manipulating the individual sounds (phonemes) in spoken and written words ("Say /fat/ without the /at/").

The teaching of letter–sound and phonological awareness skills should also be accompanied by activities that begin to attune the children to the larger clusters of letters that appear in many words—that is, pronounceable and redundant spelling units and word families that occur with a high degree of frequency in written English (*at* in *cat* and *rat*; *ight* in *right* and *light*; *sh*, *ch*, etc.). The ultimate objective of such activities is, of course, to provide readers with the ability to use pronounceable letter "chunks" (e.g., *ch* + *est* to decode *chest*) and analogy strategies to aid word identification (e.g., knowing *flop* and *chunk* helps in decoding *flunk*). Practice in using letter chunks to help decode new words will also facilitate the development of orthographic awareness and more efficient decoding and spelling skills. The sooner the child learns to search for redundant spelling units and word families, the sooner he or she will be able master the alphabetic code. More detailed and comprehensive accounts of effective approaches to phonics, phonological awareness, and orthographic awareness instruction, in both classroom and remedial settings, can be found elsewhere (e.g., Bear, Invernizzi, & Templeton, 1995; Cunningham, 1995; Stahl et al., 1998; Vellutino & Scanlon, 2002).

Teach Whole Word Identification

Because written English contains many irregularly spelled words that cannot be readily identified using phonological decoding strategies, it is essential to provide children with a great deal of practice ("drill") in whole (sight) word identification, apart from text reading as well as during text reading. Such practice is especially important for beginning (or remedial) readers who must acquire an initial set of words to help make reading meaningful and functional. Practice in whole word identification is also important for developing fluency in word recognition, even with regularly spelled words. Thus, every lesson should include time spent on whole word identification. The most effective approach to learning new (sight) words, especially in the beginning periods of reading development, is to present the learner with words that appear with a high degree of frequency in children's reading materials. Two published word lists that we found to be useful for this purpose in an intervention study we conducted (Vellutino & Scanlon, 2002) have been compiled by Harris and Jacobson (1982) and Eeds (1985). The reader will also find many useful suggestions in Hiebert and Martin (2001).

Teach Spelling

Templeton and Morris (2000) have recently pointed out that many, if not most, classroom teachers do not systematically teach spelling as an integral component of the language arts program. And, aside from encouraging invented spelling in beginning readers, some do not teach spelling at all, except on an "as needed" basis in conjunction with process writing. Moreover, I submit that those who do regularly include spelling in the language arts program typically do not teach it in conjunction with the teaching of word recognition, phonological awareness, and phonological decoding skills, given that the basal reading, phonics, and spelling programs used in most classrooms do not guarantee that children are learning to read and decode the same words they are learning to spell. A more integrated approach to the acquisition of word-level skills is what some reading scholars have called "word study" (Templeton & Morris, 2000). Word study is essentially "a means of looking at words from a variety of perspectives that serve reading, writing, and vocabulary development" (p. 537). Word study serves to integrate word recognition, phonological decoding, and spelling through structural analysis of words and spelling patterns common to many words, using a variety of activities such as word sorting and semantic mapping, in which children learn to categorize words according to their common orthographic features (e.g., *at* in *fat, cat, rat*) and/or semantic features (*bomb* in *bomb, bombard, bombardier*). Word study also helps concretize the reading–spelling connection and is based on a comprehensive theory of spelling development (Henderson, 1990) that provides an excellent framework for teaching word-level skills to children across a broad age/grade spectrum (see also Bear et al., 1995). Other useful word study activities may include oral and written spelling of words supported by analysis of their component sounds ("Say the sounds in *cat* and then say and write its letters") and using new spelling words in the context of written sentences. Such activities should always entail corrective feedback.

Teach Conjoint Use of Decoding and Context Cues

In order to become independent readers, children need to acquire a variety of strategies for word identification, especially when reading text that contains a fair number of words they may not recognize on sight. An approach that we found useful with struggling readers (Vellutino & Scanlon, 2002) was to give them a great deal of practice using their developing decoding skills in conjunction with cues provided by semantic context. This kind of practice required that the children be constantly encouraged to monitor their comprehension of the text to help them flag instances when a word they read in a sentence "didn't make sense." If they had the decoding skills to sound out the misidentified word, they were encouraged to do so and then reread the sentence to see if the decoded word now "made sense" in the context of the sentence. To give the children practice in using newly acquired decoding skills in context, we looked for text that contained new words that they could decode with their acquired skills. We found that such practice not only helped to consolidate the children's decoding skills, but it also helped them better understand the logic behind phonics instruction.

Provide Activities That Help Develop Fluency

The ultimate objective of teaching word-level skills in beginning reading instruction is, of course, to facilitate the development of fluent word recognition. As I have already indicated, practice in whole word identification and spelling, both out of context and in the context of reading and writing, are related strategies that can be used to help accomplish this objective. Such strategies can be especially useful with irregularly spelled words, many of which are noncontent words that appear in text with a high degree of frequency. Repeated and teacher-assisted reading of familiar texts is another important way to promote fluency. Stahl and Kuhn (2002) reviewed research evaluating different approaches to repeated reading of text to promote fluency and concluded that reading and rereading texts for fluency is more effective when teachers monitor and model fluent reading. They also described a promising approach to fluency instruction (Fluency-Oriented Reading Instruction [FORI]) based on five principles: (1) Lessons should be comprehension oriented, even when smooth and fluent oral reading is being emphasized, so that children never lose sight of the importance of understanding what they read; (2) children should read as many texts at their "comfort" level as possible; (3) children should be supported in their repetition of the text until that text becomes fluent; (4) children should have an opportunity to read with partners in order to increase the amount of time spent reading in school; and (5) children should increase the amount of reading they do at home (p. 583). Stahl and Kuhn (2002) also suggest that the texts children are asked to read should follow what they call the "Goldilocks principle"— they should not be too easy or too difficult, but just right—meaning that they should be at the child's instructional level (see also Hiebert & Martin, 2001, for research documentation of this idea). Suggested activities to implement these principles include the use of curriculum-based materials, teacher modeling, shared reading, choral reading, and echo reading, along with daily free-reading periods at school, during which children are provided with high-interest materials they can read comfortably, in addition to a home reading program that is structured and monitored by the teacher.

These ideas make sense to me. They speak for the need to provide children with as many opportunities to read as possible, both at school and at home. They also dictate that the materials children are asked to read should be challenging enough to facilitate new learning, but not so challenging as to cause frustration and disengagement.

Facilitate Development of Linguistic Competencies

I pointed out earlier that the foundations of proficient reading comprehension are linguistic competencies, including vocabulary knowledge, comprehension of syntax, and syntactic and pragmatic awareness. Vocabulary knowledge is basic, not only for learning to read new words, but also for comprehending texts that contain new words. Although most teachers would attest to the importance of teaching vocabulary, they tend to teach vocabulary superficially (Blachowicz & Fisher, 2000), typically as a prereading activity to aid new text reading. Yet, as pointed out by Blachowicz and Fisher (2000), there is ample reason for teachers to provide more in-depth vocabulary instruction to aid comprehension, especially in content areas (Alvermann & Swafford, 1989), and they identify four main principles, or requisites, justified by the research to guide such instruction: (1) that students be active in developing their understanding of words, (2) that students personalize word learning, (3) that students be immersed in words, and (4) that students build on multiple sources of information to learn words through repeated exposures (p. 504). Blachowicz and Fisher (2000) discuss research that justifies these principles and provide concrete examples of how they can be implemented in vocabulary instruction. These scholars stress the need for a flexible approach to vocabulary instruction that takes account of the reader's task (e.g., prereading vs. content learning). They also suggest that teachers must play an active role in selecting and in helping students select new vocabulary words for different purposes and in generating activities to help them understand and retain new words (see also Beck & McKeown, 1983, 1991, and Harris & Sipay, 1990, for more "how to" detail on vocabulary instruction).

In regard to syntactic and metalinguistic competencies of the types discussed earlier, it will suffice to point out that teachers can help facilitate development of these competencies through language enrichment activities, such as shared and interactive reading and writing; encouraging the active use of oral and written language through such activities as sharing experiences, expressing opinions, and storytelling; modeling and feedback to help students distinguish between appropriate and inappropriate uses of language in different contexts, including social situations, storytelling, and information sharing; allowing ample time for and encouraging creative and technical writing that is closely monitored by the teacher; and providing opportunities for extensive and diverse reading.

Encourage Extensive and Diverse Reading

As I have just indicated, one way to develop linguistic competencies is through extensive and diverse reading, because it is largely through reading that one encounters the more complex, more abstract, and more varied forms of language. Extensive and diverse reading is also the primary means by which children acquire discourse knowledge, that is, knowledge about the structural characteristics of different types of text (e.g., narrative vs. informational) that is so important for interpreting and organizing the text.

Extensive and diverse reading is also an important way to acquire world knowledge and domain-specific knowledge and to increase reading fluency and proficiency.

Teach Text Processing Strategies

The reading literature that has emerged over the past two decades or so is replete with studies documenting the utility of cognitive and metacognitive strategies in facilitating reading comprehension and the child's ability to learn from text. Such activities have been found to be useful in navigating through and comprehending text at every phase of reading development, as exemplified in the use of semantic context to aid word identification and monitor text processing at the beginning phase of acquisition, contrasted with the use of critical thinking and self-regulated knowledge acquisition skills at more advanced phases. Pressley (2000) has summarized the recent literature in this area of inquiry and points out that skilled readers use a variety of text processing strategies, which include awareness of the purpose of reading a text; surveying the text to determine which portions are relevant and which are not; reading selectively so as to pick out the most relevant information; using prior knowledge to interpret the text; generating questions that structure reading; revising prior knowledge; using a variety of devices to make text salient and more memorable, such as note taking, underlining and paraphrasing, and so forth.

It should be clear from these examples that critical, logical, and reflective analysis of text, in relation to the reader's purpose for reading the text, is one general comprehension strategy that teachers should attempt to foster. Pressley (2000) suggests encouraging students to do such things as asking themselves "why questions"—that is, questions about why related ideas in text make sense—to help them to generate critical thinking strategies. Pressley (2000) also advocates teaching children self-regulatory and interactive comprehension strategies through reciprocal teaching and transactional strategies instruction. Reciprocal teaching is an approach to text processing whereby students take turns as discussion leaders in helping their classmates survey and raise questions about the text, make predictions about its content, seek clarification when needed, and summarize ideas in the text (Palincsar & Brown, 1984). Transactional strategies instruction is similar to reciprocal teaching, except that it involves more direct explanation and teacher modeling of effective and flexible strategies, followed by guided practice in the use of task-relevant strategies. There is extensive research support for both types of strategy instruction, and the reader is encouraged to explore them further (Palincsar & Brown, 1984; Pressley et al., 1992; see Palincsar, Chapter 6, in this book).

CONCLUSIONS

Reading is a complex process, and therefore it is important for teachers to acquire a solid understanding of the multiple components of proficient comprehension in order to appreciate and accommodate to student differences in acquiring this skill. Most comprehension problems in elementary school readers are caused by inadequate word recognition skills, so teachers should become thoroughly acquainted with the various skills and abilities that may contribute to individual differences in word recognition. Yet some children have reading comprehension problems despite having basically good word recognition skills; thus, teachers should become thoroughly acquainted with the different types of knowledge, the linguistic and nonlinguistic abilities, and the different text processing strategies that may contribute to individual differences in language and reading comprehension in such children.

However, teachers need to prioritize instructional activities in accord with the level of reading development in the children they are teaching. Because adequate word recognition is a basic prerequisite for adequate reading comprehension, the primary objective of reading instruction with beginning readers should be the development of increasing fluency in word recognition, which presupposes teaching of the various word recognition subskills in ways that facilitate consolidation of these subskills. Once the children have acquired a sufficient degree of fluency in word recognition to read independently, the primary objective of reading instruction should be the development of comprehension and knowledge acquisition skills and the focus of instruction should shift accordingly.

Reading instruction must also be individualized. Given the demands of classroom instruction, it would be unrealistic to expect that teachers would be able to provide any of their children with a great deal of one-to-one tutoring, even struggling readers. It is realistic, however, to expect teachers to become thoroughly acquainted with the individual strengths and weaknesses of each and every one of their students in order to frame individualized instructional programs for these students. Moreover, individualized instruction, for most children, does not necessarily require one-to-one tutoring. This has been clearly established in recent intervention studies demonstrating that many impaired readers can be remediated quite successfully in small groups (Elbaum, Vaughn, Hughes, & Moody, 2000; Vellutino, et al., 1996). Individualized instruction would, however, require that children be grouped according to their instructional needs and that groupings of given children be flexible enough to allow for individual differences in reading growth among those in a particular group. This, of course, would mean that whole class instruction be abandoned as an exclusive approach to reading instruction. As will always be the case, some children will need supplemental instruction outside the classroom, but the number of these children will be greatly reduced if the teacher takes account of the unique instructional needs of each of the students and keeps abreast of individual differences in their responses to instruction. It is worth noting, in this context, that reading difficulties, in most children, are caused by inadequate instruction rather than basic deficits in reading-related cognitive abilities (Vellutino et al., 1996).

Finally, the instructional program should help children to become engaged, motivated, and purposeful readers who enjoy reading. Obviously, instruction that capitalizes on children's inherent interests and surrounds them with high-interest reading materials at their level of proficiency is more effective than instruction that does less. However, in my opinion, the best means of motivating children to read is to ensure that they become independent readers who enjoy reading.

ACKNOWLEDGMENTS

Some of the research reported in this chapter was supported by grants awarded to me by the National Institute of Child Health and Human Development (Nos. R01HD09658, P50HD25806, and 5RO1HD34598). I wish to express my sincere gratitude to the teachers, students, and secretarial and administrative staff in schools that were involved in this research. Special thanks are due also to my colleagues Dr. Donna Scanlon, Sheila Small, and Diane Fanuele, who devoted many years of their lives to the research.

REFERENCES

Adams, M. J. (1990). *Beginning to read: Thinking and learning about print*. Cambridge, MA: MIT Press.

Alvermann, D. E., & Swafford, J. (1989). Do content area strategies have a research base? *Journal of Reading, 32*, 388–394.

Anderson, R. C., & Pearson, P. D. (1984). A schema-theoretic view of basic processes in reading. In P. D. Pearson, R. Barr, M. L. Kamil, & P. Mosenthal (Eds.), *Handbook of reading research* (pp. 255–291). New York: Longman.

Baddeley, A. D., & Logie, R. H. (1999). Working memory: The Multiple Component Model. In I. A. Miyake & P. Shah (Eds.), *Models of working memory: Mechanisms of active maintenance and executive control* (pp. 28–61). New York: Cambridge University Press.

Bear, D. R., Invernizzi, M., & Templeton, S. (1995). *Words their way: Word study for phonics, vocabulary, and spelling instruction*. Englewood Cliffs, NJ: Prentice-Hall

Beck, I. L., & McKeown, M. G. (1991). Conditions of vocabulary acquisition. In R. Barr, M. L. Kamil, P. B. Mosenthal, & P. D. Pearson (Eds.), *Handbook of reading research* (Vol. II, pp. 789–814). New York: Longman.

Beck, I. L., & McKeown, M. G. (1983). Learning words well–A program to enhance vocabulary and comprehension. *Reading Teacher, 36,* 622–625.

Blachman, B. A. (2000). Phonological awareness. In M. L. Kamil, P. B. Mosenthal, P. D. Pearson, & R. Barr (Eds.), *Handbook of Reading Research* (Vol. III, pp. 483–502). Mahwah, NJ: Erlbaum.

Blachowicz, C. L. Z., & Fisher, P.(2000). Vocabulary instructon. In M. L. Kamil, P. B. Mosenthal, P. D. Pearson, & R. Barr (Eds.), *Handbook of reading research* (Vol. III, pp. 503–523). Mahwah, NJ: Erlbaum.

Bradley, L., & Bryant, P. E. (1983). Categorizing sounds and learning to read: A causal connection. *Nature, 303,* 419–421.

Clay, M. M. (1985). *The early detection of reading difficulties* (3rd ed.). Auckland, New Zealand: Heineman.

Cunningham, P. M. (1995). *Phonics they use* (2nd ed.). New York: Harper.

Duke, N. K., & Kays, J. (1998). "Can I say 'once upon a time'?" Kindergarten children developing knowledge of information book language. *Early Childhood Research Quarterly, 13*(2), 295–318.

Eeds, M. (1985). Bookwords: Using a beginning word list of high frequency words from children's literature K–3. *Reading Teacher, 38,* 418–423.

Ehri, L. C. (1991). Development of the ability to read words. In R. Barr, M. L. Kamil, P. B. Mosenthal, & P. D. Pearson (Eds.), *Handbook of reading research* (Vol. II, pp. 384–417). New York: Longman.

Elbaum, B., Vaughn, S., Hughes, M. J., & Moody, S. W. (2000). How effective are one-to-one tutoring programs in reading for elementary students at risk for reading failure? A meta-analysis of the intervention research. *Journal of Educational Psychology, 92*(4), 605–619.

Ericsson, K. A., & Kintsch, W. (1995). Long-term working memory. *Psychological Review, 102*(2), 211–245.

Foorman, B. R., Francis, D. J., Novy, D. M., & Liberman, D. (1991). How letter-sound instruction mediates progress in first-grade reading and spelling. *Journal of Educational Psychology, 83,* 456–469.

Frith, U. (1980). Unexected spelling problems. In U. Frith (Ed.), *Cognitive Processes in Spelling.* New York: Academic Press.

Frith, U. (1985). Beneath the surface of developmental dyslexia. In K. Patterson, J. Marshall, & M. Coltheart (Eds.), *Surface dyslexia: Neuropsychological and cognitive studies of phonological reading* (pp. 301–330). London, U.K.: Erlbaum.

Gathercole, S. E., & Baddely, A. D. (1989). Evaluation of the role of phonological STM in the development of vocabulary in children: A longitudinal study. *Journal of Memory and Language, 28,* 200–213.

Guthrie, J. T., Wigfield, A., & Von Secker, C. (2000). Effects of integrated instruction on motivation and strategy use in reading. *Journal of Educational Psychology, 92*(2), 331–341.

Gyselinck, V., & Tardieu, H. (1999). The role of illustrations in text comprehension: What, when, for whom and why? In H. van Ostendoorp and S. R.

Goldman (Eds), *The construction of mental representations during reading* (pp. 195–218). Mahwah, NJ: Erlbaum.

Harris, A. J., & Jacobson, M. D. (1982). *Basic reading vocabularies.* New York: Macmillan.

Harris, A. J., & Sipay, E. R. (1990). *How to increase reading ability* (9th ed.). New York: Longman.

Henderson, E. H. (1990). *Teaching spelling* (2nd.ed.). Boston: Houghton Mifflin.

Hiebert, E. H., & Martin, L. A. (2001). The texts of beginning reading instruction. In S. B. Neuman & D. K. Dickinson (Eds.), *Handbook of early literacy research* (pp. 361–376). New York: Guilford Press.

Hoover, W., & Gough, P. B. (1990). The simple view of reading. *Reading and Writing: An Interdisciplinary Journal, 2,* 127–160.

Just, M. A., & Carpenter, P. A. (1992). A capacity theory of comprehension: Individual differences in working memory: *Psychological Review, 99,* 122–149.

Levin, J. R. (1993). Mnemonic strategies and classroom learning: A twenty-year report card. *Elementary School Journal, 94,* 235–244.

Liberman, I. Y. (1983). A language-oriented view of reading and its disabilities. In H. Myklebust (Ed.), *Progress in learning disabilities* (Vol 5, pp. 81–101). New York: Grune & Stratton.

Mandler, J. M., & Johnson, N. S. (1977). Remembrance of things parsed: Story structure and recall. *Cognitive Psychology, 9,* 111–151.

Morris, D. (1993). The relationship between children's concept of word in text and phoneme awareness in learning to read: A longitudinal study. *Research in the Teaching of English, 27,* 133–154.

Olson, D. R. (1994). *The world on paper.* Cambridge, U.K.: Cambridge University Press.

Paivio, A. (1986). *Mental representations: A dual coding approach.* New York: Oxford University Press.

Palincsar, A. S., & Brown, A. L. (1984). Reciprocal teaching of comprehension-fostering and comprehension-monitoring activities. *Cognition and Instruction, 1,* 117–175.

Pearson, P. D., & Fielding, L. (1991). Comprehension instruction. In R. Barr, M. L. Kamil, P. B. Mosenthal, & P. D. Pearson (Eds.), *Handbook of reading research* (Vol. II, pp. 815–860). New York: Longman.

Perfetti, C. A. (1985). *Reading ability.* New York: Oxford University Press.

Perfetti, C. A., Beck, I, Bell, L., & Hughes, C. (1987). Phonemic knowledge and learning to read are reciprocal: A longitudinal study of first grade children. *Merrill Palmer Quarterly, 33,* 283–319.

Pressley, M. (2000). What should comprehension instruction be the instruction of? In M. L. Kamil, P. B. Mosenthal, P. D. Pearson, & R. Barr (Eds.), *Handbook of reading research* (Vol. III, pp. 545–560). Mahwah, NJ: Erlbaum.

Pressley, M., El-Dinary, P. B., Gaskins, I., Schuder, T., Bergman, J., Almasi, L., & Brown, R. (1992). Beyond direct explanation: Transactional instruction of reading comprehension strategies. *Elementary School Journal, 92,* 511–554.

Scanlon, D. M., & Vellutino, F. R. (1996). Prerequisite skills, early instruction, and success in first grade reading: Selected results from a longitudinal study. *Mental Retardation and Developmental Disabilities, 2,* 54–63.

Shaywitz, B. A., Fletcher, J. M., & Shaywitz, S. E. (1995). Defining and classifying learning disabilities and attention-deficit/hyperactivity disorder. *Journal of Child Neurology, 10*(Suppl.), S50–S57.

Snow, C. E., Barnes, W., Chandler, J. Goodman, I., & Hemphill, L. (1991). *Unfulfilled expectations: Home and school influences on literacy.* Cambridge, MA: Harvard University Press.

Snow, C. E., Burns, M. S., & Griffith, P. (1998). *Preventing reading difficulty in young children.* Washington, DC: National Academy Press.

Stahl, S. A., Duffy-Hester, A. M., & Dougherty Stahl, K. A. (1998). Everything you wanted to know about phonics (but were afraid to ask). *Reading Research Quarterly, 33*(3), 338–355.

Stahl, S. A., & Kuhn, M. R. (2002). Making it sound like language: Developing fluency. *Reading Teacher, 55*(6), 582–584.

Stanovich, K. E. (1986). Matthew effects in reading: Some consequences of individual differences in the acquisition of literacy. *Reading Research Quarterly, 21,* 360–407.

Stanovitch, K. E. (1991). Word recognition: Changing perspectives. In R. Barr, M. L. Kamill, P. B. Mosenthal, & P. D. Pearson (Eds.), *Handbook of reading research,* (Vol. II, pp. 418–452). New York: Longman.

Stein, N. L., & Trabasso, T. (1981). What's in a story: Critical issues in comprehension and instruction. In R. Glaser (Ed.), *Advances in the psychology of instruction* (Vol. II). Hillsdale, NJ: Erlbaum.

Sticht, T. G., & James, J. H. (1984). Listening and reading. In P. D. Pearson, R. Barr, M. L. Kamil, & P. B. Mosenthal (Eds.), *Handbook of reading research* (pp. 292–317). New York: Longman.

Stone, C. R., & Burton, A. E. (1960). New practice readers (Book A). New York: McGraw-Hill.

Sweet, A. P., Guthrie, J. T., & Ng, M. M. (1998). Teacher perceptions and student motivation. *Journal of Educational Psychology, 90*(2), 210–223.

Templeton, S., & Morris, D. (2000). Spelling. In M. L. Kamil, P. B. Mosenthal, P. D. Pearson, & R. Barr (Eds.), *Handbook of reading research* (Vol. III, pp. 525–543). Mahwah, NJ: Erlbaum.

Torgesen, J. K. (2000). Individual differences in response to early intervention in reading: The lingering problem of treatment resisters. *Learning Disabilities Research and Practice, 15*(1), 55–64

Tunmer, W. E., Herriman, M. L., & Nesdale, A. R. (1988). Metalinguistic abilities and beginning reading. *Reading Research Quarterly, 23,* 134–158.

van Ostendoorp, H., & Goldman, S. R (1999). *The construction of mental representations during reading.* Mahwah, NJ: Erlbaum.

Vellutino, F. R. (1987). Dyslexia. *Scientific American, March,* 34–41.

Vellutino, F. R., & Scanlon, D. M. (1987). Phonological coding, phonological awareness, and reading ability: Evidence from a longitudinal and experimental study. *Merrill-Palmer Quarterly, 33,* 321–363.

Vellutino, F. R., & Scanlon, D. M. (2002). The interactive strategies approach to reading intervention. *Contemporary Educational Psychology, 27,* 537–635.

Vellutino, F. R., Scanlon, D. M., & Lyon, G. R. (2000). Differentiating between difficult to remediate and readily remediated poor readers: More evidence against the IQ achievement discrepancy definition of reading disability. *Journal of Learning Disabilities, 33*(3), 223–238.

Vellutino, F. R., Scanlon, D. M., Sipay, E. R., Small, S. G., Pratt, A., Chen, R., & Denckla, M. B. (1996). Cognitive profiles of difficult to remediate and readily remediated poor readers: Early intervention as a vehicle for distinguishing between cognitive and experiential deficits as basic causes of specific reading disability. *Journal of Educational Psychology, 88*(4), 601–638.

Vellutino, F. R., Scanlon, D. M., Small, S. G., & Tanzman, M. S. (1991). The linguistic basis of reading ability: Converting written to oral language. *Text, 11*, 99–133.

Vellutino, F. R., Scanlon, D. M., & Spearing, D. (1995). Semantic and phonological coding in poor and normal readers. *Journal of Experimental Child Psychology, 59*, 76–123.

5

What Do Readers Need to Learn in Order to Process Coherence Relations in Narrative and Expository Text?

ARTHUR C. GRAESSER
DANIELLE S. McNAMARA
MAX M. LOUWERSE

Perhaps we should start with some questions. What do you need to learn to understand the title of this chapter? What does "processing coherence relations" mean? Why should a teacher, let alone a student, care about coherence? We care about coherence because we believe, based on years of research, that processing coherence relations is a cornerstone of comprehension. Coherence breaks down when there are gaps in the text and the reader has trouble handling them. The text is less coherent when there are many conceptual and structural gaps in the text and the reader does not possess the knowledge to fill them. At the other end of the continuum, the text is progressively more coherent to the extent that there are few gaps and the reader has the prerequisite knowledge. This chapter identifies the specific cues or characteristics of text that fortify coherence.

Our research, and that of many others, has pointed to various properties of the text as one important foundation for improving readers' comprehension. The recent RAND report *Reading for Understanding* (Snow, 2002) has communicated the pressing need to improve reading comprehension in schools throughout the country. Students' ability to understand the complex material presented in textbooks is indeed suffering. For teachers, the urgent need for change may have seemed evident for many years and certainly did not require an official report. However, the report also documents a remarkable evolution in our understanding of reading comprehension. It is now quite evident that a critical aspect of reading is the comprehension of meaning. Indeed, the centerpiece of the RAND report was *comprehension*. This contrasts with the historical focus on lower-level decoding processes, such as the processing of letters, sound units, syllables, words, and syntax. This change marks not only a better understanding of these lower-level processes, but also the increased recognition of the importance of comprehension in addition to decoding processes.

The RAND report's framework for thinking about reading comprehension included four interactive components: The *reader*, the *text*, comprehension *activities*, and the *sociocultural context* (see Chapter 1). This chapter focuses on the *coherence relations* that organize text content. A text is perceived to be *coherent* to the reader when the ideas hang together in a meaningful and organized manner. How is this accomplished? Coherence *relations* are constructed in the mind of the reader with the help of linguistic and discourse markers. A *marker* is an explicit word, phrase, sentence, or feature that guides the reader in interpreting the substantive ideas in the text, in connecting ideas with other ideas, and in connecting the ideas to higher-level global units (such as the overall theme of the text).

An excellent way to clarify the meaning of coherence relations is through examples. Consider J. K. Rowling's *Harry Potter* series, which is the top-selling children's series in the United States and is now featured in blockbuster movies. The first book in the series, *Harry Potter and the Sorcerer's Stone* (1997), begins with the following paragraph.

> Mr. and Mrs. Dursley, of number four, Privet Drive, were proud to say that they were perfectly normal, thank you very much. They were the last people you'd expect to be involved in anything strange or mysterious, because they just didn't hold with such nonsense. (p. 1)

The substantive ideas capture the facts and events in the story. These include: Mr. and Mrs. Dursley live at number four, Privet Drive; the Dursleys were perfectly normal; the Dursleys didn't get into anything strange and mysterious; and the Dursleys believed that the strange and mysterious were nonsense. In addition to these substantive ideas, this beginning paragraph contains coherence relations that vary in type and subtlety. *Text-connecting* relations connect words or clauses in the text. For example, pronouns signal a frequent type of text-connecting relation. *They* refers to Mr. and Mrs. Dursley in the preceding example. *They* serves as a bridge that links the two clauses in the first sentence with the two clauses in the second sentence.

Conjunctions are another frequent type of text-connecting relation. For example, *because* is a conjunction that connects the two clauses in the second sentence. More specifically, *because* is a signal to the reader that the second clause (the Dursleys believed the strange and mysterious were nonsense) is an explanation of the first clause (the Dursleys were the last people to be involved in the strange and mysterious). The *because* conjunction always means that there is a *causal* coherence relation. The excerpt that begins Chapter 14 of *Harry Potter* has a large number of conjunctions and other expressions that connect clauses in text.

> Quirrell, however, must have been braver than they'd thought. In the weeks that followed he did seem to be getting paler and thinner, but it didn't look as though he'd cracked yet. (p. 228)

However, but, and *in the weeks that followed* help the reader connect the clauses in this excerpt. *However* and *but* are *adversative* conjunctions that signal that a clause has information that is different from a claim or expectation. *In the weeks that followed* signals a *temporal* relation. Discourse analysts have proposed a number of taxonomies that classify these conjunctive coherence relations into subcategories (Halliday & Hasan, 1976; Mann & Thompson, 1986).

Some coherence relations are pitched at more global levels of organization and require the reader to make many inferences. The first sentence of the first Harry Potter example ends with *thank you very much*. This would be a confusing expression to a young reader if taken literally. Who is thanking whom? And for what deed? In fact, no one is being thanked at all. Instead, *thank you very much* is a vernacular expression that conveys an attitude. Children and adolescents use the expression frequently as a somewhat derogatory reply to anyone who challenges them with a question or request. But who is expressing the attitude to whom in the story? Perhaps the narrator wishes to convey that the Dursleys are very proud of being normal and would dramatically defend their attitude to any imaginary person who might question their normalcy. Perhaps the narrator is expressing this attitude to the reader. This example illustrates two facts about narrative discourse. First, there are multiple levels of dialogue to worry about in narrative. Not only are there explicit speech acts between characters in the plot, but there are implicit acts of communication between characters, implicit dialogues between the narrator and audience, and implicit dialogues between the writer and reader. Second, many of these implicit levels of communication are largely invisible to the reader and require sophisticated forms of world knowledge. Indeed, background knowledge and the process of making inferences are crucial to successful comprehension.

Harry Potter is replete with excerpts that illustrate how inferences and world knowledge are necessary for connecting sentences and clauses in text. The beginning of Chapter 8 in *Harry Potter*, for example, illustrates this in a simple dialogue between characters.

> "There, look."
> "Where?"
> "Next to the tall kid with the red hair."
> "Wearing the glasses?"
> "Did you see his face?"
> "Did you see his scar?" (p. 131)

This beginning of Chapter 8 clearly relies on the previous chapters for the reader to reconstruct the speaker and listener of each speech act in the dialogue. The text has minimal cues for directing a coherent mental picture of the dialogue. There are only quote symbols and turn-taking conventions for two-party dialogues. The child learning to read must learn what quote symbols mean and that writers sometimes leave out *who says what*. The child must learn how to recognize embedded conversations between characters and that people take turns speaking in dialogue.

The previous excerpt also illustrates the use of *deictic* coherence relations. These are words that point to characters, locations in space, and points in time in conversation and communication (Clark, 1996; Halliday & Hasan, 1976). Sometimes references to a particular person, place, or time are expressed with many words. For example, there is a rich description of the Dursleys in Chapter 1, a reference to the location of a face in Chapter 8 (*the face with the scar and glasses, located next to the tall kid with red hair*), and to a point in time in Chapter 14 (*in the weeks that followed*). At other times, however, deictic markers are semantically depleted references to people (*I, you, he, she, him, his, her*), to people or things (*this, that, these, those*), to locations (*here, there, from, to, nearby*), and to times (*now, then, whenever*). Speakers in a conversation often use gestures to point to people, locations, and points in time, but all of this needs to be reconstructed by the reader when text is read. Once again, world knowledge and inferences are needed to accomplish these reconstructions.

Most children have an impressive amount of world knowledge and capacity for generating inferences when reading children's stories (Mandler, 1984; Trabasso & Magliano, 1996; Van den Broek, 1996). The information in stories has a comparatively high similarity to experiences in everyday life (Bruner, 1986; Graesser, Singer, & Trabasso, 1994). A story is a *microworld* with characters who perform actions in pursuit of goals, events that present obstacles to goals, conflicts between characters, emotional reactions, spatial settings, objects and object properties, traits of characters, and mental states of characters. This sort of content has a high correspondence to what the child experiences in everyday life. Of course, there are some violations of everyday life when the story embarks on the supernatural. But even the supernatural must have verisimilitude. When stories and other forms of narrative text are read, the reader wants to be entertained and to learn about the wisdom of life. All of this is buttressed by a rich set of experiences and world knowledge.

In contrast to narrative stories, expository text is written to inform readers about ideas with which they are unfamiliar. Young readers normally have much less world knowledge about the ideas in expository text. Expository texts describe objects and parts in complex systems, the functions of these components, causal mechanisms that explain how mechanisms work, procedures for accomplishing objectives, and logical justifications of claims. Much of this content is abstract and technical, far removed from everyday experiences. For example, a popular expository textbook on technology and science, David Macaulay's *The Way Things Work* (1988), provides illustrated texts on hundreds of everyday devices, ranging from screws to steam engines. Consider the following excerpt about a button battery.

> The zinc loses electrons as it becomes zinc oxide, while the mercury atoms gain electrons as the mercury oxide changes to mercury. The battery produces a current of 1.35 bolts. (p. 288)

This expository text has a high density of unfamiliar terms, which is typically the case with expository texts designed to teach readers about technical material. Whereas the temporal connectives (*as, while*) explicitly clarify the timing events in the first sentence, it is notable that there are no causal conjunctions and there are no substantive words that overlap between the first and second sentences. Therefore, the learner will have to infer the relationship between these two sentences. Does the battery produce a current of 1.35 bolts *because* the mercury oxide changes to mercury? Or are these clauses not linked by causal relations? These types of inferences are necessary to understand expository texts. However, such inferences rely heavily on the reader's ability to draw on previous knowledge—knowledge that most readers do not have.

When there are more conjunctions and overlapping terms given explicitly in the text, the text is often more coherent and most readers process it more easily. Numerous studies have reported that increasing the explicit coherence relations in expository texts improves memory and comprehension (Beck, McKeown, Sinatra, & Loxterman, 1991; Britton & Gulgoz, 1991; McNamara, 2001). Paradoxically, expository texts often lack the necessary linguistic and discourse markers (and resulting coherence) that are needed for most students to successfully comprehend them. Moreover, the comprehension deficits that arise from texts with low coherence are particularly problematic for readers with less knowledge about the domain

(McNamara, Kintsch, Songer, & Kintsch, 1996; McNamara, 2001). This combination of factors results in the common situation of frustrated learners faced with nearly incomprehensible textbooks.

There are many different types of relations that improve the coherence of expository text. We have already described the referential, causal, temporal, spatial, adversative, logical, and deictic coherence relations. There are two additional classes of coherence relations. There are headers, subheaders, and highlighted words that help organize the content hierarchically and that signify the type of expository text. These *signaling devices* can unveil the organization and purpose of the expository text very quickly. Texts about dishwashers have very different signaling devices when written for a school course than for a repair manual or for an advertisement. It is interesting to note that narrative texts do not have the prevalent array of headers, subheaders, and word highlighting that occurs in expository texts.

The final class of coherence relations, particularly in expository text, consists of paragraph conventions. It is a good policy for expository text writers to follow a Topic Sentence + Elaboration rhetorical format. The first sentence identifies the main topic or theme of the paragraph, whereas the subsequent sentences supply additional detail that is relevant to the topic sentence. In contrast, the paragraph conventions for narrative are different and less constrained, because narratives often map onto our own experiences in the world. One reason that paragraph conventions are more frequent in expository text is that they reduce the number of conceptual gaps, which is more important when reading the less familiar information in such texts.

Now that we have described and illustrated coherence relations, we turn to the more practical questions of what educators need to consider when teaching children how to proficiently master coherence relations during reading. We discuss this in three parts. First, we briefly identify the mental representations and processes that researchers believe are part of the comprehension of meaning. Second, we present a comprehensive set of coherence relations that teachers and young readers need to learn. There are differences in the difficulty of mastering the various classes of coherence relations, which presents challenges for students and teachers. Third, we discuss the implications of this research on reading instruction.

MENTAL REPRESENTATIONS AND PROCESSES

When readers comprehend text, they mentally build meaning representations at multiple levels. Each level has its own special characteristics. Most researchers who investigate text and discourse comprehension talk about five levels (Graesser, Millis, & Zwaan, 1997; Kintsch, 1998):

1. *Surface code.* The exact wording and grammar of the sentences.
2. *Text base.* The meaning of the clauses that are explicitly given in the text.
3. *Mental model.* The ideas or microworld of what the text is about. Inferences based on world knowledge are needed to construct the mental model; that is, the meaning in the mental model goes beyond the explicit text.
4. *Text genre.* The category of the text. The major genre categories are narrative, expository, persuasive, and descriptive texts, but some texts are combinations of these basic categories. Each genre has its own rhetorical structure. For example, simple folktales have a Setting + Plot + Moral rhetorical structure, whereas an expository text on a scientific argument may have a Claim + Evidence rhetorical structure.
5. *Communication channel.* The act of communication between the reader and writer, or narrator and audience. Such acts of communication normally require a global theme, message, point, or purpose in writing the text. The ground rules for the communication differ among the various genres, such as arguments, tutoring sessions, jokes, and newspaper articles.

A text is coherent when there are adequate connections and harmony both within levels and between levels.

It should be perfectly obvious that children need to master each of these levels in order to be proficient readers. They need to learn the meaning of the words, the grammatical forms, the subject matter, the rhetorical structure, and the communication conventions. Moreover, it may not be enough merely to learn all of this; they may have to overlearn it. That is, they may need extensive practice, in diverse contexts, so that the codes, structures, and processing skills become automatic (Perfetti, 1985). Children become *proficient* with a level of representation when they know what the code is (called *awareness*), they can mentally build the code reliably (called *mastery*), they know when to construct the code (called *tuning*), and they know how to execute and monitor the construction of code very quickly (called *skill*). Reading proficiency is not instilled by merely lecturing to a child. There must be extensive practice, with guidance and feedback from the teacher (or peers or a computer), so that there is active application of the knowledge. Frequent reading is arguably the most critical gateway to improving reading skill, but high-quality feedback from a teacher on the reading process presumably is also important.

Reading researchers have traditionally focused on reading proficiency at the levels of the surface code and, to some extent, the text base. Children receive drill and practice on letter–sound correspondence, phonemic awareness, syllable composition, meanings of words, and sometimes grammatical form. The development of reading proficiency at the deeper levels of comprehension have been comparatively neglected, although there have been more serious attempts to fill this gap in recent years (Cornoldi & Oakhill, 1996; Palincsar & Brown, 1984; Pressley & Afflerbach, 1995; Trabasso & Magliano, 1996; Van den Broek, 1996; Williams, 1993). Part of the reason for this neglect was the lack of scientific research on the deeper levels of comprehension 25 years ago. Fortunately, times have changed. Researchers in the field of *discourse processes* have dissected the deeper levels of comprehension in rich detail and have made some impressive progress. It is beyond the scope of this chapter to reference all of the important research that has investigated deeper levels of comprehension. However, we do recommend a number of books that review this literature (Graesser, Gernsbacher, & Goldman, 2003; Kintsch, 1998; Louwerse & Van Peer, 2002; Otero, Leon, & Graesser, 2002). At the same time, we acknowledge that there are considerable gaps in the available research literature.

It is worthwhile to consider some of the key assumptions about how the mind functions in theories of reading and discourse processing (Graesser et al., 1994, 1997; Kintsch, 1998). Familiarity with these assumptions will, it is hoped, allow the reading teacher to better understand why some coherence relations are easier to master than others. The following nine assumptions are routinely adopted by discourse researchers.

1. *Information sources.* Three important information sources are the explicit text, relevant background knowledge, and the communication context that situates the reading of the text. Background knowledge includes both general knowledge (e.g., what the reader knows about door locks in general) and specific experiences (e.g., the reader's previous experience of being locked in the bathroom).

2. *Memory stores.* The three memory stores are short-term memory, working memory, and long-term memory. Short-term memory holds the current clause being processed, and working memory holds a handful of recent important clauses. It is difficult for some readers to link the immediate clause being read in the text to sentences and paragraphs several pages earlier, because the earlier content has either left short-term memory and working memory or it takes too much time to fetch it from long-term memory. These difficulties are more severe for readers with less knowledge of the topic.

3. *Discourse focus.* The discourse focus is the idea that is directly in consciousness. Content in the discourse focus can be referred to with pronouns (*he, she, this, it*). The content outside the discourse focus must be described in more words so that the reader can easily recognize what the writer is referring to.

4. *Harmony within and among levels.* Confusion is elicited by disharmony among information sources and levels of mental representation. The disharmony stimulates additional thought and mental effort to resolve such contradictions. For example, an explicit coherence relation that does not mesh with the substantive ideas requires more reading time and thought by a diligent reader.

5. *Repetition and automaticity.* Repeated activation of a word or idea increases the speed of accessing it from long-term memory. After many repetitions, the word or idea is automatically fetched from long-term memory with very little mental effort.

6. *Satisfaction of reader goals.* Readers are motivated by one or more comprehension goals when reading a text. The goals are either idiosyncratic to the reader or are appropriate for the text genre. For example, a skilled reader of a mystery novel knows that an apparently irrelevant fact (e.g., a character's scar mentioned by the author) may have explanatory significance later in the narrative. Good readers allocate their mental efforts to explicit information and inferences that address their comprehension goals.

7. *Local and global coherence.* The comprehender's goal is to construct a meaningful representation that establishes local and global coherence among clauses given in the text. Local text coherence is established when clauses next to each other in the text can be connected coherently. Global coherence links larger chunks of text.

8. *Explanation.* A proficient reader attempts to explain *why* events in the text occur and *why* the author explicitly mentions particular information in the text. Such explanations include motives of characters' actions, causes of events, and justifications of claims. Why-questions guide comprehension to a greater extent than other types of questions (e.g., where, when, how, and what happens next). Explanation of expository text is particularly important. Readers who consistently attempt to explain what the content means, rather than passively processing the text, understand the text better and at a deeper level.

9. *Levels of mental representation.* As mentioned earlier, there are multiple levels of understanding during comprehension. Five levels were listed and described earlier in this section (surface code, text base, mental model, text genre and communication channel). Among these, understanding at the level of the mental model has particularly important implications for comprehension, because this is the level at which many readers struggle.

It is important to reiterate the RAND panel's view that comprehension has four interactive components, namely, the text, the reader, comprehension activities, and sociocultural context. Empirical studies of reading have uncovered some intriguing, and sometimes counterintuitive, interactions among the text, reader, and task variables (Cote, Goldman & Saul, 1998;

McNamara et al., 1996; McNamara, 2001). For example, McNamara et al. (1996) manipulated text coherence (high vs. low), measured readers' knowledge about passage topics (high vs. low knowledge about science), and administered several tests that tapped different levels of mental representation. High-coherence texts benefited readers with low knowledge, regardless of the type of comprehension test (to no one's surprise). However, when tests of deep comprehension were analyzed, high-knowledge readers showed substantial benefits from having read texts with *low* cohesion (to the surprise of many). The low-coherence texts encourage knowledgeable readers to work harder and actively build richer mental representations. Comprehension researchers are currently discovering and explaining many such higher-order interactions (e.g., Cote, et al., 1998; McNamara et al., 1996; McNamara, 2001). Such complexities, of course, present challenges for those who teach comprehension skills.

CLASSES OF COHERENCE RELATIONS

The purpose of this section is to identify a comprehensive set of coherence relations. There are special challenges in becoming proficient in mastering each of these classes of coherence relations. Some of these challenges are discussed in this section and the subsequent section.

Coreference

Coreference occurs when two words (or verbal expressions) refer to the same person, thing, abstract concept, or idea. Pronouns constitute a textbook case of coreference. *They* is a coreference with *Mr. and Mrs. Dursley* in the first *Harry Potter* example. A proficient reader needs to figure out the coreferent whenever there is a pronoun in the text: *he, she, him, her, his, hers, they, their, it, this, that, which, what, who*—the list goes on. Pronoun comprehension is complicated and takes longer to achieve when the coreferent of the pronoun is ambiguous (the pronoun can refer to two or more entities) or is vague (it is impossible to precisely resolve the pronoun) (Clark, 1996; Gernsbacher, 1997). Many pronouns are indeed ambiguous or vague in naturalistic discourse, particularly the pronouns *it* and *they*. What does *it* refer to in *It is raining*? What individuals are involved when a child says *They don't like me*?

When an entity is first introduced in a text, a good writer grounds it with a rich description (e.g., *a big bad wolf*). A subsequent reference to it can be made with a pronoun (*it, he*) or a noun (*the wolf*) unless there are multiple wolves that need to be discriminated. If the entity has not been mentioned for several sentences or pages, a good writer has to reintroduce the entity with a rich description (e.g., *the big bad wolf that had earlier been lurking in the forest*). Beginning readers need to learn these conventions of coreference in English. They often need to use them when writers are not particularly simple and systematic in following the conventions.

Inferences are also needed when a different noun is used to refer to a previous entity or event. Consider the following examples.

> The musician brought the bassoon, but the woodwind was never played.
> Pakistan is fighting India. The conflict is escalating.

A bridging inference is needed to link *woodwind* to *bassoon* and to link *conflict* to the *fight* between Pakistan and India. As mentioned earlier, low-knowledge readers have trouble making these bridging inferences, so it is a good policy to have explicit coreferences in texts for such readers (Britton & Gulgoz, 1991; McNamara et al., 1996; McNamara, 2001).

Deixis

As discussed earlier, deictic references point to the people, locations, and time in a conversation among participants. The conversation may be between the writer and reader, between the narrator and the audience, or between two characters in a story. There are pronouns that refer to people (*I, you, we*), to locations (*here, there, over there*), and to time (*now, then, later*). As in the case of coreference, a good writer makes sure that the referents are in the *common ground* before these pronouns and adverbs are used. A referent is in the common ground when both the writer and the comprehender understand who or what it is (i.e., it is shared knowledge).

Given and New Cues

The content of every sentence in a text can be segregated into *given* (old) information and *new* information. Given information has already been introduced, mentioned, or inferred from the previous text (i.e., prior to the sentence being read). New information advances the discourse with new content. Consider the following sentence from *Harry Potter*: *The table was almost hidden beneath all Dudley's birthday presents* (p. 19). Some of the given and new ideas are enumerated in the following list:

> There is a table (given).
> There are birthday presents (given).
> Dudley exists (given).
> The birthday presents are for Dudley (given).

There are several birthday presents (given).
The table is almost hidden (new).
The table is beneath the presents (new).

Given information is frequently tucked in the nouns and noun modifiers in the sentences, whereas the main verb and its modifiers capture the new information. It is beyond the scope of this chapter to discuss the many cues that contrast given and new (see Clark, 1996), but we do advocate that children learning to read be given exercises that will develop their understanding of this distinction.

Conjunctive Relations

Conjunctive relations are text-connecting relations that normally link adjacent clauses or sentences. These relations can be classified according to particular characteristics of world knowledge, mental models, and communication. Among the subcategories of conjunctive relations are the additive (*and, also, moreover*), temporal (*and then, then, when, before, after, during, while*), causal (*because, consequently, as a result*), intentional (*in order to, by means of*), adversative (*but, although, however*), and logical (*therefore, so*) (Halliday & Hasan, 1976).

Sometimes proficient readers are able to infer the relations without the presence of the conjunctions. How do they do this? They can reconstruct the relations on the basis of world knowledge in conjunction with the various levels of meaning representation. However, beginning readers and low-knowledge readers benefit from the conjunctions being explicitly used in the text. The inclusion of conjunctions tends to lengthen sentences, which has the unwanted side effect of taxing working memory. However, the benefits of clarifying the coherence relation between the clauses normally outweigh the penalties of increasing the load on working memory. Available research suggests that the trade-off should be tipped toward clarity for low-knowledge readers (McNamara et al., 1996).

Verb Tense and Chronology

The events in stories unfold in a chronological order. Similarly, expository texts that describe event chains unfold in a sequential order. In the vast majority of texts, the order of mentioning the events corresponds to the chronological order. This correspondence is indeed assumed when explicit temporal cues are absent; if the author mentions events A, B, and C, then it is assumed that A occurred before B and B occurred before C. A good writer adds explicit temporal cues when there are deviations from this chronological order, as in the case of flashbacks and flash forwards. The tense of the verbs (i.e., past, present, future) also plays an important role in keeping track of the chronological order of events. A cooperative writer gives rich reorienting descriptions when there are major shifts in the time line, such as *last week at the Sunday dinner* or *later on in his career*. It is safe to assume that the next event described in a text is the next step on the chronological time line unless there are linguistic or discourse cues that signal temporal deviations. Such deviations take additional time for the reader to process (Zwaan & Radvansky, 1998).

Scene Changes

A scene is a spatial context that houses the characters who interact in a story or the entities that exist in an expository text. Scene changes are explicitly signaled by a good writer (e.g., *meanwhile, back at the ranch* or *the governments in other countries such as China*). It takes additional processing time for the mental camera to shift from one scene to another (Rinck, Williams, Bower, & Becker, 1996).

Headers and Highlighting

As discussed earlier, headers, subheaders, and highlighted words serve numerous discourse functions. They help organize the text and allow the reader to recognize the relevant text genre. They guide the reader's attention and comprehension strategies in a top-down fashion. These signaling devices are particularly helpful to low-knowledge readers.

Topic Sentences

A rhetorical convention for expository text is that the first sentence in a paragraph should capture the main topic or theme of the paragraph. Subsequent sentences embellish the topic sentence. Writers who deviate from this convention run the risk of confusing the reader.

Punctuation

We have already discussed the importance of quotation marks to signify speech acts of characters in stories. Speech acts in quote marks (*John said to Mary, "I hate lasagna"*) can alternatively be articulated without quote marks (*John told Mary that he hated lasagna*). Speech acts in quotes emphasize the performance, experience, and timing of the conversation (how it was said), whereas forms of indirect address settle for the bare bones meaning (what was said). Aside from quote marks, there are other forms of punctuation that have well-established conventional meanings, namely periods (.), colons (:), semicolons (;), commas (,), exclamation points (!), and dashes (—). Beginning readers may not fully understand the discourse function of these forms of punctuation.

Signals of Rhetorical Structure

There are different subclasses of narrative and expository texts that have distinct rhetorical structures. Coherence relations play a prominent role in the recognition and organization of the rhetorical structure. Consider the different types of expository texts that follow and the associated explicit coherence relations.

Lists and orderings (*First, Second, Third; a, b, c*)
Procedures (*The first step is, The second step is*)
Compare–contrast (*On one hand, On the other hand, whereas*)
Claim + Evidence (*The primary claim is, support for*)

There are distinctive words for recognizing other major subtypes of expository texts: Problem + Solution, Data + Conclusions, Explanations, Logical Syllogisms, Definition + Examples, and Introduction + Methods + Results + Discussion. Obviously, it is not sufficient for the reader to simply memorize what discourse markers are distinctively associated with each particular rhetorical structure. The reader also needs to understand the world knowledge and communication function associated with each subtype of genre.

IMPLICATIONS FOR READING INSTRUCTION

How do we improve the reader's proficiency in handling coherence relations? This is not an easy agenda. Very few teachers are aware of the broad landscape of coherence relations, because the field of discourse processes has only a 25–year history. Most researchers who have studied text coherence have not yet considered the implications of coherence for teaching reading.

An obvious first step is to increase the reader's awareness of the different types of coherence relations. Just as there are reading programs that promote phonemic awareness, there should be those that emphasize coherence awareness. There should be a cottage industry of workbooks, computer software, and teacher training workshops that identify the different types of coherence relations. There should be definitions, examples, and extensive drill and practice for each class of relation. It is not sufficient to spend a day or two giving a lecture on the taxonomy of coherence relations. The process of identifying and interpreting such relations will need to be *overlearned* to the point of being automatic. There are likely to be benefits from coordinating the writing of the coherence relations with proficiency in reading them. However, it remains to be seen what sort of curriculum will optimize reading proficiency for different types of learners.

We have emphasized throughout this chapter that world knowledge plays a major role in constructing most of the coherence relations. The importance of coherence relations becomes more critical to the extent that the reader knows less and less about the subject matter. A teacher's selection of topics for the reader is likely to be a bit tricky. If the reader knows a great deal about the topic, then attention to the coherence relations will have small payoffs. If the reader's knowledge about the subject matter is bankrupt, then there will not be enough foundation to generate the inferences that must accompany the explicit relations. We suspect that an intermediate amount of world knowledge may be optimal—at the reader's *zone of proximal development*.

There presumably are advantages to exposing readers to a variety of text genre and coherence relations. If they read fairy tales, mysteries, scientific texts, persuasive essays, newspaper articles, recipes, memos, jokes, and so on, these texts should provide a balanced repertoire of all 10 classes of coherence relations enumerated in the preceding section. The resulting reading proficiency will, it is hoped, be broad and flexible.

The purpose of this chapter is to identify what readers need to learn about coherence relations in narrative and expository texts. We have provided a glimpse of what needs to be known. Our claims have been grounded in empirical scientific research on text comprehension, but it is informative to note that the vast majority of this research has been on high school and college students rather than children. There must be more attention to investigating effective methods of teaching such relations in classrooms, tutoring sessions, computer-based training, and other learning environments. It is time for teachers and reading researchers to roll up their sleeves and get started.

ACKNOWLEDGMENTS

This research was partially supported by grants to one of us (A.C.G.) from the Department of Defense Multidisciplinary University Research Initiative (MURI) administered by the Office of Naval Research (N00014-00-1-0600) and the National Science Foundation (SES 9977969, REC 0106965, REC 0126265). The research was partially supported by a grant to another of us (D.S.McN.) from the National Science Foundation IERI (REC 0089271) and by a grant awarded to the authors by the Institute of Education Sciences (R305G020018-02). Any opinions, findings, conclusions, or recommendations expressed in this material are those of the authors and do not necessarily reflect the views of the funding agencies.

REFERENCES

Beck, I. L., McKeown, M. G., Sinatra, G. M., & Loxterman, J. A. (1991). Revising social studies text from a text-processing perspective: Evidence of improved comprehensibility. *Reading Research Quarterly, 26,* 251–276.

Britton, B. K., & Gulgoz, S. (1991). Using Kintsch's computational model to improve instructional text: Effects of repairing inference calls on recall and cognitive structures. *Journal of Educational Psychology, 83,* 329–404.

Bruner, J. (1986). *Actual minds, possible worlds.* Cambridge, MA: Harvard University Press.

Clark, H. H. (1996). *Using language.* Cambridge, MA: Cambridge University Press.

Cornoldi, C., & Oakhill, J. (Eds.). (1996). *Reading comprehension difficulties: Processes and intervention.* Hillsdale, NJ: Erlbaum.

Cote, N., Goldman, S.R ., & Saul, E. U. (1998). Students making sense of informational text: Relations between processing and representations. *Discourse Processes, 25,* 1–54.

Gernsbacher, M. A. (1997). Two decades of structure building. *Discourse Processes, 23,* 265–304.

Graesser, A. C., Gernsbacher, M. A., & Goldman, S. (Eds.). (2003). *Handbook of discourse processes.* Mahwah, NJ: Erlbaum.

Graesser, A. C., Millis, K. K., & Zwaan. R. A. (1997). Discourse comprehension. *Annual Review of Psychology, 48,* 163–189.

Graesser, A. C., Singer, M., & Trabasso, T. (1994). Constructing inferences during narrative text comprehension. *Psychological Review, 101,* 371–395.

Halliday, M. A. K., & Hasan, R. (1976). *Cohesion in English.* London: Longmans.

Kintsch, W. (1998). *Comprehension: A paradigm for cognition.* Cambridge, MA: Cambridge University Press.

Louwerse, M. M., & Van Peer, W. (Eds.). (2002). *Thematics: Interdisciplinary studies.* Amsterdam/Philadelphia: John Benjamins.

Macaulay, D. (1988). *The way things work.* Boston: Houghton Mifflin.

Mandler, J. M. (1984). *Stories, scripts, and scenes: Aspects of schema theory.* Hillsdale, NJ: Erlbaum.

Mann,W. C., & Thompson, S. A. (1986). Relational propositions in discourse. *Discourse Processes, 9,* 57–90.

McNamara, D. S. (2001). Reading both high and low coherence texts: Effects of text sequence and prior knowledge. *Canadian Journal of Experimental Psychology, 55,* 51–62.

McNamara, D. S., Kintsch, E., Songer, N. B., & Kintsch, W. (1996). Are good texts always better? Interactions of text coherence, background knowledge, and levels of understanding in learning from text. *Cognition and Instruction, 14,* 1–43.

Otero, J., Leon, J. A., & Graesser, A. C. (Eds.). (2002). *The psychology of science text comprehension.* Mahwah, NJ: Erlbaum.

Palincsar, A. M., & Brown, A. L. (1984). Reciprocal teaching of comprehension-monitoring activities. *Cognition and Instruction, 1,* 117–175.

Perfetti, C. A. (1985). *Reading ability.* New York: Oxford University Press.

Pressley, M., & Afflerbach, P. (1995). *Verbal protocols of reading: The nature of constructively responsive reading.* Mahwah, NJ: Erlbaum.

Rinck, M., Williams, P., Bower, G. H., & Becker, E. S. (1996). Spatial situation models and narrative understanding: Some generalizations and extensions. *Discourse Processes*, *21*, 23–56.

Rowling, J. K. (1997). *Harry Potter and the Sourcerer's Stone*. New York: Scholastic.

Snow, C. (2002). *Reading for understanding: Toward an R&D program in reading comprehension*. Santa Monica, CA: RAND Corporation.

Trabasso, T., & Magliano, J. P. (1996). How do children understand what they read and what can we do to help them? In M. Graves, P. van den Broek, & B. Taylor (Eds.), *The first R: A right of all children* (pp. 160–188). New York: Columbia University Press.

Van den Broek, P. W. (1996). Discovering the cement of the universe: The development of event comprehension from childhood to adulthood. In P. W. Van den Broek, P. J. Bauer, & T. Bourg (Eds.), *Developmental spans in event comprehension and representation* (pp. 321–342). Mahwah, NJ: Erlbaum.

Williams, J. P. (1993). Comprehension of students with and without learning disabilities: Identification of narrative themes and idiosyncratic text representations. *Journal of Educational Psychology*, *85*, 631–641.

Zwaan, R. A., & Radvansky, G. A. (1998). Situation models in language comprehension and memory. *Psychological Bulletin*, *123*, 162–185.

6

Collaborative Approaches to Comprehension Instruction

ANNEMARIE SULLIVAN PALINCSAR

As the previous chapters have suggested, reading comprehension is the result of the reader's *constructing meaning*—as contrasted with *retrieving information*—from text. In this chapter we consider how teachers might support students in learning how to construct meaning from text. Rather than giving an exhaustive review of approaches, we have chosen to compare and contrast three instructional procedures, each of which engages teachers and their students in a collaborative approach to text comprehension in the context of a discussion. The three approaches are *Reciprocal Teaching*, *Questioning the Author*, and *Collaborative Reasoning*.

Before describing these approaches, we present a general framework for thinking about comprehension instruction. Our assumption is that the ultimate goal of any form of instruction is to enable students to function independently; this notion is captured in the idea of "teaching for self-regulation." There are certain features of instruction that promote self-regulation on the part of learners—for example, the teacher's mindfulness regarding transferring responsibility for the learning activity to students. In the case of teaching comprehension, a teacher who is teaching for self-regulation is mindful of sharing with his or her students the authority for determining what is worth knowing in the text or how the text might be interpreted.

A second tenet of teaching for self-regulation is a focus on the processes, rather than products, of learning. For example, in a traditional recitation-style lesson, in which the teacher is asking questions, the students are responding to these questions, and the teacher is evaluating the accuracy or acceptability of the responses, there is little opportunity for the learners to discern how the teacher determined what questions were worth asking or how the teacher evaluated their responses. A teacher engaged in teaching for self-regulation is attentive to making explicit the processes of constructing meaning from text—for example, by disclosing to students how she or he made decisions about the key points in the text, or by identifying what she or he regards as evidence for a particular interpretation of the text. Similarly, the teacher is mindful of determining how students set about comprehending text.

Complementing a focus on the processes—rather than the products— of comprehension, is the notion of teaching students to be strategic in their reading of text. Strategies are planful approaches that learners bring to organizing and monitoring their activity as readers. There are particular strategies that have gained currency in the comprehension instruction literature; among them are self-questioning, predicting upcoming information or events, visualizing ideas in the text, paraphrasing ideas in the text, using text structure to organize the information, and using context clues to define unknown words. Integral to thinking about the place of strategy instruction in comprehension instruction is mindfulness that strategies are but a means to an end; they are a means of providing students entrée to the text, a means of checking on one's understanding, and a means of taking corrective action when experiencing difficulty in understanding the text. As we explore specific methods of teaching comprehension for self-regulation, we will revisit these three tenets.

RECIPROCAL TEACHING

Reciprocal Teaching (RT) is an instructional procedure designed to enhance students' reading comprehension. The procedure typically engages teachers and students in a dialogue, the purpose of which is to jointly construct the meaning of the text. The dialogue is supported with the use of four strategies: question generating, summarizing, clarifying, and predicting. When students are initially introduced to RT, the teacher models the application of these strategies for both actively bringing meaning to the written word and monitoring one's own thinking and learning from text. Over the course of time, the students assume increased responsibility for leading the dialogues. By focusing on the processes requisite to successful comprehension, RT is designed to provide students with tools for learning independently.

The Four RT Strategies

When students first begin RT dialogues, they are encouraged to use its strategies with each segment of text; later, as the students become more familiar with them and the purposes for each, the strategies are used opportunistically (e.g., predictions are used only when the text does indeed support making a prediction).

Summarizing provides an opportunity to identify, paraphrase, and integrate important information in the text. Text can be summarized across sentences, across paragraphs, and across the passage as a whole. When the students first begin the RT procedure, their efforts are generally focused at the paragraph level. As they become more proficient, they are able to integrate larger portions of text.

Questioning reinforces the summarizing strategy and carries the learner one more step along the comprehension activity. When students generate questions, they first identify the kind of information that is significant enough to provide the substance for a question. Then they pose this information in question form and self-test to ascertain that they can indeed answer their own question. Question generating is a flexible strategy to the extent that students can be taught and encouraged to generate questions at many levels. For example, some school situations require students to identify andrecall details in the text; others require students to infer from text or apply information from text to novel problems or situations.

Clarifying is an activity that is particularly important when working with students who may believe that the purpose of reading is saying the words correctly; they may not be particularly uncomfortable that the words, and, in fact the passage, are not making sense. As students are taught to clarify, their attention is called to the many reasons that a text is difficult to understand—for example, new vocabulary, unclear referent words, and unfamiliar or difficult concepts. They are taught to be alert to the effects of such impediments to understanding and to take the necessary steps to restore meaning (e.g., reread, read ahead, ask for help).

Predicting requires students to hypothesize about what the author might discuss next in the text. To do this successfully, students must activate the relevant background knowledge they already possess regarding the topic. The students then have a purpose for reading: to confirm or disprove their hypotheses. Furthermore, an opportunity has been created for the students to link the new knowledge they will encounter in the text with the knowledge they already possess. The predicting strategy also facilitates use of text structure as students learn that headings, subheadings, and questions imbedded in the text are useful means of anticipating what may occur next.

Using the Strategies in RT Dialogues

A typical discussion may follow this pattern: The group reads a section of text silently on their own or reads along as someone in the group reads orally (depending on the decoding skills of the students). The discussion leader (a teacher or student) generates a question to which the other members respond. Other members of the group are invited to ask questions they thought of while reading the text. The leader then summarizes the text and asks the group if they would like to elaborate on or revise the summary. Necessary clarifications may be discussed throughout the dialogue or all at once. Finally, in preparation for moving on to the next segment of text, the group makes predictions.

The following dialogue is presented to illustrate the use of the four strategies in a typical RT lesson. In this case, a small group of first-grade students were taught the RT procedure to improve their listening comprehension abilities. The group listened as their teacher, Mrs. Mackey, read aloud text about the pipefish, a fish that mimics and is camouflaged by surrounding plants. Clare is the discussion leader for this portion of the text.

Text: The pipefish change their color and movements to blend with their surroundings. For example, pipefish that live among green plants change their color to a shade of green to match the plants.

CLARE: [*Question*] One question that I had about this paragraph is: What is special about the way that the pipefish looks?

KEITH: [*Clarification*] Do you mean the way that it is green?

ANDY: It's not just that it's green; it's that it's the same color as the plants around it, all around it.

CLARE: [*Summary*] Yes. That's it. My summary is this part tells how the pipefish looks and that it looks like what is around it. [*Prediction*] My prediction is that this is about its enemies and how it protects itself and who the enemies are.

MONTY: [*Addition to summary*] They also talked about how the pipefish moves . . .

KEITH: It sways back and forth.

ANDY: Along with the other plants.

TEACHER: What do we call it when something looks like and acts like something else? The way that the walkingstick was yesterday? We clarified this word when we talked about the walkingstick.

ANGEL: Mimic.

TEACHER: That's right? We said . . . we would say . . . that the pipefish mimics the . . .

STUDENTS: Plants.

TEACHER: Okay! Let's see if Clare's predictions come true.

The Learning Principles Underlying the Use of RT

RT is founded on progressive reconceptualizations of reading and of effective reading instruction. One feature of traditional reading instruction that has proven problematic is that strategies are typically presented as a set of isolated skills. For example, in teaching summarizing, students may be asked to underline a topic sentence in a series of disconnected passages; this type of task does not reflect the nature of summarization, which involves analyzing and synthesizing information. A second characteristic is that strategies are seldom practiced in the actual context in which they will be useful—specifically, while reading extended text. As a result, students, as well as teachers, may lose sight of the purpose of strategy instruction as a means to better comprehension. Finally, the isolated practice of individual strategies does not reinforce their flexible and opportunistic use. Hence, traditional reading instruction has typically provided inadequate opportunities for children to acquire the conditional as well as procedural knowledge regarding the use of strategies.

RT was developed on the basis of alternative conceptions of reading instruction. First, the instruction focuses on helping students to understand the factors that interact and influence their comprehension of text. Second, students are taught to apply the strategies in meaningful contexts, that is, while reading extended text, rather than in isolation and while using artificial tasks. Third, students are encouraged to use the strategies flexibly and opportunistically; in other words, students learn to use the strategies as opportunities arise in which they will assist comprehension, rather than routinely applying the strategies. The strategies are taught as a means for enhancing comprehension, rather than as an end in themselves.

Underlying the model of RT is the notion that expert-led social interactions play an important role in learning and can provide a major impetus to cognitive development. This idea can be found in the writings of Vygotsky (1978), Dewey (1910/1933), and Piaget (1967), who emphasized the role of guided learning in social contexts as a key to developmental change. Dialogue is a critical element of socially mediated instruction inasmuch as it is the means by which experts provide and adjust support to novice learners.

Socially mediated instruction is sometimes referred to as *scaffolded* instruction. A scaffold is a structure that provides support; however, that support is temporary and can be adjusted to meet one's needs. The metaphor of a scaffold appropriately characterizes this kind of instruction, as the teacher and group provide support, which is temporary and adjusted over time, for individual learning (Bruner, 1978; Wood, Bruner, & Ross, 1976). In the initial phase of instruction teachers provide a great deal of support to students as they learn about the strategies and how to use the RT procedure. Teachers scaffold student learning by providing explanation regarding the four strategies and how the strategies can be applied. Teachers further support students by modeling the application of the strategies, thereby making their own problem solving public. During the dialogues there is a conscious effort on the part of the teachers to gradually decrease the amount of support provided to the students over time. Eventually, the teachers provide minimal support or scaffolding and their role becomes more like that of a coach, providing feedback and prompting as necessary.

Finally, RT takes into consideration the influence of motivation on student learning and the kinds of attributions typically made by students who have a history of academic difficulty. Students who are anxious and feel helpless in school are inclined to attribute success with a task to "luck" and to attribute failure with a task to their own lack of ability. Students making these kinds of attributions need to make connections between engaging in strategic activity and the outcomes of this activity. RT enhances motivation by increasing student awareness of the kinds of factors that influence learning outcomes; furthermore, as students become experienced with RT dialogues, they come to appreciate the relationship between their activity as readers and the outcomes of this activity. RT also enhances motivation because students typically enjoy interacting with their peers and collaborating with their teachers.

RT and Knowledge Building

When RT was first designed, it was conceptualized principally as an intervention for supporting students who were significantly challenged in their ability to comprehend and learn from text. Over time, the researchers became increasingly interested in how RT dialogues might support knowledge building and subject matter learning. Palincsar, Brown, and Campione (1993) and Brown et al. (1993) reported on the use of RT dialogues that engaged students in using the dialogues to understand scientific "themes," such as changing populations, by studying specific subtopics (e.g., extinct, endangered, and artificial populations). Analyses of learning in these studies indicate that students made important gains in knowledge building, as well as gains on comprehension measures.

The following transcript illustrates a group fifth graders engaged in RT learning about a process called terraforming.

TEACHER: Let's begin with some predictions about what this passage, called "Living in Space," might tell us about.

RICARDO: It might tell us about the kinds of activities people might have to do to live on Mars.

KEITH: How it would be physically to live on Mars—like what the atmosphere is and how it changes.

SHANNON: How you would have to dress and breathe to live on Mars.

TEACHER: These are all interesting ideas. I notice too that there is a subheading, "Terraforming." Has anyone ever heard that word? Do you know a word that sounds like this that reminds you of "terraforming"? Terrarium? Extraterrestrial? Well, let's begin reading and see what we can learn about this process called terraforming.

(*Students and teacher silently read text, and Jay leads the discussion.*)

JAY: My question is: What is one way to create a greenhouse effect?

SHANNON: Put fluorocarbons in the air?

JAY: Yes. Does anyone have a different question?

KEISHA: What if it gets too hot?

RICARDO: Yes, what if they put too many fluorocarbons in the air?

TEACHER: What do you think of that question? Does the text tell us?

JAY: No, but probably the scientists would know enough about how much it would take.

TEACHER: I have a clarification question that I would like to ask. I was really surprised when I read this, because I know that on earth we are trying to reduce the release of fluorocarbons in the air, so people are asked not use aerosol cans and other sources of fluorocarbons. Why would they want to create a greenhouse effect on Mars?

KEITH: To warm it up. To make the temperature hotter.

TEACHER: Good for you! Because what do we know about the temperature on Mars?

STUDENTS: It is really cold.

TEACHER: All right. If there are no more questions, could Jay summarize for us now?

JAY: This was about how they would pump gases into the air on Mars so that they could make a greenhouse effect and heat up the planet.

TEACHER: That's excellent, and I might add to the summary that creating this greenhouse effect is one part of the terraforming process that they are describing. Any predictions before we go on?

TARA: Maybe more about the air and what they would need to do to breathe the air on Mars?

In this transcript, we see an interesting blend of learning about interpreting text, as well as learning about making an inhospitable environment conducive to human habitation.

Research into the Effectiveness of RT

Most research regarding RT has been conducted in reading and listening comprehension by general, remedial, and special educators. Approximately 300 middle school students and 400 primary grade students participated in the research conducted by Palincsar and Brown (1984, 1989) on RT, designed especially for students who were at risk for academic difficulty or who were already identified as remedial or special education students. Participants in the research typically scored below the 40th percentile on nationally normed measures of reading achievement. To evaluate the success of the intervention, criterion-referenced measures of text comprehension were administered as one of several assessments of student learning. These assessments were designed to evaluate students' ability to recall information, draw inferences, identify the gist of a passage, and apply information presented in the text to a novel situation. The criterion level of performance was defined as the ability to score 75–85% on four out of five consecutive assessments. Prior to instruction, students typically scored approximately 30% on these criterion-referenced measures of text comprehension (averaging 3 of 10 questions correct). However, at the conclusion of instruction (typically 20 days) approximately 80% of both the primary and middle school students achieved the criterion level of performance. Furthermore, participants demonstrated maintenance of these gains for up to 6 months to a year following instruction (Palincsar & Brown, 1984, 1989).

Rosenshine and Meister (1994) conducted a meta-analysis of 16 studies of RT, conducted with students from age 7 to adulthood, in which RT was compared with traditional basal reading instruction, explicit instruction in reading comprehension, and reading and answering questions. They determined that when standardized measures were used to assess comprehension, the median effect size, favoring RT, was .32. When experimenter-developed comprehension tests were used, the median effect size was .88. Furthermore, the researchers found no significant relationship between the number of sessions (which ranged from 6 to 25), nor for the number of students in each instructional group (which ranged from 2 to 23).

Essential Components of RT

Comparative studies have been conducted to determine the essential features of RT. Specifically, the studies were designed to evaluate the role of dialogue in teaching students to be self-regulated learners and to determine whether all four strategies were needed to improve students' comprehension of text. To compare RT with other kinds of instruction that focused on teaching the same set of strategies, not in a dialogic manner, students were randomly assigned to one of four conditions: (1) modeling, in which the teacher demonstrated how to use the strategies while reading text and the students observed and responded to the teacher's questions; (2) isolated skills practice, in which students were taught the RT strategies, using worksheet activities, with extensive teacher feedback regarding their performance; (3) RT/independent practice, in which students were taught RT for only 4 days, followed by 8 days of independently applying the strategies in writing while reading text. Only (4) the traditional RT procedure that incorporated dialogic instruction was effective in bringing about large and reliable changes in student performance (Brown & Palincsar, 1987).

A second comparative study was conducted to determine whether all four strategies were needed to improve students' comprehension abilities or whether a subset would suffice. The performances of students who were taught 10 days of reciprocal questioning alone, and students who were taught 10 days of reciprocal summarizing alone, were compared with the performance of students who were taught 10 days of the traditional RT procedure, in which they were taught all four strategies concurrently. Neither of the individual strategy conditions was as effective as using the full set of strategies to support the dialogue (Brown & Palincsar, 1987).

QUESTIONING THE AUTHOR

Questioning the Author (QtA) (Beck, McKeown, Worthy, Sandora, & Kucan, 1997; Beck, McKeown, Hamilton, & Kucan, 1997), like RT, takes the form of a discussion that unfolds as students are reading a text for the first time, so that they collaborate in the experience of constructing the meaning of the text. The analogue to the strategies used in RT are "queries." The queries serve a broad range of purposes, which include promoting interaction with the text, grappling with ideas, investigating with the text, and clarifying ideas in the text.

There are several ideas key to understanding the design of QtA; one is the notion that text is a human creation; as such, it is subject to the flaws and limitations of any human endeavor. This disposition toward the text is important because it frees the reader to find the text challenging or incomprehensible, not because of the reader's limitations, but because of the fallibility of the author. The efforts of the reader can then be committed to making sense of the text, rather than attempting to mask his or her challenges or making non-productive attributions about his or her ability to read with understanding.

A second key idea is that reading is an ongoing process of constructing meaning; the meaning unfolds and builds with each new piece of text. QtA is designed to provide the teacher with a means of modeling this process and guiding students to approach the text in this way.

A third key idea is that integral to learning about text comprehension is the activity of discussing, during which each participant makes unique contributions to the construction of meaning for the targeted text. Just as strategy instruction is not the ultimate goal of RT, neither is discussion the ultimate goal of QtA. Rather, the goal is the collective understanding of the text.

The Process of Using QtA

There are two sets of tools that are featured in QtA, queries and discussion moves (Beck, McKeown, Hamilton, et al., 1997). Isabel Beck, Margaret McKeown (1997), and their colleagues draw the following distinction between questions and queries. They propose that whereas questions are used to assess student understanding following the reading of a text, queries are designed to support students as they make sense of the text. They describe two sets of queries: initiating queries and follow-up queries. Sample initiating queries, following the reading of a segment of text, include:

- What's going on here?
- What has the author told us so far?
- What do you understand about what the author is saying here?

Follow-up queries that are designed to help focus the content and direction of a discussion and support students in the activity of integrating ideas in the text include:

- That is what the author said, but what did the author mean?
- Does that make sense to you?
- How does what the author said here connect to what we read yesterday?

In recognition of the different demands and opportunities associated with narrative text, the designers have also developed four queries that are specific to narrative text:

- How do things look for this character now?
- Given what the author has already told us about this character, what do you think he's up to?
- How has the author let you know something has changed?
- How has the author settled this for us?

Complementing the use of queries is a repertoire of discussion moves that teachers can opportunistically employ to support and advance the conversation. These moves are identified, described, and illustrated in Table 6.1.

Investigating the Effectiveness of QtA

There have been a number of investigations of QtA. One set of studies has investigated the use of QtA with more than 120 students in the upper elementary grades. The focus of these studies has been a comparison of the nature of the discourse in reading and social studies classes before and after the implementation of QtA. Beck et al. (1996) and McKeown, Beck, & Sandora (1996) report the following changes in classroom discourse:

- Question asking that focuses on constructing and extending meaning, rather than information retrieval.
- Teacher responsiveness to students that is designed to extend the conversation, rather than merely evaluate student contributions.

TABLE 6.1. Discussion Moves in QtA

Marking	Drawing attention to an idea and emphasizing its importance: *Did you hear what Liz just said? Please say that again, Liz. That's a very important idea.*
Turning Back	Turning back responsibility for thinking/explaining to students: *Why do you think that way, Eileen? Do you agree with what Bonnie said? Why or why not?* Turning back to the text to locate information *Let's find the place where the author explained that for us.*
Revoicing	Interpreting what students are struggling to express and rephrasing the ideas so that they can become part of the discussion: *So, Nicole, you seem to be talking about the length of the wires in the diagram and the distance and resistance. Are you saying that the distance can act like a resistor?*
Modeling	Thinking aloud, rereading, expressing confusion: *After reading this part about the complex circuit, I'm confused. Is only part of the current going through the light bulbs in the second circuit? Molly, will you help me out on this?*
Annotating	Providing information that is not in the text: *You should know that filaments can be made of different materials.*
Recapping	Summing up: *So, Rachael, will you please sum up what we've understood so far?*

Note. I gratefully acknowledge Linda Kucan for the specific illustrations included in this table.

- Twice the amount of student talk during QtA discussions.
- Frequent student initiation of questions.
- Frequent student-to-student interactions.

A study conducted by Sandora (1994) compared QtA with another discussion method in which sixth- and seventh-grade students first read and then discussed whole text selections. The results indicated that the students in the QtA condition recalled more from each selection and more successfully responded to interpretation questions.

COLLABORATIVE REASONING

A third approach to comprehension instruction, Collaborative Reasoning, was developed and investigated by Clark Chinn, Richard Anderson, Martha Waggoner, and colleagues (Chinn & Anderson, 1998; Chinn, Anderson, & Waggoner, 2001). Like RT and QtA, its design is informed by a social constructivist perspective suggesting that in the context of a group discussion, readers bring together their diverse interpretations, responses to the text, and connections with prior texts (including personal experiences), which will enrich the process of interpreting the shared text. In Collaborative Reasoning, the analogue to the strategies of RT and the queries in QtA is reasoned argumentation. The expectation is that as students participate in developing and responding to arguments and counterarguments, they internalize this way of thinking and reasoning about text.

Collaborative Reasoning has been investigated exclusively with narrative text and is intended to support students' engagement in critical reading and thinking about a piece of literature. Furthermore, unlike RT and QtA, it is designed to be used following independent reading of the story.

In Collaborative Reasoning discussions, students take positions on a key question related to the story. This key question is typically posed by the teacher. After the question has been framed, each student in the group takes an initial position relative to that question. The group then proceeds to develop the arguments for their various positions, drawing on the literature and related texts as sources of evidence to support their arguments or to dispute those of others.

Teachers are encouraged to be sparing with their own talk during the discussion; however, as is true with RT and QtA, the teacher plays a primary role in providing a scaffold for the discussion (see the next section). The expectation is that the authority for interpreting the text rests with the group and is determined by the strength of the argument(s) framed in support of the interpretation.

Implementing Collaborative Reasoning

The first decision the teacher confronts is the selection of literature. Ideally, the story should support a central question or issue to which students can reasonably bring diverse perspectives. The procedure begins with students independently reading the story. Small heterogeneous groups (eight or nine students) then gather for the discussion, which begins with the teacher framing a central question about a significant issue in the story. For example, one story this research group has used is entitled "Making Room for Uncle Joe" (Litchfield, 1987). The story concerns a family's dilemma when an uncle who has Down syndrome needs a new home. The central question the teacher frames regarding this story is whether the family has made the right decision in making room for Uncle Joe in their home. As is true in most real-life situations, there are reasonable pros and cons for the decision the family reaches. Following silent reading of the text, the teacher poses the central question and cedes the discussion to the students, providing support only as needed. For example, the teacher asks questions that will lead the students to clarify their thinking, prompts the students to provide reasons for their positions and elaborate on their evidence, and models the process of generating and supporting arguments and counterarguments.

Students are encouraged to take turns in the discussion, without raising hands or being called on by the teacher, and they are urged to address one another. As the discussion unfolds, the students are engaged in weighing the various positions with their associated evidence and counterevidence. At the conclusion of the discussion, students are provided a chance to indicate whether they wish to maintain their initial positions or to change their positions.

Investigating the Effectiveness of Collaborative Reasoning

Research on Collaborative Reasoning, like research on QtA, has been conducted primarily with upper elementary students. The purposes of the research have been to determine the feasibility of this procedure and to compare the effects of Collaborative Reasoning with those of traditional recitations, in which the authority for interpreting the text rests principally with the teacher. The studies have been conducted by doing close analyses of the student and teacher talk in the course of both instructional conditions.

In Chinn et al. (2001), the researchers report on a broad array of measures. Although there were differences across the participating classrooms, they found that, generally, student talk increased significantly in the context of Collaborative Reasoning. Interesting differences in the number and nature of questions were found in comparing the two conditions. In the context of Collaborative Reasoning, the teachers asked half as many questions as they did in recitation lessons and the proportion of open-ended questions increased from 30 to 56%; furthermore, the teachers generated fewer questions that tapped explicit or inferred information during Collaborative Reasoning and asked more questions seeking reasons for a student's position and clarification of student thinking. When the content of talk was compared across the two conditions, the researchers observed more talk in the recitation condition focused on specific information in the text, in contrast to the Collaborative Reasoning condition, in which the talk was more analytic.

The authors concluded from this and related studies (Anderson, Wilkinson, & Mason, 1991) that teachers were most successful at handing over more control of interpretation to students. Teachers were more challenged at turning over control of the topic and turn taking.

CONCLUSION

In this chapter we have presented three instructional procedures designed to support students in learning how to comprehend text. Although there are similarities across the three procedures, there are also important differences; hence, teachers need to consider the opportunities and constraints of each procedure and how these match with their own instructional goals and with the profiles of their students.

Each of the procedures acknowledges the key role of the reader in interpreting text and recognizes the power of social interaction in supporting students to learn the processes of interpreting text. Each procedure engages students in learning about comprehension as they read and respond to the types of text (subject matter and literature) that are characteristic of the types of text they will encounter in school contexts. The ultimate goal of each procedure is to cede control of text interpretation to the student and support the student in learning ways of interpreting text that can be internalized and independently applied. The teacher plays a prominent role in each instructional approach, modeling the means of interacting with text, supporting students to appropriate these means, and providing students feedback regarding their progress.

Reciprocal Teaching, which was specifically designed for students who encounter significant challenges in comprehending text, is the most explicit form of instruction of the three. The scaffolding, via the strategies of RT, is initially very transparent. The strategies provide a metascript for organizing and sustaining the conversation; over the course of time, as the students acquire the disposition to be interactive with the text, the strategies are less significant and are called up only when students are challenged in their understanding of the text. RT is perhaps ideally suited to engaging students who are significantly challenged, vis á vis comprehension, in the process of knowledge building from text.

Questioning the Author is designed for use with both content and narrative text; it too is a good match for supporting students to read for information, although it also lends itself to engaging in critical analytic thinking about the text. Because the teacher's queries serve an important organizing function in the discussions, the teacher has a significant measure of control over both the topic and turn taking. The interpretive authority for the text is shared between the teacher and the students, with increasing amounts of authority transferred to the students over time.

Collaborative Reasoning is designed for use with narrative text. With its focus on a major dilemma or problem represented in the story, it is a particularly good match for supporting students to engage in critical/ analytic thinking with text. Although the teacher plays a key role in modeling the activity of generating arguments and counterarguments, the authority for interpreting the text rests exclusively with the students, whose decisions are guided by how compelling the evidence is for the various interpretations put forth in the group discussion.

Although systematic comparisons across these three instructional approaches have not been conducted, it is likely that teachers will want to think of these approaches, as well as others, in terms of a repertoire of practices they draw upon in support of students' learning how to interpret, learn from, and reason with text.

REFERENCES

Anderson, R. C., Chinn, C., Chang, J., Waggoner, M., & Yi, H. (1997). On the logical integrity of children's arguments. *Cognition and Instruction, 15*, 135–167.

Anderson, R. C., Wilkinson, I. A. G., & Mason, J. (1991). A microanalysis of the small-group guided reading lesson: Effects of an emphasis on global story meaning. *Reading Research Quarterly, 26*, 417–441.

Beck, I. L., McKeown, M. G., Hamilton, R. L., & Kucan, L. (1997). *Questioning the author: An approach for enhancing student engagement with text.* Newark, DE: International Reading Association.

Beck, I. L., McKeown, M. G., Worthy, J., Sandora, C. A., & Kucan, L. (1996). Questioning the Author: A year-long classroom implementation to engage students with text. *Elementary School Journal, 96*(4), 385–414.

Brown, A. L., Ash, D., Rutherford, M., Nakagawa, K., Gordon, A., & Campione, J. C. (1993). Distributed expertise in the classroom. In G. Salomon (Ed.), *Distributed cognitions* (pp. 188–228). Cambridge, MA: MIT Press.

Brown, A. L., & Palincsar, A. S. (1987). Reciprocal teaching of comprehension strategies: A natural history of one program for enhancing learning. In J.

Borkowski & J. D. Day (Eds.), *Intelligence and cognition in special children: Comparative studies of giftedness, mental retardation, and learning disabilities.* New York: Ablex.

Brown, A. L., Palincsar, A. S. (1989). Guided cooperative learning and individual knowledge acquisition. In L. B. Resnick (Ed.), *Knowing, learning, and instruction: Essays in honor of Robert Glaser* (pp. 393–451). Hillsdale, NJ: Erlbaum.

Bruner, J. (1978). The role of dialogue in language acquisition. In A. Sinclair, R. J. Jarvella, & W. J. M. Levelt (Eds.), *The child's conception of language* (pp. 241–256). New York: Springer-Verlag.

Chinn, C. A., & Anderson, R. C. (1998). The structure of discussions that promote reasoning. *Teachers College Record, 100,* 315–368.

Chinn, C. A., Anderson, R. C., & Waggoner, M. (2001). Patterns of discourse in two kinds of literature discussion. *Reading Research Quarterly, 36*(4), 378–411.

Dewey, J. (1910). *How we think.* Boston: Heath. (2nd ed., Heath, 1933)

Litchfield, A. B. (1987). Making room for Uncle Joe. In B. E. Cullinan, R. C. Farr, W. D. Hammond, N. L. Roser, & D. Strickland (Eds.), *Crossorads* (pp. 22–23). Orlando, FL: Harcourt Brace Jovonovich.

Palincsar, A. S., & Brown, A. L. (1984). Reciprocal teaching of comprehension fostering and comprehension monitoring activities. *Cognition and Instruction, 1,* 117–175.

Palincsar, A. S., & Brown, A. L. (1989). Classroom dialogues to promote self-regulated comprehension. In J. Brophy (Ed.), *Advances in research on teaching* (pp. 35–71). New York: JAI Press.

Palincsar, A. S., Brown, A. L., & Campione, J. C. (1993). Dialogues among communities of first grade learners. E. Foreman, N. Minnick, & A. Stone (Eds.), *The institutional and social context of mind: New directions in Vygotskian theory and reseach* (pp. 43–57). Oxford University Press.

Piaget, J. (1967). *Biologie et connaissance [Biology and knowledge].* Paris: Gallimard.

Rosenshine, B., & Meister, C. (1994). Reciprocal teaching: A review of the research. *Review of Educational Research, 64,* 479–530.

Sandora, C. A. (1994). *A comparison of two discussion techniques: Great Books (post-reading) and Questioning the Author (on-line) on students' comprehension and interpretation of narrative texts.* Unpublished doctoral dissertation. University of Pittsburgh, Pittsburgh, PA.

Vygotsky, L. (1978). *Mind in society: The development of higher psychological processes.* Cambridge, MA: Harvard University Press.

Waggoner, M., Chinn, C., Yi, H., & Anderson, R. (1995). Collaborative reasoning about stories. *Language Arts, 72,* 582–589.

Wood, P., Bruner, J., & Ross, G. (1976). The role of tutoring in problem solving. *Journal of Child Psychology and Psychiatry, 17,* 89–100.

7

Concept-Oriented Reading Instruction

Practices of Teaching Reading for Understanding

JOHN T. GUTHRIE

The foundation of knowledge about reading comprehension based on the report on *Reading for Understanding* emphasizes reading processes and instructional practices. Many classroom practices might be created from these fundamental insights. In this chapter we describe the instructional framework of Concept-Oriented Reading Instruction (CORI), which is built on the knowledge and principles of this report. In addition, CORI contains practices that go beyond the empirically verifiable research base. CORI draws on research literature on subjects such as knowledge development and reading motivation that extend beyond the RAND project (Guthrie & Wigfield, 2000). Such topics, however, are necessary to a classroom plan that is sufficient to ensure reading comprehension development in children.

The cornerstone of CORI is a view of reading comprehension that is highly compatible with the definition offered in the RAND report. In this chapter, the view is most like definitions of reading comprehension found in Kintsch's (1998) research on reading comprehension, and in publications by van den Broek and Kremer (2002), Williams (2002), and Guthrie and

Cox (1998). *Our view is that reading comprehension consists of constructing knowledge contained in text through interaction and involvement with the text.* We place an emphasis on building new understanding through intensive work with text.

We believe that the language and cognitive processes outlined in the RAND report, including phonemic awareness, phonics instruction, vocabulary, and fluency, are necessary for text comprehension. It is not possible to comprehend text without recognizing words within it. However, the aforementioned processes are not sufficient for text comprehension. If a reader is fluent in orally reading a text aloud, he or she will not necessarily be competent in comprehending that text. It is well established that training in vocabulary or fluency does not produce improvements in reading comprehension without explicit instruction in comprehension.

Beginning with this definition, we identify two needs that are vital to learners if they are to comprehend text. The first need is interaction with text. The second is involvement with text, which includes knowledge development that enables text to be understood and a classroom context that sustains motivation for these reading processes. CORI is designed to meet these needs.

STRATEGY INSTRUCTION IN CORI

Interaction with text refers to the use of language systems for translating the printed word into spoken language, which enables a text to be understood. These language systems include vocabulary and word meanings; they emphasize the structure of sentences—the relationships of subjects, predicates, modifiers, and meanings denoted by punctuation.

Most important within a person's interaction with text is the use of cognitive strategies. As indicated in the National Reading Panel report and recent publications on comprehension instruction (Pressley, 1997), there are several cognitive strategies that improve reading comprehension that are incorporated in CORI:

1. Activating background knowledge, which refers to the reader's recalling what he or she knows prior to reading a text with new information.
2. Questioning, which may occur before and during reading in order to focus the learner's attention.
3. Searching for information, which refers to an attempt to locate critical important information in a long text.
4. Summarizing, which may be performed for information within one section, on one page, or in an entire book.

5. Organizing graphically, which refers to making concept maps, diagrams, or charts of information from a text.
6. Structuring stories, which refers to providing a diagram or chart of the plot, character development, and development of theme within a story.

These cognitive strategies have two important attributes. First, they distinguish good readers from poor readers in the elementary grades. Good readers use these strategies frequently; poor readers do not know them or do not use them frequently. In addition, these strategies have been shown to be teachable. Within usual instructional and classroom settings, teachers can enable children to learn these strategies, given sufficient time.

In CORI, our first instructional practice is to *provide explicit systematic instruction for all reading comprehension strategies.* Here we are referring to strategies that were presented earlier. All of the strategies such as questioning, summarizing, and organizing graphically should be taught to students systematically. There are several aspects of each strategy that are necessary if the strategies are to become tools in the comprehender's tool kit.

The first aspect is competence. Students must be in command of using the strategy. They must be able to implement it effectively with a text suited to their reading levels. Second, learners need awareness of the reading strategy. Students need to know when, where, and how to apply the strategy, which requires them to be aware of it as a tool and conscious of their own deliberate use of it to help them understand. The third attribute of the strategic reader is self-initiation. A strategic reader begins using a strategy when it is appropriate and ceases the strategy when it is not useful. For example, if a learner is confused he or she may attempt to summarize what has been learned thus far in the text. Thus, the summarizing strategy comes into play to help reduce confusion. Self-initiation refers to students voluntarily deciding to use a strategy to help themselves. This quality is just as important as competence, because the student who *does not* use a strategy is no better in comprehension than the student who *cannot* use the strategy.

Explicit strategy instruction refers to a sequence of activities well established in the research literature. This sequence begins with modeling each strategy. As he or she models, the teacher shows students how to perform the strategy, such as asking questions during reading. Second, the teacher scaffolds that strategy. *Scaffolding* refers to doing the strategy with the students. The teacher may say, "Let's work together on questioning with this text," and then proceed to join the students in forming questions that will help them learn. The third process is guided practice, which refers to ensuring that students practice a strategy, with a sufficient number of texts, to gain command of it.

To provide suitable amounts of modeling, scaffolding, and guided practice, teachers in effective comprehension programs spend a minimum of 30 minutes daily with a class. Struggling readers receive a total of 60 minutes daily. Many effective strategy instruction programs provide single-strategy instruction initially. That is, questioning is taught until students are comfortable with it. Then another strategy, such as organizing graphically, is taught until students are comfortable with it. This single-strategy instruction may continue for 6–10 weeks. Next, multiple strategy instruction is provided. Here students are taught to combine strategies, such as questioning and organizing graphically. Teaching students the process of combining and integrating strategies may last 6–10 weeks.

Scaffolding Novices and Experts

An extremely high level of teacher support is necessary for the novice learner. At the highest level of teacher support, the teacher provides the full process of using the strategy. The teacher demonstrates or models to the students. At a slightly lower level of support, the teacher provides a scaffold and the students begin to participate in the strategy-using process. Here, the teacher may provide examples of partial strategy use. He or she frequently asks questions and guides student participation closely. The teacher is doing 90% of the strategy use, and the students are contributing 10%.

At a moderate level of scaffolding, the teacher may request that students perform key aspects of the strategy, but does not display the strategy or model it for them. At this level, the teacher may structure the task, for example, by selecting one page of text to be used. The teacher may direct the students' attention by suggesting that they read two boldface headings on this page of text. Further, the teacher may request that the students write their outcomes of using the strategy in their journals. This moderate level of scaffolding does not include a display or a model but, rather, directed attention, selected tasks, and guided performance.

At the lowest level of scaffolding, the teacher may simply request the students to perform the strategy. For example, the teacher may say, "We will begin the new book on peoples of the rainforest. You should use your strategy of questioning for this book." In this case, the teacher expects students to peruse the book briefly, to think of questions they have about the topic, to share questions with their friends, and to record several key questions in their strategy journals. If students are successful at this low level of scaffolding, the teacher will probably have spent many previous weeks or months in instruction on the questioning strategy.

It is possible to scaffold strategies for either novices or experts with a particular text. Good teachers provide a high level of scaffolding when:

- The students are low achievers.
- The particular text is difficult.
- The strategy has not been learned.
- The content of the text is unfamiliar.

Under these conditions, a high level of scaffolding is needed. The teacher then provides extensive support, possibly modeling. On the other hand, if students are relative experts on the topic of a given text, know the material, can read the words, and can perform the strategy easily, the teacher uses a low level of scaffolding. In this case, it may be sufficient to simply request students to use the strategy. For students in grades 3–5, scaffolding may occur across these levels. Even relatively expert readers in grades 3 and 5 can benefit from low levels of scaffolding to increase their use of strategies across different reading situations.

Adapting Scaffolding

An essential process in effective strategy instruction is adjusting the scaffolding. When students are frustrated because strategy learning seems difficult or unproductive, it is likely that the level of scaffolding has been too low. For third graders, a low level of scaffolding for summarizing consists of requesting, "Please write a summary." This will frustrate many learners. In addition, a scaffold that is, in fact, moderate when it should be high, will also be frustrating. Likewise, students who are relatively expert with a given text on a given topic will not want a highly detailed and explicitly displayed model on how to use a strategy that is familiar to them. Too much scaffolding can be boring and counterproductive.

Adapting the scaffold is vital not only for student learning, but also for motivation. If students are learning under the right level of scaffolding, they will be successful. Gaining competence in a strategy helps students become aware, and thus proud, of their work. A scaffold that is attuned to the learner's needs ensures the student's progress in a complex task. From their newfound skills, students gain a sense of confidence and self-efficacy. Under the opposite conditions of a misaligned scaffold that is too high or too low for learners, students will be disaffected. They become frustrated or bored. In the extreme case, they will likely withdraw from literacy learning activities.

Comprehension of a book is more than a collection of cognitive strategies. Acts of understanding are pursuits toward meaning. Interacting with a text, a reader "changes his or her mind," perhaps forever. A shift so significant is not made against the will of the reader. Just the opposite: The reader's will and intention drive comprehension. Motivation fuels the quest to learn from text. In a word, comprehension is at the service of motivation, which is unfolded more fully in the principles. All of the following guidelines provide the motivational energy and conceptual focus for strategic, engaged reading. Using these principles enables students to become purposeful readers, a characteristic that is emphasized repeatedly in the RAND report.

CONCEPTUAL KNOWLEDGE IN CORI

The second instructional practice is to *use knowledge goals for reading instruction*. Reading comprehension instruction should be conducted within a content domain that is clear to students. Dominated by "big ideas" associated with supporting information, these goals take the form of conceptual knowledge structures that contain concepts, supporting facts, and interrelationships among them. For example, one big idea often taught in life sciences in the elementary grades is survival. Concepts that are related to this overarching theme of survival include eating, defense, locomotion, competition, communication, predation, reproduction, adaptation to habitat, and niche. Students read about animals and how they live as they learn these concepts. Strategies for reading comprehension such as questioning and graphic organizing are taught within this knowledge domain in a long-term program of 5–30 days, depending on the complexity of the knowledge area.

The main point is to avoid teaching cognitive strategies in isolation from deep content. A student cannot know whether a summary is adequate unless he or she has an understanding of the content being summarized. Students cannot ask intelligent questions or monitor their understanding for contents that are unfamiliar or confusing to them.

Reading comprehension of texts on ecology—or how animals and plants survive—can occur at many levels. We have observed that children's comprehension develops from lower to higher levels of knowledge gained from text. The following rubric of developmental benchmarks was based on children's writing about their reading of multiple texts on a diversity of animals and how they live in various biomes (e.g., lions live as predators in the grassland). Some students in grades 3–5 are at the lower levels and others are at the higher levels (see Figure 7.1).

> *Level 1. Facts and associations: Simple.* Students present a very few simple characteristics of either biomes or organisms. Their statements exclude ecological concepts or definitions.
> *Level 2. Facts and associations: Extended.* Students correctly present several relevant facts, appearing in the form of a list. In ecology, they may have classified several organisms.
> *Level 3. Concepts and evidence: Simple.* Well-formed, fully elaborated

Performance Assessment Reading Comprehension Levels

Level 1 Facts and Associations: Simple
Students' writing consists of very few characteristics of either biome or organisms. The statement excludes ecological concepts or definitions and may only consist of the student's name as identifying information.

Level 1

Fish live in the Oceans.

Level 2 Facts and Associations: Extended
At this level, students correctly classified several organisms. Limited definitions and universal plant-animal concept statements are often presented. The overall information included at this level is factual and often appears in the form of a list.

Level 3 Concepts and Evidence: Partial and Limited
A well-formed, fully elaborated definition of both biomes is often accompanied by a substantial number of organisms accurately classified. Students will often present one or more ecological concepts with minimal supporting information in a disorganized statement.

Level 3

What I know is, Golden Wheel spider cartwheels
Gorillas can crawl when 2 months old. Roadrunner
22 MPH. Water boatman uses legs like oars,
diving beetle larva eats tadpoles.

Level 4 Concepts and Evidence: Complete and Well-Formed
Students display conceptual understanding of organisms and their survival mechanisms in one or more biomes. The student presents specific organisms and the physical characteristics or the behavioral patterns that facilitate these organisms' survival. The student begins to include higher-level principles, such as food webs or interactions among ecological concepts with supporting information.

Level 5 Pattern of Relationships: Moderate and Supported
At this level, students show command of ecological concepts. They present highly detailed descriptions of relationships among and between different organisms and the biomes they inhabit. These interactions are the central to the statement.

Level 5

A river is different from a grassland because a river
is a body of water and a grassland is land.
A river is fast flowing. Grasshoppers live in
a grassland. A grasshopper called a locust
lays its eggs in a thin case. One case could
carry 100 eggs. The largest herbivore in the
grasslands is an elephant. In the african
savannah meat eaters prey on grazing animals
such as a zebra. Many animals live in a grassland.
The river is a home to many animals. In
a drop of river water millions of animals
can be living in it. Many fish live in the
river. Many birds fly above the grasslands
and rivers. A river is called a freshwater
because it has no salt in it.

Level 6 Pattern of Relationships: Complex and Elaborate
Students describe complex relationships among multiple organisms and their habitats. The concepts and principles presented are thoroughly supported by statements directly relating them to specific organisms' behaviors or physical adaptations. Elaborate food webs and detailed discussions of principles are the fundamental components of a Level 6 statement.

FIGURE 7.1. Guthrie and Scafiddi's reading comprehension rubric.

definitions of one or two important concepts are given with minimal supporting information in the text. In ecology, definitions of several biomes are often accompanied by a substantial number of organisms accurately classified. The student states a concept such as predation or competition necessary to survival, with some minimal support.

Level 4. Concepts and evidence: Extended. Students present multiple concepts central to the text with support and exemplification of each. In ecology, students display conceptual understanding of organisms and their survival mechanisms in one or more biomes. They present specific organisms and the physical characteristics or the behavioral patterns that facilitate these organisms' survival. Students may include higher-level principles, such as food webs or interactions among ecological concepts, with limited supporting information.

Level 5. Pattern of relationships: Simple. Students present multiple concepts explicitly linked together, with at least minimal evidence. In ecology, students show command of ecological concepts with highly detailed descriptions or relationships among different organisms and the biomes they inhabit. Interactions are central to the statement.

Level 6. Pattern of relationships: Extended. Students present many concepts, elaborately interrelated, with detailed examples and supporting information. In ecology, students describe complex relationships among multiple organisms and their habitats. The concepts and principles presented are thoroughly supported by statements directly relating them to specific organisms' behaviors or physical adaptations.

To illustrate gaining conceptual knowledge from text, consider Jeffrey, a third grader. Before reading the text, Jeffrey wrote his prior knowledge about how animals live in grasslands and rivers. This was his statement:

"Cheetahs, lions, zebras, grass, trees, leopards, and many other things live in grasslands. Fish, alligators, and plants live in rivers."

After reading several information texts in two 30–minute periods, Jeffrey's understanding of life in grasslands and rivers increased to the following:

"Grasslands and rivers are very different. Rivers are bodies of water. Rivers have salmon, fish, and other animals unable to live on land. Grasslands have hyenas, lions, zebras, hippos, and other animals that can't permanently live underwater. Grasslands have mostly grass, and rivers have several types of plants. Otters (river animals) hunt for shellfish, crayfish, and fish. They can chuckle, giggle, and make many other noises. They can stay underwater for two minutes. The salmon (fish) life cycle goes: egg, fry, parr, smolt, adult. That's what I learned about grasslands and rivers."

Jeffrey included good definitions of both biomes. For each biome, he correctly identified species of plants and many animals that dwell there. He proceeded to describe the concept of predation among otters, with an enumeration of their prey. He conveyed various communications of otters, and indicated their proficiency for holding their breath, showing how their respiration restricts their hunting. He briefly depicted the life cycle of the salmon, alluding to the basic phases of reproduction, even though the detail is minimal.

Jeffrey began the reading with information about a few *facts and asso-*

ciations, Level 2. He departed the reading assessment with knowledge of multiple survival *concepts and evidence*, which is Level 4. He conveyed a beginning understanding of the life cycle network. Not only did he understand, but he built a substantial amount of new knowledge.

The CORI goal is to enable students to gain knowledge from text. In other words, the students and teachers are "concept-oriented." Gaining knowledge (expository or literary) is the point of reading, and enabling students to gain such knowledge the main aim of reading instruction. The cognitive strategies mentioned previously are tools. They are means to the end, but not the purpose of reading, which is understanding. As reading comprehension is a form of cognitive expertise, it is sensible to scaffold children gradually toward higher levels of expertise. Research on scaffolding has found that it is counterproductive to attempt to teach novices to become experts immediately. A more sensible approach is a tactic of moving novices slowly through a progression of increasing levels of competence.

Teaching for knowledge building is vital to reading comprehension instruction. If students in a classroom are predominately at Levels 1 and 2, understanding a few simple facts and associations after reading, it will be most valuable to help the students focus on a single concept with supporting information. Knowledge goals for instruction can be linked to the students' benchmarks on the reading comprehension rubric. Level 1 students can be encouraged to move to Level 2; reading to learn a few simple facts can be followed by reading to learn a wider number of appropriate facts and associations of the topic domain. If the classroom has many Level 5 students who can build a rich array of concepts that are linked to one another, the teacher may expand their reading comprehension by enabling them to widen the network of concepts and interrelationships and to deepen the supporting information for all of them. This would move those students toward Level 6.

TEXTS FOR INSTRUCTION

The third instructional practice in CORI is to *employ an abundance of diverse, interesting texts for reading instruction*. Diverse texts means various types of materials. For example, narrative texts are appealing to young children. But information texts are also being published for the early elementary grades that are readable and effective for reading instruction. Documents such as maps, posters, and pictures with captions are valuable parts of a diet of diverse materials. Diversity is also related to the difficulty of the text in relationship to the student's reading ability. It is vital to match text difficulty to students' reading levels in comprehension instruction. Students should be attempting to comprehend text for which their oral reading fluency is well established. Teachers can use multiple texts to teach the same strategy, enabling students to see that a strategy such as activating background knowledge can be used for nearly everything they encounter in print. Reading an abundance of books is an important behavioral manifestation of motivation for reading (Wigfield & Guthrie, 1997).

Interesting texts are well organized, illustrated, and aligned with the child's conceptual knowledge base. The features of such texts include a table of contents, an index, headings, bold print for new words, captioned illustrations, a clear macro structure, and strong topic sentences. Vivid details are included, but do not detract from the conceptual theme of the content. A diversity of such literature used for instruction enhances comprehension (Morrow, Pressley, Smith, & Smith, 1997).

In 12 weeks of CORI for a class of 25 third-grade students, the following books are recommended: Six class sets, that is, six trade books of 25 pages each for all members of the class or group being taught; 10 team sets, that is, 10 titles of books of about 25 pages, one for each member of a team of 6 students; 40 individual titles; and 5 copies of 12 titles of lower difficulty for struggling readers in the classroom. That is a total of 310 books in the program for 12 weeks of instruction.

Using an abundance of texts for instruction is supported by various types of scientific evidence, including a meta-analysis of experiments on questioning by Rosenshine, Meister, and Chapman (1996) and a meta-analysis of instructional effects on reading achievement by Guthrie, Schafer, VonSecker, and Alban (2000). This research establishes unequivocally that using abundant diverse texts for reading instruction produces higher achievement than using fewer, more constrained materials.

STUDENT CHOICES IN THE CLASSROOM

The fourth instructional practice is to *optimize student choices in reading instruction.* This refers to the importance of active learning, thinking, and effort during reading activities. The word *optimize* should not be mistaken for *maximize*. Maximizing student choice usually occurs at recess. During learning, however, students should be supported in making choices, taking control, and exercising their autonomy as learners (Sweet, Guthrie, & Ng, 1998).

The importance of student centeredness is based on the need for high effort during reading comprehension activities. Learning to use cognitive strategies is demanding and may be frustrating. Therefore, student motivation is crucial. Optimized student centeredness increases motivation. The evidence for this principle is based on strong experiments conducted in the scientific tradition, as well as structural equation models that link this structural practice with reading achievement through mediating variables of strategic reading and sustained engagement with text.

In providing support for student centeredness, for example, students may be supported in choosing which page to read during questioning instruction. Students may be given a menu of two to three pages, asked to read one page of their choice, and to form a question about the information on the page. This choice provides them ownership of the text and the question. With a sense of investment, the students' cognitive efforts are increased and their attention is focused on the difficult task of thinking and writing a good question on the text. Students can be given options for reading sections, selecting books, choosing a topic to read on a given day, choosing a topic to read across a period of one week, displaying their understanding in different ways (i.e., writing or speaking), or responding to text through alternative modes (i.e., speaking, writing, or drawing).

Degrees of choice and control must obviously be provided within a narrow scope for younger learners. The range can be wider for older students. In other words, student centeredness should be provided in a way that is developmentally responsive. Student centeredness should be given at levels that optimize cognitive challenge. Students should be given the choice among tasks that are appropriately challenging. We are not suggesting that students should be given the choice to perform tasks that are trivial or will not produce new learning. Choice within a menu of cognitively challenging options provides both student investment and learning opportunities.

COLLABORATION IN READING

The fifth instructional practice in CORI is to *ensure collaboration for learning from text*. Enabling students to discuss the content of a text with each other is vitally important. For example, student pairs can be asked to summarize a paragraph together. They can identify the central ideas, locate supporting information, attempt to ignore weaker supporting details, and develop a summary as a team. Groups of students or teams can perform the more complex strategy of building a concept map from a four-page text. For example, a team assigned a more complex activity may be asked to synthesize "how falcons survive." One team member may be given the responsibility of reading about how falcons eat and what foods are in their diet. Another student may be assigned to read about nesting, a third member to read about locomotion, a fourth to read about falcon predation, a fifth to focus on the competitors a falcon contends with, and a sixth to learn about how falcons defend themselves from enemies. When these students discuss what they have learned from texts, they synthesize their knowledge of falcon survival. Such social collaboration enables them to perform complex cognitive processes of integrating information across multiple texts.

Evidence supporting the practice of social collaborating for learning from text is drawn from systematic observations of effective teachers, effective classrooms, and exemplary programs. At present, this variable of social collaboration has not been vigorously subjected to experimental tests. However, it is a consistent feature of the work of exemplary programs and outstanding teachers.

REAL-WORLD CONNECTIONS

The sixth instructional practice in CORI is to *connect texts to students' real-world experiences*. Young learners are attentive to concrete, tangible objects and events. Teachers refer to such interactions with concrete objects as hands-on activities. Numerous surveys show that well-formed samples of teachers rate hands-on activities as one of their highest priorities for helping students to comprehend by linking texts to experience. Students are attracted to a pet bird in the classroom, not to mention a terrarium housing a snake or an iguana. When experiences can be linked to reading, students' comprehension increases dramatically.

A substantial number of studies show that students' long-term commitments to learning through text originate in specific situational interests (Hidi & Harackiewicz, 2000). Within a classroom, a child who observes a bird's nest will be more likely to effectively comprehend a bird book. However, the ratio of time for such activities is relatively low, at 1 (observe) to 10 (read). One hour of observing will be satisfactory to generate 10 hours of intensive reading activity related to the observational experience. Although they are powerful, these real-world experiences need not require a substantial amount of time away from text interaction during reading instruction. Evidence for this practice in reading comprehension instruction is derived from systematic observation and surveys of expert practitioners. The practice awaits further experimental investigation.

A CORI VIGNETTE
ON SUMMARIZING INSTRUCTION

This following vignette is a transcription of a videotape taken in October 2001, in Frederick, Maryland.

Ann Duncan is teaching third-grade students a unit on aquatic life. The students have taken a trip to a pond and have brought back specimens to the classroom. They are observing an aquarium with guppies and snails while jotting their notes in science journals. Along with this activity, Ann is teaching the reading strategy of summarizing.

Ann opens the lesson by explaining what summarizing is and how it helps children with their reading. She begins:

> "The strategy I am teaching today is summarizing, and actually being able to write a summary and understand what to write. They kind of go together . . . you're reading, you're understanding, and you're thinking about what you're reading. You're making those connections to your real life. On top of that, I'm going to then take you through the summarizing process. How do you summarize? What is a summary? The first part of our strategy is going to involve our actually understanding what we read.
>
> "Actually, this past week, we've been talking about organisms that live in our aquarium. And we've observed one of the organisms, which is the snail. We came up with lots of ideas about what a snail does, what helps it to do a lot of these aspects of survival, such as what does it do to defend itself, what body parts does it have that helps it to defend itself. I also hear people talking about the locomotion part of the snail. What helps it move from one place to another?"

Ann walks to the side of the classroom. Ecology concepts are posted on display boards. They include eight core concepts that have been studied since the beginning of the year, including (1) feeding, (2) locomotion, (3) predation, (4) reproduction, (5) respiration, (6) communication, (7) defense, and (8) competition. An icon is associated with each of these abstract terms to help the third graders remember them. For instance, a telephone represents communication and a baby in a cradle represents reproduction. Ann has explained the human analogies for these concepts in relation to the students' study of animals, birds, insects, and now aquatic life. Having laid the conceptual foundation for this lesson on summarizing, Ann introduces the text.

> "We observed snails in our aquaria early this morning. As I walked around the classroom, I heard students talking about how they move and how they eat. Now, we will read about the food for a snail. We will use this book, *Snails*, and read one page from it now. In front of you is a page that I photocopied for us to read. I will read it aloud and you follow along with me, now. I'm going to stop at certain points, and I'm going to say stop and talk. You talk about what we just read with your partner, at those times."

Ann organizes and pairs a few students who do not have partners at their tables. Then she reads aloud:

> "Snails are herbivores. Herbivores are animals that eat plants. Land snails eat grass, leaves, and dried plants. Freshwater snails eat algae and other plants. Algae are small floating plants. Ocean snails eat seaweed."
>
> "Stop and talk."

Now students chat about the meaning of what they just read. The classroom is alive with interchange. After three "read-and-discuss" cycles, Ann proceeds to her summarizing lesson.

> "Now please look here, and I want your attention. Look at this page on the overhead projector. Now, I am going to give you some strategies for summarizing what you just read. A summary, first of all, should give you an understanding of what you just read, OK? It tells me, Mrs. Duncan, that you know what? That Sarah, she understands what she just read. There are two parts to a summary, OK? First of all, there is the main idea, OK. You have a main idea in your summary. Secondly, you have what is known as supporting ideas, ideas that support that main idea of your summary. And, lastly, your summary is only about three to four sentences."

A student responds to Ann's last statement by saying, "That's fun, because you don't have to write very many sentences."

Ann Duncan places the first paragraph from the text on the overhead projector and proceeds.

> "In this paragraph, I want us to circle the most important point, which is the main idea. This is about snails and food, so *food* is the most important word. This is my main idea, and I will circle it. You do this on your page."

All of the students find the word in the first paragraph on their photocopied page and circle it.

Ann continues her instruction.

> "You never want to underline whole sentences. You want to underline key words that help you understand what you just read. What other word in the first sentence will help me understand about snails and feeding?"

Andres, another student, replies, "Herbivores."

"Yes," Ann responds.
"That is an important word. Let's underline it. A herbivore is an animal that eats plants. Are there any important ideas that are going to help me understand how snails feed and eat? OK, so you want to underline each plant. Any important supporting ideas about snails and how they feed or what they feed on? *Plankton* is another important word. Plankton are small flat worms. We are underlining supporting words or supporting ideas in each sentence there that help us make sense of how a snail feeds. Now, you're going to take your main ideas and we are going to actually write a summary with our main ideas."

Ann walks to a different side of the classroom to a large white sheet of paper hanging on a chalkboard. She asks students for information and writes their summary on the paper. She asks class members for the main ideas and supporting details in each paragraph. She writes one sentence for each paragraph in her summary on the paper in large words.

Ann asks a student to read the paragraph, which she does, but the final sentence is unclear. Ann questions the student, "Does that last sentence make sense?"

"No," the class choruses in response.

"How can we fix it?" Ann asks. Students make various suggestions as Ann enters them on the chart.

Denise reads the summary:

"Our main idea is about snails and how they eat and how they use their body parts to eat. Some snails are carnivores they eat meat and others herbivores they eat plants. Snails have long black tongues called radulas. A radula is covered with tiny sharp teeth that help to bring the food into its small body."

Ann asked the students to write a summary of the next page in pairs. Students followed her model. They identified the main idea by circling key words. Next, they underlined supporting information in the form of key words and phrases. Finally, they placed a line through unimportant details. Then, in pairs, students wrote a three-to-four sentence summary of this page from the book. Individuals read their summaries aloud to the class. As they worked, Ann circulated among the pairs, answering questions, coaching, and encouraging. Students were able to follow her framework; they easily read and took their initial steps in this exceptionally challenging job of summarizing a page of print. As they progressed and gained self-assurance, their confidence slowly increased and their smiles were shared. Students placed the notes from their summary activity into their reading journals. Their pages with key words circled, supporting information underlined, and less important information deleted, were placed in their journals. Their written summary was retained as a reminder of their first step toward learning to summarize a text.

In this vignette, the CORI principles were in action. Ann was teaching toward knowledge goals in the life science topic of ecology. She preceded the lesson by a "real-world" interaction, which consisted of a trip to a pond, and having simple aquaria in the classroom. The books were suitable to her summarizing instruction. On one page, the content was sufficiently complete to invite a summary. Yet it was not too long or complex. The headings were clear and the illustrations were informative, but did not replace text-based information. Ann spent considerable time, energy, and attention on teaching well.

Instruction for summarizing is a challenge. With her scaffolding, Ann's students took a first step. Much additional scaffolding with other texts would be needed for students to gain competence. Notice that awareness of the strategy and the conditions for using it were not taught at this early stage. Self-initiation of the strategy could not be emphasized yet. However, Ann taught toward those phases of development at later points in the year.

In this lesson, a few choices were provided, and collaboration was evident as learners thought together about the "key words" and supporting information. More liberal choices and collaboration would be offered at a future stage of instruction.

INFRASTRUCTURE FOR INTEGRATED INSTRUCTION

At an organizational level, ensuring the success of CORI requires *providing infrastructure for teaching*. To support CORI practices, an instructional leader in a school is necessary. This person may be a reading specialist, a principal, or a coordinator whose job it is to facilitate reading comprehension programs. This leader has uniquely important responsibilities:

- Ensuring that a full supply of books and appropriate texts are available to the teachers.
- Ensuring that schedules allocate adequate time for instruction and are not interrupted by distracting activities.

- Ensuring that teacher training is complete for all educators.
- Providing time for teacher planning, daily and weekly, for comprehension.
- Aligning assessments with instructional goals for comprehension, knowledge, and reading motivation.
- Facilitating school-wide coordination so that instruction is not piecemeal.

TEACHER EXPERTISE

At the core of CORI is the expert educator. A reading comprehension program with goals, materials, activities, assessments, and instructional guides cannot possibly anticipate the response of every learner to every text or teaching action. Crucial to the delivery of effective comprehension instruction is the process of coordinating a program with students' needs. The professional teacher understands the reading processes, selects texts effectively, delivers explicit strategy instruction, and coordinates students' competencies with these teaching processes.

Relatively little is known about the most effective approach to teacher preparation for reading comprehension instruction. In our current project, funded by the Interagency Education Research Initiative (IERI) (Guthrie, Wigfield, & Barbosa, 2002), we provide 100 hours of intensive teacher preparation for comprehension instruction. This includes initial workshops, ongoing monitoring, videotaped interviews, and performance-based monitoring of program implementation.

One source of evidence for this instructional practice is data from program implementation studies. As shown in a wide range of implementation research and program evaluations, teacher variation is extensive. A given program may be well implemented or poorly implemented as a consequence of the level of teacher expertise. Therefore, at the center of effective comprehension instruction is teacher expertise, which must be developed with the same attention to detail and commitment to excellence that instructional practices for children are conducted.

These instructional practices are mutually supportive. To provide sustained explicit instruction, an infrastructure in the school is invaluable. Further, when instructional designs are well formulated, it is more obvious how to provide infrastructure administratively. Although all these practices are important, they can be phased into a program. A reading program can be judged on the number of these practices that are implemented, as well as the quality of each individual practice that is being provided to learners.

BENEFITS OF CORI FOR CHILDREN'S LEARNING AND DEVELOPMENT

CORI is an educational design intended to make children good comprehenders. To investigate the benefits of this instruction, we need data on children. We need information on all the aspects of their learning and development we are trying to foster. To justify the costs of CORI, or any reading program, it is valuable to document its advantages over traditional reading instruction. Our empirical studies are being directed toward two questions:

1. Does CORI improve children's reading comprehension and reading motivation in comparison to traditional forms of reading instruction?
2. Which instructional practices within CORI are most important to its effectiveness?

In the following sections, we put emphasis on the first question, while briefly noting findings and literature pertaining to the second question.

Does CORI Improve Children's Reading Comprehension and Reading Motivation in Comparison to Traditional Forms of Reading Instruction?

Perhaps the most global question we can ask is whether CORI increases children's reading comprehension more than traditional reading instruction. From a practical educational perspective, this question has obvious value. It is worth knowing whether CORI increases comprehension, because evidence on instructional effectiveness is important to policy makers, principals, and teachers alike. In other words, if CORI "works," in the sense of increasing reading comprehension in comparison to other traditional interventions, it is worth implementing in classrooms and schools.

From a theoretical viewpoint, it is important to identify the constituents of CORI clearly. If the main ingredients of an instructional intervention cannot be identified, described, and measured, then the teaching program cannot easily be transferred. Without knowing the centrally important practices within an intervention such as CORI, it is extremely unlikely that the program can be implemented successfully by a range of educators. As indicated previously, the constituents of CORI are defined as follows:

1. Explicit instruction in cognitive strategies for reading in the context of the practices consisting of constituents 2 through 6;
2. Knowledge goals for reading instruction;

3. Interesting texts;
4. Optimal student choices in reading instruction;
5. Collaboration for comprehension; and
6. Real-world connection for reading.

To compare CORI with traditional instruction is to examine the effect of this composite of instructional practices as it increases reading comprehension and other aspects of development.

We compared CORI with traditional reading instruction in three large experiments. Although the experiments varied slightly, they usually included six classrooms with CORI and six classrooms with traditional instruction in the same schools. Students in grades 3 and 5 were included in both instructional programs. In this instruction, CORI teachers provided three 10–week units of instruction during the school year. Pretests in September and posttests in March were given to all of the students. The results were that CORI students scored higher than traditional students on an extended reading comprehension task. This task required students to read multiple texts, take notes, and answer a global question in writing. CORI students showed an effect size of 0.91 in one investigation (Guthrie et al., 1998) and an effect size of 0.66 in another investigation (Guthrie et al., 1996). This showed that CORI students were 0.5 to 1.0 standard deviations higher than traditional students on these reading- strategy-based comprehension activities. Not only were these differences statistically significant, but they were substantial by educational criteria.

Several of our investigations have examined motivation for reading along with students' amount and breadth of reading. In these controlled experiments, CORI students scored higher than traditional students on intrinsic motivation, especially curiosity. CORI students had an advantage over traditional students, with an effect size of 2.35 on measures of their interest in learning from new texts. CORI students also showed more desire to "get lost in books" and involved themselves in extensive reading activities. In a measure of this aspect of motivation, CORI students showed an effect size of 1.60, which is markedly higher than that of traditional students. In other words, the benefits of motivation resulting from CORI when previous achievement and knowledge of the content of reading were controlled, have been substantiated (Guthrie, Wigfield, & Von Secker, 2000).

Which Instructional Practices within CORI Are Most Important to Its Effectiveness?

In making global comparisons, previous investigations have shown an advantage of CORI over programs of traditional, basal-centered instruction for reading comprehension. We now pose a new question about which parts of CORI are most important to ensure its benefit. As indicated previously, CORI can be partitioned into two broad aspects. The most distinctive aspect is its motivational support system, which consists of the instructional practices related to:

1. Knowledge goals
2. Real-world connections
3. Optimal student choices
4. Interesting texts
5. Collaboration for comprehension

These practices represent a context within which the sixth practice is embedded. The sixth principle refers to explicit instruction in cognitive strategies for reading.

At present, we are posing the question, "To what extent are these motivational context supports contributing to CORI's benefits for students?" As we have suggested, CORI is a merger of explicit cognitive strategy instruction and motivational support practices. In asking this question we are inquiring whether these motivational practices are indeed beneficial for reading comprehension. One method of addressing this question is to compare CORI to a program of reading instruction that provides explicit strategy instruction, but does not provide the motivational support base for reading. In the current study, we compared CORI, which provides (1) motivational support for reading and (2) explicit strategy instruction, with an instructional model of explicit strategy teaching that includes strategy instruction only and no explcit motivational support. In this comparison, if CORI produces an advantage over strategy instruction for reading comprehension, we conclude that the motivational aspect of CORI is important in accounting for its benefits for children.

To investigate whether students receiving CORI increase in reading comprehension in comparison to students receiving explicit strategy instruction, we conducted an experiment in four schools. Two schools were assigned to CORI. They included all 10 teachers in Grade 3. Two schools were assigned to strategy instruction, consisting of 11 teachers in Grade 3. District administrators judged the schools to be comparable in socioeconomic status, prior reading achievement, leadership by the principal, and teacher quality. In each of the treatment groups, one school was more affluent and more highly achieving than the other school. To provide professional development in CORI and strategy instruction, extensive summer workshops were held and one full day per month of professional development was provided for teachers in both instructional frameworks. Teaching both models occurred for 12 weeks, from September to December 2001, with pretests in the first week of September and posttests in the second week of December.

The measures of students' reading consisted of a 4–day performance assessment lasting 50 minutes per day. In the assessment, the children were given the following subtests: prior knowledge of the topic of reading, questioning, searching for information in multiple texts, organizing knowledge from reading, reading comprehension based on constructive responses, reading comprehension based on a computerized assessment, motivation for reading questionnaire, and a reading activity questionnaire. The students' questions and their written responses to the multiple texts were coded according to rubrics that are described elsewhere (Guthrie, Wigfield, & Barbosa, 2002).

Reading Comprehension

CORI students scored higher than strategy instruction students in growth of reading comprehension. The children's growth was measured by examining their posttest scores in December, while controlling for their pretest scores of reading comprehension from September. On the rubric, students in CORI, in December, were able to construct fundamental concepts of the text topics supported by text-based evidence. However, students who received strategy instruction were likely to make factual statements. They showed less conceptual organization and a weaker grasp of the main ideas in text. The CORI advantage over strategy instruction on this measure was statistically significant (see Figure 7.1). CORI was higher than strategy instruction in gain of reading from September to December.

Reading Comprehension from Computer-Based Assessment

In the performance assessment, students read a 600–word text and completed a computer-based assessment known as Pathfinder. In this assessment, the computer draws a concept map of the children's knowledge, based on students' judgments of the relatedness among key words in text. This concept map is correlated with the concept map of an expert. CORI students showed higher correlation with the concept map of experts than did traditional students. CORI students had an advantage in building coherent knowledge structures from text. This statistically significant advantage for CORI students is depicted in Figure 7.2. Therefore in two different measures, one demanding extensive writing and one that was free of a writing requirement, CORI students scored higher than strategy instruction students in reading comprehension.

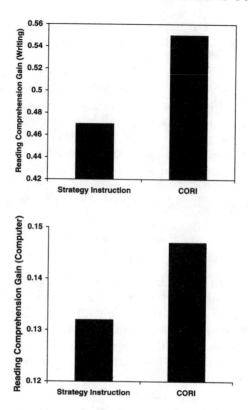

FIGURE 7.2. Growth in reading comprehension.

Engagement Effects on Reading Comprehension

In addition to examining whether CORI students scored higher than strategy instruction students on reading comprehension, we examined the role of reading engagement. As indicated previously, we refer to reading engagement as the joint functioning of motivation for reading and strategies for reading. Students who are engaged are both intrinsically motivated to read and strategic in their approach to text. We found that each of the cognitive strategies correlated with the reading comprehension measure in this investigation. That is, the quality of students' questioning predicted their reading comprehension (0.45); students' abilities to search for relevant information predicted their reading comprehension (0.24); students' abilities to retrieve their background knowledge predicted their reading comprehension (0.39); and students' organization of knowledge gained during reading predicted reading comprehension (0.19). All of these were significant at ($p < .05$).

Motivation for reading in this investigation was a combination of students reporting reading motivations merged with the amount and breadth of their reading activities. This motivational composite predicted reading comprehension with a correlation of 0.29. Therefore, all of the reading strategies and reading motivations we measured were correlated to reading comprehension outcomes.

On the motivation measure, students who received CORI scored significantly higher than students who received reading strategy instruction. This difference was statistically significant and practically substantive. It showed an advantage for motivation growth, as the postassessment scores in December were corrected for the students' levels of preexisting motivations in September.

A fascinating result was that CORI students did not score higher than strategy instruction students on the reading strategies as a group. In other words, when all of the strategies, consisting of questioning, searching, organizing, and activating background knowledge, were clustered to form one "strategic reading" composite, strategy instruction was just as effective as CORI. There was no CORI advantage on this measure of composite strategies. This outcome is completely reasonable in view of the focus on reading comprehension strategies by the teachers in this strategy instruction model.

This leads us to conclude that the CORI advantage for reading comprehension was due to the combination of the CORI students' level of motivation and their substantial learning of strategies. When CORI students were able to combine their enhanced motivations for reading with their well-developed strategies for reading, they exhibited high performance on the reading comprehension measures. Although the strategy instruction students had acquired cognitive strategies, their relatively lower motivations limited their application of these strategies in the extended reading task and, consequently, limited their demonstration of comprehension of texts.

Our findings show that reading engagement is a link between instruction and comprehension. The evidence is that when the student's level of motivation and strategic reading are held constant, CORI did not have an advantage over strategy instruction. In terms of teaching practices, this suggests that CORI teachers benefit their students' reading comprehension by increasing the students' reading engagement. In turn, this increases students' reading comprehension outcomes. Of course, some strategy instruction teachers were effective in increasing reading engagement in their classrooms. When their increases in engagement equaled the increases shown in CORI classrooms, the benefits for reading comprehension were just as high as in CORI classrooms. However, the difference is that the CORI classrooms more frequently and more substantially facilitated reading engagement, thus producing the overall reading comprehension benefits for learners in CORI classrooms. These data support the mediated model of the effects of instruction on reading comprehension. This model has been described and supported in our previous investigations (Guthrie et al., 1998), as well as in research conducted on learning in general by other investigators (Skinner & Belmont, 1993; Skinner, Wellborn, & Connell, 1990).

CONCLUSION

Teaching reading for understanding is a vital challenge. It cannot be performed routinely nor ritually. It cannot be accomplished casually nor nonchalantly. Such teaching demands the fusion of a set of instructional practices that meet young learners' language, cognitive, motivational, and social needs. The CORI practices presented here are offered as one set of instructional principles for this purpose. While initially supported in experimental comparisons with traditional instruction and calling for deeper investigation, they consist of the following:

1. Provide explicit systematic instruction for all reading comprehension strategies.
2. Use knowledge goals for reading instruction.
3. Employ an abundance of diverse, interesting texts for reading instruction.
4. Optimize student choices in reading instruction.
5. Ensure collaboration for learning from text.
6. Connect texts to students' real-world experiences.
7. Provide infrastructure for teaching.

REFERENCES

Alexander, P. A., & Jetton, T. L. (2000). Learning from text: A multidimensional and developmental perspective. In M. L. Kamil, P. B. Mosenthal, P. D. Pearson, & R. Barr (Eds.), Handbook of reading research (Vol. 3, pp. 285–310). Mahwah, NJ: Erlbaum.

Baker, L. (2002). Metacognition in comprehension instruction. In C.C. Block & M. Pressley (Eds.), Comprehension instruction: Research-based best practices (pp. 77–95). New York: Guilford Press.

Chi, M. T. H., De Leeun, N., Chiu, M., & Lavancher, C. (1994). Eliciting self-explanations improves understanding. Cognitive Science, 18, 439–477.

Guthrie, J. T., & Anderson, E. (1999). Engagement in reading: Processes of motivated, strategic, knowledgeable, social readers. In J. T. Guthrie & D. E. Alvermann (Eds.), Engaged reading: Process, practices, and policy implications (pp. 17–45). New York: Teachers College Press.

Guthrie, J. T., Anderson, E., Alao, S., & Rinehart, J. (1999). Influences of Concept-

Oriented Reading Instruction on strategy use and conceptual learning from text. *Elementary School Journal, 99*(4), 343–366.

Guthrie, J. T., & Cox, K. (1998). Portrait of an engaging classroom: Principles of Concept-Oriented Reading Instruction for diverse students. In K. Harris (Ed.), *Teaching every child every day: Learning in diverse schools and classrooms* (pp. 70–130). Cambridge, MA: Brookline Books.

Guthrie, J. T., & Scaffidi, N. T. (in press). Reading comprehension for information text: Theoretical meanings, developmental patterns, and benchmarks for instruction. In J. T. Guthrie, A. Wigield, & K. C. Perencevich (Eds.), *Concept-oriented reading instruction*. Mahwah, NJ: Erlbaum.

Guthrie, J. T., Schafer, W. D., Von Secker, C., & Alban, T. (2000). Contributions of instructional practices to reading achievement in a statewide improvement program. *Journal of Educational Research, 93*(4), 211–225.

Guthrie, J. T., Van Meter, P., Hancock, G. R., McCann, A., Anderson, E., & Alao, S. (1998). Does Concept-Oriented Reading Instruction increase strategy use and conceptual learning from text? *Journal of Educational Psychology, 90*(2), 261–278.

Guthrie, J. T., Van Meter, P., McCann, A. D., Wigfield, A., Bennett, L., Poundstone, C. C., Rice, M. E., Faibisch, F. M., Hunt, B., & Mitchell, A. M. (1996). Growth of literacy engagement: Changes in motivations and strategies during Concept-Oriented Reading Instruction. *Reading Research Quarterly, 31*, 306–332.

Guthrie, J. T., Wigfield, A., & Barbosa, P. (2002). *http://www.cori.umd.edu/Research/Papers/IncrRead.htm*

Guthrie, J. T., & Wigfield, A. (2000). Engagement and motivation in reading. In M. L. Kamil & P. B. Mosenthal (Eds.), *Handbook of reading research* (Vol. III, pp. 403–422). Mahwah, NJ: Erlbaum.

Guthrie, J. T., Wigfield, A., & VonSecker, C. (2000). Effects of integrated instruction on motivation and strategy use in reading. *Journal of Educational Psychology, 92*(2), 331–341.

Hidi, S., & Harackiewicz, J. M. (2000). Motivating the academically unmotivated: A critical issue for the 21st century. *Review of Educational Research, 70*(2), 151–179.

Kintsch, W. (1998). *Comprehension: A paradigm for cognition.* New York: Cambridge University Press.

Morrow, L. M., Pressley, M., Smith, J. K., & Smith, M. (1997). The effect of a literature-based program integrated into literacy and science instruction with children from diverse backgrounds. *Reading Research Quarterly, 32*, 54–76.

Pressley, M. (1997). The cognitive science of reading. *Contemporary Educational Psychology, 22*, 247–259.

Rosenshine, B., Meister, C., & Chapman, S. (1996). Teaching students to generate questions: A review of the intervention studies. *Review of Educational Research, 66*, 181–221.

Skinner, E. A., & Belmont, M. J. (1993). Motivation in the classroom: Reciprocal effects of teacher behavior and student engagement across the school year. *Journal of Educational Psychology, 85*, 571–581.

Skinner, E. A., Wellborn, J. G., & Connell, J. P. (1990). What it takes to do well in school and whether I've got it: A process model of perceived control and children's engagement and achievement in school. *Journal of Educational Psychology, 82*, 22–32.

Sweet, A. P., Guthrie, J. T., & Ng, M. (1998). Teacher perceptions and student reading motivation. *Journal of Educational Psychology, 90*(2), 210–224.

van den Broek, P., & Kremer, K. E. (2000). The mind in action: What it means to comprehend during reading. In B. M. Taylor, M. F. Graves, & P. van den Broek (Eds.), *Reading for meaning: Fostering comprehension in the middle grades* (pp. 1–31). Newark, DE: International Reading Association.

Wigfield, A., & Guthrie, J. T. (1997). Relations of children's motivation for reading to the amount and breadth of their reading. *Journal of Educational Psychology, 89*, 420–432.

Williams, J. P. (2002). Using the theme scheme to improve story comprehension. In C. C. Block & M. Pressley (Eds.), *Comprehension instruction: Research-based best practices* (pp. 126–139). New York: Guilford Press.

8

Taking Charge of Reader, Text, Activity, and Context Variables

IRENE W. GASKINS

A goal of schools is to provide instruction that enables all students to read with appropriate comprehension. As outlined by the RAND Reading Study Group (RRSG), reading comprehension, the act of simultaneously extracting and constructing meaning from text, consists of three elements: the reader, the text, and the activity or purpose for reading (RRSG, 2002). These elements interact with each other and with a larger sociocultural context that shapes and is shaped by the reader. Thus, if schools are to provide their students with the optimum opportunity to comprehend what they read, it appears that instruction should address these elements of comprehension. The purpose of this chapter is to describe a reading comprehension program developed to teach students strategies for taking charge of reader, text, activity, and context variables. The ultimate goal of the program is to create proficient readers who, as a result of engaging in the reading process and reflecting on what is being read, are capable of acquiring new knowledge, understanding concepts, and appropriately applying textual information (RRSG, 2002).

Good comprehension, the hallmark of proficient reading, develops over many years, is manifested different at different phases of development, and is greatly influenced by the quality of classroom instruction. These facts suggest several challenges for schools. One is to provide explicit instruction related to the elements of comprehension during both language arts and content area instruction, in at least grades 1–8. A second challenge is to address developmental differences, because not all students at the same age and grade are ready to comprehend the same text, at the same time, and at the same pace. Thus, comprehension instruction must be geared to meet students where they are and at the pace at which they are able to respond. A third challenge is to ensure that the comprehension instruction children receive is of high quality and that it is based on what we know works in improving comprehension.

We have learned a lot about comprehension instruction in the past 20 years, and some of what we know is being implemented in classrooms across the United States—but there is still room for improvement (Pressley, 2002). We know that if comprehension strategies are taught, they are taught during the daily reading period, or language arts block, using basal readers or trade books. The transfer of these strategies, however, is a concern. If students are taught and coached to use the strategies only during the reading period, using basals and trade books, they may not recognize occasions when they can transfer these strategies to content area reading or to out-of-school reading—for example, when reading directions for building a model or baking a cake or when researching a topic on the Internet. For this reason, the goal of comprehension instruction in all areas of the curriculum should be to explicitly teach students how to comprehend the variety of texts they encounter in and out of school. Thus, teaching reading comprehension means teaching students how to take charge of the elements of reading comprehension throughout the day, across the curriculum, and for accomplishing a variety of activities.

During the past 15 years the staff of Benchmark School, a school for bright, struggling readers in grades 1–8, has developed an across-the-curriculum reading comprehension program to teach students strategies for taking charge of reader, text, activity, and context variables related to constructing meaning from text (Gaskins, 1988; Gaskins & Elliot, 1991; Gaskins, 1998). In this chapter, I discuss how the Benchmark staff teaches students to be aware of and take charge of these variables. As part of this discussion, I describe the ways in which teachers foster student engagement and reflection,[1] key ingredients of comprehension. The degree and depth of engagement and reflection are often attributed to reader variables. Thus, I begin the discussion of Benchmark's reading comprehension program by

---

[1] As defined by the RRSG, engagement results from the interaction of motivation, cognitive strategies, background knowledge, and social interchanges (RRSG, 2002). Reflection is taking time to think about what is read. It may involve relating what is being read to what is known, as well as interpreting, critically analyzing, summarizing, or thinking about a possible application.

delineating reader variables that affect comprehension and describing some of the methods Benchmark teachers use to guide students to be aware of and take charge of these variables.

READER VARIABLES

Reader variables that affect comprehension can be categorized in many ways. One possible schema for thinking about reader variables is outlined in Figure 8.1. When a student is experiencing difficulty in comprehending, a teacher may initially wonder whether the problem can be explained by physical factors such as health problems or failure to achieve important developmental milestones. If these are ruled out, the teacher may ponder whether the student's difficulty is related to emotion-laden attributes such as values, attitudes, interests, or beliefs. Other areas of consideration are cognitive style and motivation. Difficulties in comprehension may also be the result of a lack of knowledge about how to comprehend or a lack of declarative knowledge, such as vocabulary, world or domain knowledge, linguistic knowledge, discourse knowledge, or cognitive and metacognitive strategy knowledge. More than likely, a difficulty in comprehension is the result of an interaction between several reader variables, as well as text, activity, and context variables. Difficulties in comprehension are seldom the result of one factor. In this section about reader variables, I discuss cogni-

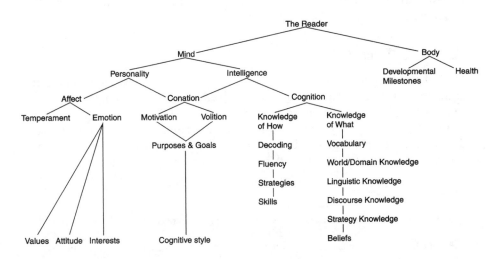

FIGURE 8.1. Reader variables. Parts of the mind outline are adapted from Snow, Corno, and Jackson (1996).

tive style,[2] beliefs, motivation, and procedural and declarative knowledge. These are the variables that tend to be most problematic for Benchmark's struggling readers.

Cognitive Style

Since the inception of Benchmark School in 1970, teachers have consistently identified five specific style characteristics that are primary roadblocks to their students' ability to comprehend what they read (Gaskins, 1984). These are passivity, inattention, nonpersistence, impulsivity, and inflexibility. In the early years of the school, teachers dealt with these maladaptive cognitive styles by implementing various renditions of behavior modification. However, behavior modification did not produce lasting results. As an alternative, in the early 1980s we conducted research with Jonathan Baron to evaluate the benefits of teaching our struggling readers a more cognitive approach for coping with maladaptive styles (Gaskins & Baron, 1985), an approach in which students were taught to use self-talk to take charge of maladaptive styles. This approach, an adaptation of Meichenbaum's (1977) cognitive-behavior modification, produced significant, as well as long lasting, results and is one part of our current approach to helping students deal with personal characteristics that interfere with learning and comprehension. Our goal is for students to gain awareness of, and control over, their maladaptive cognitive styles that interfere with comprehension. Because maladaptive cognitive styles block students' responses to instruction, they are usually an initial focus of attention for Benchmark teachers.

Active Involvement

One of the first things teachers discuss with a class of new-to-Benchmark students is the need to be actively involved in understanding what they read. Teachers explain that each student is in charge of what his or her brain takes in and remembers; thus, students cannot sit back and relax. They must take action to be in charge of their understanding. As a way of convincing students of the need to replace passivity with active involve-

---

[2] Some professionals use the term *temperament* to identify most of the characteristics described here as *cognitive style* (Thomas & Chess, 1977; Carey & McDevitt, 1995), and others link some of these characteristics (e.g., attention and persistence) to the self system and motivation (e.g., Marzano, 2001). Whichever term is used, it is used to mean the way in which an individual typically behaves or responds in similar situations.

ment, teachers often illustrate the folly of passivity with a few mini-experiments or stories.

For example, one teacher pulled down a map to cover the items and messages on the chalkboard, then asked students what was on the chalkboard under the map. The students were unable to answer the question. The teacher next asked the class why they could not tell what was, just a few minutes ago, within their sight. One student commented, "It is just the same old chalkboard that is there everyday. I didn't look at it carefully or think about what I saw, so I can't remember anything." The teacher commented, "That's brilliant! You have figured out that you have to direct your brain to take action if you want to remember what you see and hear."

On another occasion a teacher told her class about a time when she headed for the grocery store and ended up in the Benchmark parking lot. She asked her class to explain how that could have happened. The students suggested that their teacher had been thinking about something else besides the grocery store. They advised her that she should have kept her mind on where she was going, then the things she saw along the road would register in her brain and make her aware that she was not on the road that led to the grocery store. Intuitively, even our youngest struggling readers realize that active involvement is part of remembering and comprehending; however, like the teacher, they need to more consciously monitor progress toward their goals. I have heard teachers explain:

> "If you want to get what you are seeing or hearing to stick in your brain, you must react in some way—take action. If you don't consciously think about the information, it will pass right through your brain without getting filed. If the information doesn't get filed in your brain, you won't be able to remember and use it to understand."

Benchmark teachers explain and mental-model for their students how to react to what they are reading. For example, as they read a text aloud, they may think aloud to model how students can make pictures, or a TV show, in their heads about what they are reading. Another action teachers may model is summarizing in their own words a paragraph or section of text they have just read. The key, the teachers point out, is for students to be actively thinking about what they are reading *as they read*. Teachers remind their students that if they merely pass their eyes over the words without doing something with the information they are reading, they are passive readers and will not have good comprehension. Active involvement is the treatment for passivity, a treatment that can be totally within the control of the reader.

Attention

Attention to the tasks of reading and discussing is an attribute that must be present for comprehension to take place. Although struggling readers are always paying attention to something, it is often to something other than the task at hand. Benchmark teachers like to help students realize, sometimes through mini-experiments, that it is impossible to give full attention to two things at the same time. For example, it is hard to pay attention to what you are reading if you are also listening to a conversation. With respect to attention during group discussions, students have found that keeping their eyes on the speaker and thinking about what the speaker is saying aids comprehension. During reading, attention to comprehension can be enhanced by jotting notes about important story elements or main ideas. Another way Benchmark teachers foster attention, particularly in an usually inattentive student, is to make the student aware of the benefits of attention, especially when it is obvious that the student is paying attention. For example, a teacher may whisper to a student during reading group, "I know your comprehension is going to be really good today because I could tell by your involvement when we surveyed, predicted, and set a purpose for reading that you were paying attention."

Persistence

Persistence is another attribute teachers encourage struggling readers to develop. Persistence, or lack of persistence, comes into play when a student encounters an unknown word or a portion of text that is confusing. When students are aware that there is a decoding or comprehension problem, Benchmark teachers encourage them to stop reading for a moment and let the teacher or the group know about the problem and how they persisted in finding a way to conquer it. The teacher's goal is to highlight instances when students have monitored for understanding, acknowledged confusion, and persisted in solving comprehension problems. Teachers also share with students the results of Joanne Murphy's (1996) follow-up study of Benchmark students, in which she found that those students rated by their teachers as persistent at the time they were graduated from Benchmark are among the most successful of our graduates.

Reflectivity

Reflectivity is a key attribute related to comprehension, yet it is impulsivity that is often characteristic of struggling readers. For example, some students have a tendency to rush through what they are reading—perhaps to appear to be fast and fluent readers, or perhaps they rush just to finish a task they regard as unpleasant. Others may rush through what they read because it is their cognitive style to respond impulsively. Whatever the cause, teachers know that reflection, rather than impulsivity, is the characteristic they want students to develop. Comprehension is almost always enhanced by taking time to reflect and pull ideas together.

A method teachers use on an almost daily basis to foster reflectivity is to ask students to self-assess their comprehension. As students finish reading, the teacher gives each one a pencil and a note card. The students write notes on their cards about the story, including the characters, setting, story problem, and resolution. If students cannot recall these elements, they realize they have not read reflectively and thus need to reread more thoughtfully to find information for their summaries. When a teacher observes that a student is frequently unable to write notes after a first reading, the teacher asks the student to identify the obstacle that seems to be getting in the way of good comprehension during the first reading and what he or she is doing differently on the second reading to achieve more complete understanding. Making students aware of the effect of impulsivity is the first step toward putting them in charge of becoming more reflective.

Flexibility

Inflexibility is another characteristic common among our struggling readers. Inflexibility may be part of a student's cognitive style, or it may be the result of believing it is "bad" to be wrong or to not know an answer. Whatever the cause, inflexibility interferes with improving comprehension. Instead of telling students outright that a response to a question is "right" or "wrong," Benchmark teachers ask students to explain their reasoning. This tends to make students less defensive and gives them an opportunity to explain their way to an improved response. However, when a student is irreparably off track in his or her response, the teacher treats it lightly, often pointing out that, for the teacher, mistakes usually prove to be opportunities to learn, and that this may prove true for students too. In fact, I have heard teachers say, "If you never make a mistake, you probably aren't learning anything new."

When a student demonstrates a pattern of responding inflexibly to teacher and/or peer feedback, the teacher may place a goal card on the student's desk, which is checked each time the student demonstrates flexibility in responding to a teacher or peer suggestion. The goal card and the checks on it make students aware of their style of response and seem to help them break the habit of responding inflexibly to feedback. At the end of each school day, teachers ask students to self-assess how well they did in achieving their goals and what the benefits of achieving their goals have been. Goal cards are not only used for shaping flexibility, but they are also used to encourage active involvement, attention, persistence, and reflectivity. No rewards are given for the checks students earn on their goal cards; rather, the checks are merely used as a way for students to self-assess how well they are doing in taking charge of a personal characteristic that may interfere with comprehension.

Beliefs

What a person believes shapes what he or she does. One way the Benchmark staff fosters students' positive beliefs about their control over successful comprehension is to present information about how the brain works and how the strategies they are learning help the brain to learn and understand. Mini-experiments and discussion of provocative questions (e.g., What determines how smart you are?) are one part of changing students' beliefs about intelligence and the value of strategies.

Beliefs about Intelligence and the Brain

In working with Benchmark's struggling readers, teachers have concluded that concerns with failure and attempts to avoid appearing incompetent often result from students believing that an achievement task measures a person's intelligence, something they view as unchangeable. This makes them feel vulnerable and concerned about investing in success. The result is a tendency to pursue avoidance-oriented goals, including excessive instances of broken pencil points, trips to the nurse's office, and "lost" books, assignments, and computer files. For these students, their beliefs about challenging performance goals create motivational vulnerability. In contrast, when a task is seen as assessing the current status of a person's skills and strategies, students are more likely to attribute failure to a lack of effort or to a poor choice of strategies and there is usually not the same concern about possible failure and its avoidance. Students usually see lack of effort or a poor choice of strategies as changeable. The key issue is the meaning a student ascribes to success or failure. Does the student believe success is due to intelligence or to effort and specific strategies?

If a student believes that intelligence is fixed and that his or her difficulties in comprehension are due to lack of adequate intelligence, then the student usually fulfills that prophecy by not persisting in an attempt to comprehend. On the other hand, if a student believes that he or she has control over intelligence, that student is more likely to put forth effort toward improved comprehension. Similarly, students who believe that there is something wrong with their brains (e.g., dyslexia, learning disability, auditory processing deficit) may believe that it is impossible to comprehend as other children do and thus give up without pursuing ways in which they might cope with their learning differences. Conversely, students who believe that they are smart, but just learn differently, are more likely to persist in finding ways to cope with the difficulties they encounter in reading and understanding.

To change dysfunctional beliefs, Benchmark teachers share articles and research reports, tell personal stories, and conduct mini-experiments. For example, teachers in the lower school have presented articles from magazines and newspapers about such "dyslexic" individuals as Charles Schwab, Albert Einstein, Thomas Edison, and Winston Churchill and related how these "greats" demonstrated resilience in overcoming adversity by strategic effort and persistence. Middle school teachers tell stories of Benchmark graduates who experienced extreme difficulties in decoding, yet who during their years at Benchmark found ways to cope with these difficulties. For example, some of these students persisted in listening to audiotapes of books their classes were reading and, as a result, were able to demonstrate excellent comprehension during book discussions. Many of these same Benchmark graduates continued to persist in coping with their learning differences in undergraduate and graduate school and went on to esteemed positions such as college law professor, Ph.D. psychologist, movie producer, business owner, and medical doctor. Each year former Benchmark students are invited to return to Benchmark to share their learning differences and how they have coped with them. These successful graduates make quite an impression on our students and help to erode faulty belief systems about intelligence and how their brains work.

Beliefs about Strategies

Belief in the value of applying comprehension strategies is one key to students improving their comprehension. Implementing strategies almost always entails more effort than students are accustomed to putting forth when they read, thus it is not uncommon for teachers to need to convince students of the value of using such strategies. Teachers attempt to do this by explaining how a new strategy is tied to how the brain works. They also try to convince students of the value of strategies by conducting mini-experiments.

For example, one day I was in a fourth-grade social studies class that had set the goal of learning the capitals of all 50 states before the end of the school year. I asked the students what strategies they were using to learn the state capitals. The students confessed that their teacher had suggested some strategies, but they did not think that the strategies worked. One student said, "It is easier just to look at the state and the capital and memorize it." Addressing the class, I said, "Put up your hand if you are absolutely convinced of the truth of that statement." About half of the class did so. I asked the students who had not put up their hands to go to the library, where I would meet them in a few minutes. I gave the students who remained in the classroom a map of the United States that included the names of states and capitals and asked them to use the next 15 minutes to study for a test on the state capitals of the 10 most western states. The classroom teacher remained in the classroom with these students while I met with the others in the library.

In the library, I gave the students the same state capital assignment; however, I collaborated with this group to brainstorm meaningful associations between the names of the states and their capitals. For example, students at Benchmark know that I am from Idaho, and I told the group in the library that I like boys because I have two sons. The association I guided them to make was between my being from Idaho and my liking boys. Thus, the capital of Idaho is Boise (BOY-SEE). We studied the shape of Nevada and decided that if we turned it on its side and added wheels, we would have a car—and the capital of Nevada is CARson City. We studied the shape of California and concluded that it looked like a sack, and the capital of California is SACramento.

At the end of 15 minutes these students returned to their classroom, and all students filled in the names of the capitals of the western states on a map of the United States. The students who used the method of associating the name of each capital with the name of the state significantly outscored those who had stayed in the classroom and tried to memorize the name of each state's capital. When I attempted a mini-experiment a few weeks later, all the students wanted to go to the library with me to learn strategies. Their belief about strategies was beginning to change. Clearly, beliefs about, and the meaning assigned to, achievement affects students' motivation.

Motivation

At Benchmark, teachers tell students that they are in charge of their own motivation. They explain that motivation is a desire to do something and that desire comes from within them. Teachers also explain that it is the students' job to have the desire, curiosity, and interest to learn and understand. It is the teacher's job to meet them where they are in respect to their abilities and needs, as well as to teach and scaffold the strategies they need in order to comprehend well. We have found that when we do what we say we will do (meet their needs and support their performance), students are motivated.

Motivation, the desire to do something (e.g., read a story, participate in a discussion, or learn about explorers), rests on the fulfillment of needs, especially the needs for relatedness, competence, and autonomy (choice) (Deci, 1995). When students' basic needs are not met, they find it difficult to be motivated to read and understand. For example, if students' minds are occupied with concerns about fitting in socially or fears about their ability to perform as well as others in their class, motivation for completing school tasks is diminished. Similarly, if students believe they have no choice about what they do in school, they will feel unmotivated. Relatedness, competence, and perceived autonomy enhance motivation.

Relatedness

In the minds of many children, school is first of all a social event. They need to feel that they belong, have friends, and are liked by their teacher. If a teacher supports students in building relationships, the likelihood of their teaching motivated students increases. One way Benchmark teachers foster a sense of belonging is by placing school desks in pairs. The students who occupy each pair of desks are partners who collaborate to complete school tasks. For example, employing the Think-Pair-Share technique, teachers ask a question and give students individual think time (often with the expectation that students write brief notes on a pad of paper called a "think pad"). Then, after students have had time to formulate a possible answer, the teacher tells students they have 30 seconds to discuss their thoughts with their partners. When it is time for whole-class sharing, there are usually as many hands in the air as there are children in the class. This technique not only encourages s sense of camaraderie, but it also allows students who feel least competent to realize that they are as capable of participating as their partners because the partners have agreed on a response. Think-Pair-Share tends to alleviate students's possible inclination not to participate in academic tasks as a way to protect themselves from situations they perceive as threatening to their self-images.

Competence

Another way Benchmark teachers enhance competency-related motivation is by scaffolding for students the application of strategies they can use to successfully complete comprehension tasks and by providing specific feedback (Gaskins, Rauch, et al., 1997). Teachers also frame for students the value and purposes of each strategy and provide emotional support and encouragement during the learning process, especially when difficulties are encountered. When students know that the teacher has supports in place that keep them from failing, they become less fearful of putting forth effort to understand and become involved.

Choice

Within a scaffolded learning environment, teachers also provide choices to support autonomy-related motivation. For example, teachers of students on the fourth-grade level and above are often heard saying something like this:

> "There are several ways you might cope with your need to read slowly and thoughtfully, yet read the same amount of text the rest of your group reads prior to discussion. One alternative is to take the book home tonight and complete part of the reading before class. Another alternative would be to follow along in the text as you listen to a tape of the assigned chapter during your silent-reading time in class. Would you like to try one of these methods?"

Another situation in which choices make a motivational difference occurs when students are asked to write an essay or composition. Rather than assign a single topic, teachers allow students to choose from several topics. Allowing students to choose shows that there is room for student autonomy in the classroom.

Mastery versus Performance Goals

Another issue with respect to motivation is mastery goals versus performance goals. The crux of this matter is that a student's goal orientation often determines how he or she values teacher guidance or information; thus, Benchmark teachers guide students to value learning strategies for reading and comprehending (mastery goals) over outperforming their peers. Improvement should be the goal rather than grades.

Performance-oriented students are usually more interested in what they have to do to get the grade they want rather than how to improve their understanding. An example of a performance-oriented student is the student who attends only to the grade on his or her paper and does not use the teacher's written comments to learn how to improve understanding or competence. On the other hand, students who are mastery oriented tend to be eager to seek information and guidance from teachers and peers about how to improve. Mastery goals are particularly beneficial for struggling readers whose present capacities, especially reading level, are inadequate to meet grade-level task demands. One way for teachers to encourage mastery goal orientation is to provide information (e.g., rubrics, anchor papers, constructive help, task-specific feedback) that will orient students to evaluate how well they are doing and to seek opportunities to improve comprehension.

Relatedness, competence, autonomy, and the meaning students assign to achievement all affect motivation. Having a rudimentary understanding of how the brain works also supports motivation by providing a rationale for why students need to use strategies to take charge of their learning and understanding. Benchmark teachers explain that what students learn and understand depends not only on such student factors as control over cognitive style, beliefs, and motivation, but also on students' knowledge about and use of strategies and concepts—the how and what of comprehension.

Procedural Knowledge: How to Comprehend

Although many children in the United States learn to decode and comprehend without explicit instruction in how to do so, there is a sizeable group of students who do not figure out these things on their own and need to be explicitly taught strategies for *how* to decode and comprehend, and at a pace and level appropriate for each of them. It is this latter group of students who attend Benchmark School. To guide students in breaking the code, we have developed a word identification program (Word Detectives), which systematically introduces students to phonemic segmentation, sound–letter matches, and ways to use what they know about how our language works to figure out words they do not know (Gaskins, Ehri, Cress, O'Hara, & Donnelly, 1996–1997). To guide students in constructing meaning from text, we teach students the specific strategies they need to complete the comprehension activities we assign.

Studies that examine the comprehension of proficient readers suggest that there are between five and eight comprehension strategies that proficient readers use consistently (e.g., Gaskins & Elliot, 1991; Keene & Zimmermann, 1997; Pearson, 1993; Pressley, 2002), that each of these major comprehension strategies should be taught over a long period of time, to students from kindergarten through 12th grade, and that these strategies should be modeled by teachers and practiced by students using a variety of texts.

What are these major comprehension strategies? Pressley (2002) believes they are *predicting, questioning, making images, seeking clarification,* and *constructing summaries.* Keene and Zimmermann (1997) suggest *be metacognitive, connect the new to the known, determine importance, question, use sensory images, infer, synthesize,* and *solve reading problems.* Pearson (1993) posited three major categories of strategies: *monitor for sense, make inferences,* and *look for patterns.* To these three categories, Benchmark has added *analyze the task* (Gaskins, 2000). There seems to be general agreement about strategies that are worth teaching.

Perhaps the most important objective of strategy instruction is to create students who are metacognitive (who think about their own thinking).

To accomplish this, teachers make students aware of the components of metacognition. For example, when students are reading, they need to know what and when they are comprehending and when comprehension is not taking place. Additional components of metacognition include setting goals or purposes for reading, planning how to meet the demands of text and activity, identifying text that is unclear and determining why, and knowing how to implement fix-up strategies when meaning making breaks down.

An aspect of metacognition that is problematic for Benchmark students is time management. Like many underachievers, they have great difficulty in realistically planning how to use their time. To help students plan their out-of-school time, some Benchmark teachers of first-year middle school students ask students to come to school each day with a list of after-school plans and activities for that day. Then, sometime during the day, an adult mentor supervises students as they complete a homework plan that takes into consideration their after-school plans and activities. In discussing the previous day's plan, as well as in completing a new plan, teachers guide students to see how they can have more control and autonomy by planning exactly how they will use their out-of-school time. Teachers support students in coming to the realization that planning allows them not only to have time to accomplish their schoolwork and take part in regularly scheduled activities, but also to have free time. Teachers have discovered that after several, sometimes tedious, months of planning with students, the students begin to realize that improved time management can help them complete their required school tasks more efficiently—and provide for free time.

To teach metacognitive and cognitive strategies, Benchmark teachers, upon introducing a new strategy, explicitly explain to students *what* strategy they are going to learn, *why* the strategy is important, *when* it can be used, and *how* to implement it. (See Gaskins, Anderson, Pressley, Cunicelli, and Satlow, 1993, for a more detailed account of the Benchmark instructional model.) For example, on the first day third-grade students were introduced to summarizing fiction, the teacher placed on the chalkboard the four cards she uses in discussing strategies. Each card contained one word, either WHAT, WHY, WHEN, or HOW. Beneath the WHAT card on the chalkboard, she placed a card that explained the WHAT. She pointed to the card and said, "Today we are going to learn how to summarize fiction. A summary is a short retelling that includes the important information. Why would you want to know how to summarize fiction?" The teacher listened to the children's responses, then placed beneath the WHY card a card that explained the WHY. She said:

> "Summarizing fiction helps us focus on important information, monitor our understanding, remember what we have read, and concisely share what we have read with others. That's a lot to

remember—who can explain in their own words one reason for learning to summarize fiction?"

The teacher listened to students' responses, pointing to each part on the card as that part was discussed. Next, she asked, "When would you use this strategy?" Students made a few suggestions; then the teacher continued with the WHEN card, saying, "We can use this strategy to monitor our understanding any time we read fiction." Placing the HOW card on the chalkboard, the teacher said:

> "I am going to tell you the steps I use in summarizing fiction. First, as I read, I write notes about characters, setting, problem and resolution, and key events. Second, after I finish reading, I read through my notes to identify the most important information to include in my summary. Third, I weave the most important information together into several sentences to tell about what I have read. Let me model for you how I would do that as we read together the booklet I have given you."

The teacher read aloud as students followed in their texts. As the teacher read, she stopped to jot notes on the chalkboard about characters, setting, problem, resolution, and key events. Next, she read the notes she had written on the chalkboard and thought aloud about important items to include in her summary. She identified these with checkmarks. Finally, she thought aloud as she wove the checked notes together into a summary.

The teacher then prepared students to read a short fiction selection and asked them, as they read the first page, to think about what on that page they would include in their notes. After students finished reading the page, they suggested notes, which the teacher wrote on the chalkboard. The students proceeded through the story in this page-by-page manner. When all the notes were collected on the chalkboard, the students read them over and discussed which should be part of their summary. These were checked. The teacher asked a volunteer to summarize the story orally, using the checked notes on the chalkboard.

Students practice summarizing in this manner until they seem to have a grasp of how to complete the strategy; then the teacher releases some of the responsibility for completing the strategy by asking students to jot down notes as they read. These notes are contributed as described earlier, and an oral summary is composed. Once students are comfortable writing notes, the teacher releases more responsibility and students check their own notes for the most important ideas and then summarize their notes orally. As a last step, perhaps 6 weeks from the introduction of the strategy, the teacher supervises students as they write their first summaries on their own.

All strategies are introduced and practiced in a similar manner. Each day, after introducing a strategy, the teacher turns the WHAT, WHY, WHEN, and HOW of the strategy into questions as a way of helping students solidify the information. Then the teacher guides students as they practice implementing the strategy, first with a great deal of support and later with a gradual release of responsibility to the students for employing the strategy. Teacher modeling recurs periodically, and the teacher often illustrates by telling about a time when he or she used the strategy or asks students to tell of instances in which they have used the strategy.

Strategies, of course, are not used in isolation. When students learn how to summarize fiction, they are also practicing other strategies they have learned, such as monitoring for sense, surveying, predicting, setting purposes, identifying story elements, and so forth. In addition, they are applying metacognitive strategies to take control of cognitive styles, beliefs, and motivation issues. Sometimes they are tracking goals on a goal card or planning with a teacher how to find time to complete their independent reading or to write a report. There is lots of action in every Benchmark classroom related to students' taking control of mental processing.

Declarative Knowledge: What I Know

It is axiomatic that what a person understands is based on what he or she already knows. In reading text, a student's background of knowledge about factors such as topic, structure of the domain, genre, and topic-specific vocabulary greatly affects how well the student will comprehend. Declarative knowledge—knowledge of what one knows—is a reader variable that deserves consideration in discussing comprehension.

For most of our bright, struggling readers at Benchmark School, lack of background knowledge does not become an issue until they begin reading materials written on third- or fourth-reader level. Prior to this time, students have usually been reading about topics and in genres with which they are familiar. Even most of the nonfiction written for students reading below the third-grade level has been on topics for which they have some background knowledge. However, as students encounter unfamiliar topics and vocabulary in content-area texts, there is a need for them to develop strategies for coping with a lack of background knowledge.

For example, Benchmark teachers recommend to students that when a topic is introduced for which they have little background knowledge, they should ask the librarian to help them to find one or two books on the topic written at an easy reading level. I often tell students that when, unexpectedly and on short notice, I was given an opportunity to join my husband on a business trip to China (a country about which I knew almost nothing), the first thing I did was to ask the Benchmark librarian for books about

China written at the easiest possible level. I knew that these easy books would most likely contain the most important concepts about China, written in the simplest vocabulary. I thought that if I had the basic information about China, I could hook what I learned while in China to that basic information. My theory proved to be true. At Benchmark we have found that telling students about strategies we actually use as adults can be a powerful influence on what students do. The librarian tells me that students often confide in her, when they come to the library for an easy book on a specific topic, that it is "because it is what Dr. Gaskins does when she does not have background knowledge about a topic."

There are a number of other ways of coping with a lack of background knowledge that Benchmark teachers suggest: listen to a taped book or watch a video about the topic, then discuss the information with someone who knows more about the topic than you do; find a book about the topic with lots of pictures and study the pictures to get a sense of the topic and concrete images of the topic-specific vocabulary; read a piece of fiction in which the characters are dealing with the topic, such as a novel that takes place during the Revolutionary War as a way of understanding that war; seek information on the Internet or on a compact disk. In the middle school, teachers routinely ask students to read topic-related "easy" books before they tackle a major piece of literature such as one of Shakespeare's plays. For example, before reading *Romeo and Juliet*, middle school students read books about the time period in which the play was set, as well as about the Elizabethan theater.

Teachers' coaching students to be aware of, acknowledge, and take action when a lack of background knowledge is interfering with comprehension can help students better comprehend text. Background knowledge is a reader variable crucial to adequate comprehension.

Reader variables, as discussed in this section, are the most dominant of the four kinds of variables affecting comprehension. In the following sections the three remaining types of variables are discussed more briefly, because they are variables over which readers have less control. Nevertheless, text, activity, and context are variables about which the reader must be aware and for which they must develop ways of coping in order to comprehend what they read.

TEXT VARIABLES

A second category of variables that affects comprehension includes text variables. If the fit is good between text variables and reader capabilities, then in all likelihood comprehension will be satisfactory. If the fit is poor, comprehension may be impaired. There are many categories and dimensions of text variables that have potential to affect comprehension. Among these are level of vocabulary, proposed audience, familiarity of content, characteristics of text genre, type of text, clarity of text structure, and the nature of illustrations and graphics. Most of these text variables can be included in two categories: density of text and type of text. A teacher's role is to acquaint students with text variables as they are encountered in classroom activities and to teach students ways of coping when text variables become a roadblock to comprehension. A few examples are provided in the following paragraphs.

Density of Text

Density of text has to do with the number of concepts a reader encounters per unit of text. For example, expository text tends to be denser than narrative text because of the many concepts a reader encounters per page as compared with concepts per page in narrative text. Teachers at Benchmark have found that they have to explicitly mental model the process they use in reading expository texts and point out how it is different from the process they use for narrative text. They also have to explain that because the purposes of the two genres are different, the pace of reading and the depth of analysis will probably also have to be different. As a mini-experiment, I have had students list the unfamiliar concepts and vocabulary from a page of expository text and a page of narrative text. Students are usually surprised to discover the density of concepts and vocabulary in expository text as compared with narrative text. I follow this discovery with a discussion of strategies students can use to comprehend expository text.

Contributing to the density of concepts is the density of unknown word meanings. Rather than teach vocabulary development in isolation, Benchmark teachers put in place systems to help students acknowledge, as they read, their awareness of words for which they do not know the meaning. Students may list these words in a reading or content-area log (or even on a scrap of paper). During discussion, students share with peers their questions and hunches about word meanings and request clarification from members of the group. Seldom do students turn to the dictionary for a definition before they have first tried to extract the meaning of a word either by using context clues or through collaboration with a peer. The dictionary is consulted when verification is needed.

Type of Text

A classic problem among our students is the desire to read all forms of text (e.g., textbooks, novels, advertisements, hypertext) at the same pace and with the same level of reflectivity. Therefore, as the staff broadens the choice of texts students are given to read, they find a need to teach the comprehension strategies that each type of text necessitates. For example, middle school teachers discovered (prior to our having Internet accessibility in classrooms) that when left on their own (i.e., at home or in a library) to research a topic using the Internet, students had a tendency to accept the accuracy and appropriateness of what they read. Teachers have since begun to provide students with explicit instruction on how to determine the appropriateness of hypertext information for a topic and how to corroborate the accuracy of the information. Teachers have also learned that students do not automatically apply what they know about library research to researching a topic on the Internet; thus, search strategies often must be cued and sometimes retaught.

The interaction of text variables with reader, activity, and context variables can affect comprehension. The teacher's job is to make students aware of such interactions and to teach them strategies for coping with them. The goal is for students to be aware of the vagaries of text and to feel confident in their ability to handle them.

ACTIVITY VARIABLES

Activity refers to the purpose for reading. General purposes for reading include learning, applying knowledge, and being engaged (RRSG, 2002). Some purposes may be teacher imposed and rather limited, and other activities may require students to read for authentic purposes, such as reading a model text in preparation for writing a specific genre, reading to gain insights to share with others, and reading as part of e-mail communication. When students embrace the purpose, the reading task is more likely to be completed with satisfactory comprehension.

In school, activities are most often assigned by the teacher, with some activities being more appropriate for enhancing progress in reading comprehension than others. One of the activities highly related to progress in reading, at all levels of reading, is the amount of time a student is actively engaged in reading level-appropriate text (Anderson, Wilson, & Fielding, 1988). Thus, an activity that should be high on the priority list of each day's classroom activities is students' completion of a great deal of reading, both for pleasure and to complete tasks. Reading activities are enhanced by teaching students how to process text beyond the literal level, then expecting them to respond to what they read at these higher levels. This can be accomplished by explicitly teaching students strategies for interpreting, critically analyzing, and applying to other situations what was understood. Collaborative discussion about interpretative and critical responses to text is another activity that fosters high-level comprehension.

In the primary grades, the activity involving students' responses to reading may begin as a scaffolded response sheet for which students supply missing information about characters, setting, story problem, and resolution of the problem. Later, students progress to using this response sheet to gather information for writing a summary of the text. Another activity may involve students writing sentence responses to questions asking for inferences that are backed with evidence from the text. As students progress into the intermediate grades, the activities that are assigned often require more steps, such as the steps needed for writing an essay or report, which may include selecting a topic or theme, searching for information, analyzing information critically for appropriateness and accuracy, and organizing the information into an essay or report. By the time students are in the middle school, the activities assigned may involve multiple texts and a number of comprehension strategies that vary from just getting the facts straight to comparing themes of several novels, writing a brochure to persuade someone to travel to Alaska, or completing an author study. Clearly, the reading comprehension activities in which teachers ask students to engage will greatly affect the level of reading proficiency they achieve.

CONTEXT VARIABLES

Sociocultural context variables can be divided into three groups: cognitive, social, and cultural (S. Goldman, personal communication to the RRSG). Cognitive group variables include teacher knowledge, classroom culture, and instruction. Social group variables include socioeconomic status (SES), education, religion, and support for the school by family and peers. Cultural group variables include unique languages, customs, and values. These three groups of sociocultural variables interact with reader, text, and activity variables to determine reading comprehension. Most sociocultural variables are variables that students cannot change, but this does not mean that students must to be victims of these variables. Students can be taught how to cope with those context variables they view as interfering with reading comprehension.

Because this chapter is about what teachers can teach students to do to take charge of reader, text, activity, and context variables, I focus on the context variables over which students have some control in fostering comprehension. Teachers are familiar with hearing students comment about factors in their environment that get in the way of their being able to satisfactorily complete comprehension activities. To counter this tendency and to put control of these factors in students' hands, teachers brainstorm with students about what they can do to take charge of these variables. A few of the variables over which students have control include teachers who do not explain how to complete the activities they assign in a way a student understands, classmates who are distracting, assignments that are too difficult, homes that have no quiet space for completing assignments, families who do not value regular school attendance, and parents who are unable to support the completion of assignments because of language or economic reasons.

The strategy for solving these problems, recommended by Benchmark teachers, is for students to become self-advocates. With teacher coaching, students in Benchmark's middle school come to believe that it is their responsibility to seek out the teacher and ask for clarification when they do not understand how to complete an assignment. When classmates prove to be a distraction, it is the responsibility of the student being distracted to move away from the distraction or to ask for permission to move. Sometimes assignments are too difficult because of the level of the text or lack of background knowledge. In such cases students learn to ask a teacher, parent, mentor, or friend to read and discuss the text with them. With respect to lack of background knowledge, students cope by searching in the library or on the Internet for relevant background information at an easy level. If homes have no quiet space, students make arrangements to stay late at school, come to school early, or work in a public library. In homes where parents allow students to miss school, for instance, because they have to baby-sit a sibling or because parents overslept, students take a stand and enlist other family members or mentors in supporting the value of school attendance. Students search for mentors through participation in community youth organizations or church or synagogue activities. Encouraging and guiding students to be self-advocates is one of the greatest gifts a teacher can give students. A school staff that supports self-advocacy is preparing students for the real world. One teacher, mentor, or counselor may not be able to change the context in which reading comprehension must take place, but he or she can teach students ways to cope with it.

TAKING CHARGE

During their time at Benchmark, students are gradually introduced to the concept of taking charge of the variables that affect reading comprehension. From their entrance into the school, students are made aware of *reader* variables that affect comprehension and how they can take charge of these variables. Responsibility for taking charge of *text, activity,* and *context* variables is gradually added during the lower school years, and students are expected to deal simultaneously with all four of these variables during their middle school years. One of the goals of the middle school is for students to analyze each comprehension activity with respect to taking charge of reader, text, activity, and context variables.

For example, in first-year middle school social studies and science classes students are expected to use the ANOW strategy when answering any essay question. The "A" in ANOW stands for *analyze*. To indicate that they have analyzed the essay question, students are required to write the essay question in their own words. The "N" stands for *notes*. Rather than just begin writing the essay without planning it, students are required to write brief notes about the ideas they want to include in their essays. Once the notes are written, students complete the "O" part of ANOW. They *organize* the notes in some logical order. Finally, students *write* ("W") their essays. Should students not have sufficient time to write the essay after having analyzed, written notes, and organized, they are given credit for the essay based on the understanding indicated by their notes and how these notes are organized.

By the second year of the middle school, teachers assign activities, whether for the class period or as a 6–week project, and ask students to talk about the reader, text, activity, and context variables of which they will have to take charge and how they will do this. They are often asked to fill in a chart, with Reader, Text, Activity, and Context across the top, on which they fill in their personal roadblock in each area and how they will cope with it. If this is a long-term project, they also, with teacher guidance, fill in a time line for completing the project and self-assess their progress on an almost daily basis, using this time line.

Near the conclusion of their third year in the middle school, each student makes a presentation to an invited group of Benchmark staff, usually their mentors and former teachers. During their presentations, students tell about their journies through Benchmark, and what they have learned about themselves as learners and readers, and their plans for success in their new schools. These students could have written this chapter.

RESEARCH-BASED
INSTRUCTIONAL RECOMMENDATIONS

The following recommendations for instruction emphasize teaching students how to take charge of reader, text, activity, and context variables. Because these variables interact, some of the instructional recommendations apply to more than one variable.

Reader Variables

1. Guide students to become aware of maladaptive cognitive styles and beliefs that interfere with reading comprehension.

2. Explain and mental model strategies for active involvement, attention, persistence, reflectivity, and flexibility, including strategies for monitoring how well one is doing in achieving a specific cognitive-style goal.
3. Provide a learning environment that allows students to experience relatedness, competence, and autonomy by employing techniques such as Think-Pair-Share, scaffolding, feedback, and choice.
4. Focus on improvement goals rather than grades and competition.
5. Teach explicitly and model the cognitive and metacognitive strategies students need to complete the activities that are assigned.
6. Explain and/or illustrate via mini-experiments how the strategies being taught are related to how the brain works.

Text Variables

1. Acquaint students with text variables (e.g., density of text and type of text) as they are encountered in classroom activities, and teach students ways of coping with text variables that may become roadblocks to comprehension.
2. Teach students strategies for comprehending the variety of texts they encounter in and out of school, throughout the day, across the curriculum, and for accomplishing a variety of activities.
3. Coach students to be aware of, acknowledge, and take action when a lack of background knowledge is interfering with comprehension.
4. Put in place systems to help students acknowledge, as they read, their awareness of words of which they do not know the meaning.

Activity Variables

1. Ensure that reading comprehension activities are designed to meet students where they are and are conducted at the pace at which students are able to respond.
2. Provide opportunities for students to complete a great deal of reading in interesting, level-appropriate texts that are read both for pleasure and to complete tasks.
3. Provide meaningful opportunities for students to practice (over a long period of time and in different contexts) the five to eight comprehension strategies that proficient readers use consistently.
4. Foster collaborative discussions in which interpretative and critical responses to texts are expected.
5. Scaffold the completion of activities, especially long-term projects.

Context Variables

1. Teach students to be aware of context variables that may interfere with comprehension and to be self-advocates who know either how to cope with these context variables or how to get the support they need to be able to comprehend the text.

FINAL THOUGHTS

Developing struggling readers into students who know how to comprehend well is not achieved in 1 or 2 years. It is a process that occurs over many years. For the process to work well, the emphasis throughout the school and across the curriculum over many years must focus on how to take charge of reader, text, activity, and context variables. It is an undertaking well worth the investment of staff time and energy, with results measured in terms of competent students empowered to take charge of constructing meaning for the rest of their lives.

REFERENCES

Anderson, R. C., Wilson, P., & Fielding, L. (1988). Growth in reading and how children spend time outside of school. *Reading Research Quarterly, 23,* 285–303.

Carey, W. B., & McDevitt, S. C. (1995). *Coping with children's temperament: A guide for professionals.* New York: Basic Books.

Deci, E. L., with Flaste, R. (1995). *Why we do what we do: The dynamics of personal autonomy.* New York: G. P. Putnam's Sons.

Gaskins, I. W. (1984). There's more to a reading problem than poor reading. *Journal of Learning Disabilities, 17,* 467–471.

Gaskins, I. W. (1988). Teachers as thinking coaches: Creating strategic learners and problem solvers. *Reading, Writing, and Learning Disabilities, 4,* 35–48.

Gaskins, I. W. (1998). There's more to teaching at-risk and delayed readers than good reading instruction. *Reading Teacher, 51,* 534–547.

Gaskins, I. W. (2000). *A framework for learning and understanding.* Unpublished manuscript, Benchmark School, Media, PA.

Gaskins, I. W., Anderson, R. C., Pressley, M., Cunicelli, E. A., & Satlow, E. (1993). Six teachers' dialogue during cognitive process instruction. *Elementary School Journal, 93,* 277–304.

Gaskins, I. W., & Baron, J. (1985). Teaching poor readers to cope with maladaptive cognitive styles: A training program. *Journal of Learning Disabilities, 18,* 390–394.

Gaskins, I. W., Ehri, L. C., Cress, C., O'Hara, C., & Donnelly, K. (1996–1997).

Procedures for word learning: Making discoveries about words. *Reading Teacher, 50,* 312–327.

Gaskins, I. W., & Elliot, T. T. (1991). *Implementing cognitive strategy instruction across the school: The Benchmark manual for teachers.* Cambridge, MA: Brookline Books.

Gaskins, I. W., Rauch, S., Gensemer, E., Cunicelli, E., O'Hara, C., Six, L., & Scott, T. (1997). Scaffolding the development of intelligence among children who are delayed in learning to read. In K. Hogan & M. Pressley (Eds.), *Scaffolding student learning: Instructional approaches and issues* (pp. 43–73). Cambridge, MA: Brookline Books.

Keene, E. O., & Zimmermann, S. (1997). *Mosaic of thought: Teaching comprehension in a readers' workshop.* Portsmouth, NH: Heinemann.

Marzano, R. J. (2001). *Designing a new taxonomy of educational objectives.* Thousand Oaks, CA: Corwin Press.

Meichenbaum, D. (1977). *Cognitive-behavior modification: An integrative approach.* New York: Plenum Press.

Murphy, J. M. (1996). *A follow-up study of delayed readers and an investigation of factors related to their success in young adulthood.* Unpublished doctoral dissertation, University of Pennsylvania, Philadelphia.

Pearson, P. D. (1993). Teaching and learning reading: A research perspective. *Language Arts, 70,* 502–511.

Pressley, M. (2002). *Reading instruction that works: The case for balanced teaching* (2nd ed.). New York: Guilford Press.

RAND Reading Study Group. (2002). *Reading for understanding: Toward an R & D program in reading comprehension.* Santa Monica, CA: RAND Corporation.

Snow, R. E., Lorno, L., & Jackson, D. (1996). Individual differences in affective and cognitive functions. In D. Berliner & R. Calfee (Eds.), *Handbook of educational psychology* (pp. 243–310). New York: Simon & Schuster Macmillan.

Thomas, A., & Chess, S. (1977). *Temperament and development.* New York: Brunner/Mazel.

9

Electronic and Multimedia Documents

HELEN S. KIM
MICHAEL L. KAMIL

With the widespread use of computer and multimedia technologies has come a change in the set of skills necessary to be a competent reader. New forms of text, such as electronic documents, hypertext and hypermedia, require the reader to develop new and different abilities in addition to the skills and strategies needed to read traditional texts.

Expanding the definition of reading to include electronic and multimedia documents is a necessity, given the sheer volume of these types of text. For example, as of August 14, 2002, there were, 2,469,940,685 web pages indexed by the Google search engine (*www.google.com*). To read many of these web pages proficiently, a reader needs the same skills that are required to read any conventional printed text. In addition, however, new skills, like navigation and integration of multimedia information with print, are required to read most web pages. The development and spread of electronic text has occurred in a relatively short period of time. Yet, reading instruction has not been quick to incorporate these changes, despite the fact that many schools routinely have students doing work on the Internet, reading at computers, and even creating their own multimedia presentations.

In this chapter, we explore the characteristics of electronic and multimedia documents and reflect on some important considerations for reading and instruction. It must be remembered, however, that this chapter does not reiterate all of the conventional comprehension skills required to read electronic text. These are considered in the other chapters of this book.

Because electronic and multimedia text represent a relatively new area, the research is not as fully developed as in many other areas of comprehension. The lack of a strong research base limits the conclusions that can be drawn. There are many areas, however, in which we can make conclusions. Where appropriate, we summarize the available research and highlight areas for future investigation. We also show the implications for instruction, where appropriate.

FORMS OF ELECTRONIC TEXT

The use of computers to present text and multimedia information has become relatively common. Multimedia presentations in the form of computer texts, Internet web pages, e-mail, word processing, and even computer games are everyday occurrences. Although these represent different forms of electronic texts, it is important to note that electronic texts have a number of unique properties. In fact, there are several different types of electronic documents or texts that are displayed through the computer or other electronic media. Hypertext is text that can be expanded electronically by allowing a reader to access information beyond the scope of that which is physically present. The information can be in the form of either additional text (hypertext) or other media (hypermedia). A unique benefit of documents with hyperlinks is the ability of the writer to provide access to more information about the topic at hand. For example, readers may have the option of pursuing a link to find a definition of an unknown word, background information, or additional elaboration of the topic, such as via a video or sound clip. Documents with carefully designed hyperlinks have potential to enrich the reading experience for the reader. They can also make it possible for struggling readers to comprehend material in much more sophisticated ways.

PRIOR RESEARCH ON MULTIMEDIA AND ELECTRONIC TEXTS

Despite the appeal of using multimedia documents to enhance reading, there is much that we do not yet know about the underlying cognitive processes involved in reading and processing these types of texts (Kamil, Intrator, & Kim, 2000). Very little is known about the cognitive processes readers use with electronic documents, and most of these findings are tentative, at best. Neilsen (1997) suggests that readers only scan text on the web.

He found that 79% of the participants in his study always scanned new hypertext pages they encountered, and only 16% of the participants read the pages word for word. If this is indeed the way in which people read on the Web, it has serious implications for instruction.

Research has identified some factors that may account for successful outcomes in hypertext reading, including the ability to identify important text nodes (or links), taking time to read them more carefully (Gillingham, 1993), and utilizing a variety of learning strategies (Davidson-Shivers, Rasmussen, & Bratton-Jeffery, 1997). Davidson-Shivers et al. (1997) found that the more successful readers of hypertext engaged in more comprehension monitoring, as well as actively linking new information with their prior knowledge of the topic.

In regard to reading tasks, research has found some interesting differences in hypertext as compared with conventional text. Gillingham (1993) found that it takes adult participants longer to search for information in hypertext than in conventional text. This finding suggests that there may be important differences related to specific types of processing, such as looking for data or reading for comprehension.

One difficulty in reading hypertext is that all of the structural cues (cf. Goldman & Rakestraw, 2000) are condensed into a single dimensional cue. The signal, usually underlining or coloring a word or phrase representing the link, indicates that there is some information to be had by activating the link. The difficulty for the reader is that there is no way to know in advance what information is to be obtained by opening the link. In the absence of differentiated cues, the reader needs to know when to "gamble" that the information will be useful. Some readers also pursue links because of their interest or curiosity, and not necessarily because the link is deemed important for text comprehension. Coupled with the finding that many hypertext documents offer links based on availability of additional information, rather than relevance, readers are clearly faced with some unique strategic considerations when reading electronic documents. It appears that writers do not have consistent patterns of writing hypertext. Writers do not seem to make decisions about hyperlinks on the basis of what readers would need at any given point in the text.

The consequences of reading nonrelevant, or only peripherally related, information available through hyperlinks are unclear. At the very least, we know that the reading will take much longer. At worst, it can distract the reader who follows seemingly interesting links.

One line of research from general reading theory that may be relevant to reading electronic documents with links is the study of the inclusion of "seductive details." Seductive details are those details often included in text that are more interesting than the main topic of the text. Readers are often drawn to these details even when they do not contribute much to the overall comprehension of the text. Pursuing hypertext links that contain little or no information relevant to understanding the main topic parallels the notion of a seductive detail, or the attention to "propositions presenting interesting, but unimportant information" (Garner, Gillingham, & White, 1989, p. 41).

Garner et al. (1989) found that adults who read passages with seductive details included significantly fewer main ideas in their recall protocols, in comparison with those who read text passages without the seductive details. Applied to the area of reading hypertext, it may be that readers follow certain types of links or read text in idiosyncratic ways and do not comprehend the most conventional meaning of the text that is present. Ensuring that students understand the importance of metacognitive monitoring is clearly an instructional necessity for teaching them to read hypertext.

UNIQUE SKILLS FOR HYPERTEXT

There are many similarities between reading electronic documents and reading traditional materials. For example, reading electronic text requires several of the same basic skills such as decoding, monitoring understanding, vocabulary knowledge, and attending to structural cues. However, research on reading electronic documents suggests that there are also important differences and that electronic documents impose some unique demands. From simple reading tasks, such as searching for information, to reading for comprehension, various challenges are presented in reading electronic documents. In addition to specific strategies needed to navigate through linked text, other challenges include evaluating the relevance of additional information, reading texts in nonlinear ways, and integrating information presented in different media and of varying degrees of relevance. Apart from these important challenges, there are at least equally as many potential benefits that documents with additional links to information can provide. Instantaneous access to additional information, contextual information, fast electronic searches, and reading assistance are just a few of the many advantages provided by the use of electronic documents.

CHARACTERISTICS OF ELECTRONIC TEXT

In this section we consider some of the characteristics of electronic text and relate them to instructional needs.

The characteristics of multimedia and electronic documents can be grouped in three categories: design (how the texts are constructed), strategies (how students are able to go about the task of reading a passage), and style and difficulty (related to the information contained in the text). We focus on these issues because we believe these characteristics of electronic texts should be considered in instruction. That is, students should be taught strategies for reading electronic texts that reflect these characteristics. As each category has its own set of implications for instruction, we discuss each set of characteristics separately.

Design

There are several factors to consider when deciding whether an electronic document is well designed for a reading task. Two of the most important considerations are the *purpose of the reading task* and the *level of prior knowledge of the reader.* Electronic documents seem to be an efficient way for readers to explore new subjects and obtain a lot of background information in a very short time. However, previous research (e.g., Shin, Schallert, & Savenye, 1994) found that students with little prior knowledge of a topic may do better when options for reading are restricted. That is, students with little prior knowledge may do better when electronic documents contain fewer hyperlinks and a more controlled learning environment, such as one that guides the student to read the pages or links in a predetermined way. This suggests that students with little prior knowledge may need extra instruction before reading some documents that are not designed appropriately.

The ability to offer multimedia supports to learning, such as video or audio examples, can help students achieve a deeper understanding of the subject material. However, when students are reading electronic texts for comprehension, research tells us that particularly close attention should be given to the design of the material. The choice, relevance, and placement of hyperlinks are important considerations in reading electronic documents. Although there are not many empirically based design guidelines for increasing the text comprehension of electronic documents, a few general guidelines are suggested from the research. Irrelevant links to additional information, documents that are overloaded with hyperlinks, and chaotic presentations of material are not conducive to overall text comprehension.

An even more basic, but often overlooked, design consideration is the physical presentation of the electronic text. Even with technological advances and the relatively low cost of providing larger screen sizes and enhanced resolution, readers commonly report eye strain, difficulty in scrolling, and related difficulties when asked to compare reading electronic and conventional texts (Kim & Kamil, 2000). A unique feature of many electronic texts is the reader's control over the font and size of the print. In many electronic texts, these variables can be changed by the reader whenever the need or desire arises.

A difficulty that has been reported in regard to reading electronic texts is the inability to manipulate the text, such as by using a highlighter to underline important concepts, writing in the margins, or flipping through the pages forward and back. Although these innate problems with electronic documents are difficult to ameliorate, they underscore the need to offer reasonable alternatives, such as providing printed copies of the electronic displays for students who find it easier to work with print. For accessing electronic documents, even the most basic ergonomic design considerations should be reviewed for comfort and ease of use. Difficulties involved with reading text on the computer screen may be a problem that will be solved in the near future. Some e-books now have some of the desired features available, including the possibility of annotating the text.

As technology advances, some of the problematic issues will be ameliorated. Others will be rendered less important because of the increasing experience students will have with electronic text. The remaining problems can be remedied by providing students with appropriate explicit instruction about reading electronic texts.

Strategies

Students need to acquire some special strategies to comprehend electronic text effectively. Among these are basic computer skills, which are needed to navigate though text, find information on-line, scroll through information, and access files and folders. Although these skills are becoming increasingly common in today's school and workplace, children and adults who have not had much experience with computers, and, more specifically, with reading electronic documents, may find themselves having trouble navigating the text, getting lost on the Internet, or experiencing difficulties in searching for information. With the vast number of websites on the Internet, for example, even one incorrect letter may be sufficient to send the reader to a different website or an error message. This underscores the importance of basic skills such as typing, navigating, and spelling. Although some of these challenges can be dealt with through the careful selection of material, specific instruction in strategies and computer skills is likely to be critical in enhancing multimedia reading. Instruction in basic computer skills may help novice readers concentrate on reading the text, rather than devoting a lot of attention to technical issues.

Proficient readers of electronic documents must be able to attend to important text information in the face of numerous distractions, such as flashing images, advertisements, links to other pages, or photos and sounds that simultaneously compete for the reader's attention. As compared with traditional texts, electronic documents include far more potential sources of interruption. For example, with a click on a link, a reader can instantly leave the current page and be taken to a page where the subject matter is only slightly related. A reader can also be distracted by the multimedia options, often specifically designed to appeal to the reader's interest, such as flashing banners, advertisements that pop up in separate windows, and background music. These interruptions are likely to give students less time to process the pertinent information, especially when they do not have control over the timing or speed of the presentation of text. Given these processing demands, instruction on the strategic use of hyperlinks and the judicious timing of related opportunities to pursue additional information on the computer are important to utilizing multimedia supports effectively. Specific strategies for reading electronic documents are not commonly taught skills, and there are few guidelines for teaching them. A high priority for research is to determine the range of skills required and how they can best be taught.

Although further research is needed, it is clear that instruction should reflect the special demands of reading multimedia documents. Readers may need to learn how to adapt strategies used in reading traditional text to reading electronic documents. For example, students who are used to highlighting important sections, writing notes in the margins, or marking the text as they read traditional documents can be instructed on new ways to highlight important sections, such as highlighting text on the screen or taking notes on a separate piece of paper. Another example of such adaptation is seen among beginning readers who use their fingers to help track words as they read in traditional documents; they can be taught how to use the mouse in a similar way—a good alternative for tracking the words in electronic documents. Readers of electronic documents may also be instructed on how and when to apply different reading strategies, depending on the goals for reading and their knowledge of the topic. For instance, novice readers may benefit from reading the entire text before pursuing any hyperlinks, or performing electronic searches to locate key words and concepts before reading the text.

Style and Difficulty

In addition to the physical differences between electronic and traditional texts, previous research suggests that there are likely to be important differences between the two media in regard to the content readers are likely to encounter. For example, research on the average readability levels on the Internet (e.g., Kamil & Lane, 1998) consistently found that text on the Internet is, for the most part, very difficult. Particularly for children's websites, the average readability levels of the texts tend to be many grade levels higher than the intended audience. An implication of this finding is that children need to have access to a variety of on-line multimedia materials and texts that range in reading difficulty. When readers freely browse the Internet in search of materials, they are likely to encounter texts that are written for an audience with a fair amount of reading proficiency. Although this may not be an obstacle for many adults, it can certainly pose challenges for children and non-native speakers of English who are trying to access the information.

In addition to indicating the reading difficulty of many texts found on the Internet, research also tells us that electronic text is predominantly expository in nature (Kamil & Lane, 1998). However, research has also found that there is often a lack of time spent on reading and instruction with expository materials through the primary and elementary grades (e.g., Duke, 2000).

An important consequence of the lack of exposure to reading expository forms in the earlier grades is that many children do not become familiar with reading non-narrative texts. Expository texts demand different reading strategies of the reader, including the need to evaluate the veracity of the material and the ability to judge the credibility of different sources and arguments. These demands take on renewed importance in the context of multimedia and electronic documents found on the Internet, where the credibility and authority of information is often called into question. Moreover, children and adults who have not had much experience with reading expository material may be particularly unprepared for reading the majority of multimedia texts on the Internet. These readers are likely to benefit from specialized instruction in these areas, as well as strategies for evaluating the source and credibility of on-line references.

IMPLICATIONS OF RESEARCH FOR PRACTICE

Despite the small body of research relating to issues of electronic and multimedia text, there are conclusions that can be drawn in the three areas mentioned earlier: design, instructional strategies for reading, and the style and difficulty of the texts.

With respect to design, we conclude that electronic texts should be carefully scrutinized for readability and cohesiveness, with particularly close attention given to the match between the text and the reader. For example, electronic texts with multiple links to additional information of varying degrees of relevance, and several user-controlled options to read the text in nonsequential ways, are likely to be confusing for a novice reader. In contrast, a more structured experience, such as provided by limiting the number of links and placing them in relevant locations, as well as reducing the number of potential distractions, is likely to facilitate text comprehension and give readers more time to process the information in a cohesive way.

In addition to the careful selection of texts, instruction in strategies and skills is important for helping readers to extract significant information from multimedia documents. Students can benefit from explicit instruction in reading electronic and multimedia texts.

Finally, the style and difficulty of electronic documents are also important considerations in teaching for comprehension. Electronic documents, particularly those found on the Internet, are likely to be more difficult to read with respect to instructional level, even texts and websites written for children. In addition, texts on the Internet are likely to be expository, or informational, in nature. These two characteristics may pose reading challenges, as the difficulty and genre of the text are often unfamiliar territory for most children as well as some adults. Rather than relying solely on a website's designation of reading grade level, teachers may find it more useful to check the readability of the text by applying a readability formula to it, an option that is available in most word processing programs. If the readability level is higher than the students' ability, prior instruction in vocabulary can help prepare them for reading more difficult material. With respect to the abundance of expository material on the Internet, teachers may find it beneficial to instruct and engage their students in reading informational text in both traditional and electronic formats.

Although there are few empirical guidelines for the instruction of multimedia reading strategies, teachers and parents are likely to discover important areas for instruction through observation of the difficulties and challenges students face when reading multimedia documents. Instruction in making metacognitive judgments about necessary information (e.g., when to click on hyperlinks), conducting electronic searches for information, and evaluating electronic references are examples of specific computer skills that may be necessary. Assessments of prior knowledge may also help teachers identify areas in which students need preinstruction, such as in navigational skills or on vocabulary words relevant to an understanding of the text. Specific instruction tailored to the students' needs and addressing common problems through classroom instruction can be important in helping students read electronic texts more effectively.

CONCLUSION

In this chapter we reviewed some of the differences and similarities between reading conventional and electronic texts and offered some practical implications for instruction. We examined the impact of three factors—the design of electronic text; the strategies required to read electronic text; and the form, style, and content of electronic texts—on reading electronic texts.

When the definition of reading is expanded to include electronic and multimedia text, our conception of literacy is also fundamentally changed. No longer is reading proficiency determined solely by traditional reading skills, such as the ability to decode words and extract meaning from text, but also by a multitude of other skills that are not likely to have been included before. However, conventional skills are as important as ever. The difference is that now there are many new skills that are important to reading both traditional and electronic and multimedia texts. For example, learning to integrate information from various media· and navigating through texts with links are just two of the skills that pose new challenges to readers. These new skills and challenges require explicit instruction, as well as the careful design and selection of reading materials. Through the continued exploration of the factors that contribute to success in reading both traditional and electronic formats, we can add new and important dimensions to our students' reading instruction and literacy development in the new millennium.

REFERENCES

Davidson-Shivers, G. V., Rasmussen, K. L., & Bratton-Jeffery, M. F. (1997). Investigating learning strategies generation in a hypermedia environment using qualitative methods. *Journal of Computing in Childhood Education, 8,* 247–261.

Duke, N. K. (2000). 3.6 minutes per day: The scarcity of informational texts in first grade. *Reading Research Quarterly, 35,* 202–224.

Garner, R., Gillingham, M. G., & White, C. S. (1989). Effects of "seductive details" on macroprocessing and microprocessing in adults and children. *Cognition and Instruction, 6,* 41–57.

Gillingham, M. (1993). Effects of question complexity and reader strategies on adults' hypertext comprehension. *Journal of Research on Computing in Education, 26,* 1–15.

Goldman, S., & Rakestraw, J. (2000). Structural aspects of constructing meaning from text. In M. Kamil, P. Mosenthal, P. D. Pearson, & R. Barr (Eds.), *Handbook of reading research* (Vol. III, pp. 311–335). Mahwah, NJ: Erlbaum.

Kamil, M. L., Intrator, S., & Kim, H. S. (2000). Effects of other technologies on literacy and literacy learning. In M. Kamil, P. Mosenthal, P. D. Pearson, and R. Barr (Eds.), *Handbook of reading research* (Vol. III, pp. 771–788). Mahwah, NJ: Erlbaum.

Kamil, M. L., & Lane, D. (1998, December). *Information text, task demands For students, and readability of text on the internet.* Paper presented at the meeting of the National Reading Conference, Austin, TX.

Kim, H. S., & Kamil, M. L. (1999, December). *Exploring hypertext reading and strategy use for structured vs. unstructured texts.* Paper presented at the meeting of the National Reading Conference, Orlando, FL.

Neilsen, J. (1997). How users read on the Web. (Available at *www.useit.com/alertbox/9710a.html*)

Shin, C., Schallert, D., & Savenye, W. (1994). Effects of learner control, advisement, and prior knowledge on young students' learning in a hypertext environment. *Educational Technology Research and Development, 42,* 33–46.

10

Professional Development in Reading Comprehension Instruction

JANICE A. DOLE

I begin this chapter with a true incident that occurred when I was becoming a reader. I was part of a small reading group in my fifth-grade class. Our teacher, Mrs. Silver, asked us a question about a story we had just read. I was puzzled by the question because I didn't remember reading the answer. So I went back into the text to find several paragraphs where I thought the answer might be located. I read those paragraphs carefully, and then I read them over again. But I didn't find the answer to Mrs. Silver's question. When another child answered the question and Mrs. Silver responded, "Yes, good," I was incredulous. I had read the story carefully and had read one specific part twice, and I knew that answer was not in there. So I raised my hand and asked, "Where did he get his answer? It's not in the story." Mrs. Silver responded to me, "No, it's not. You have to read between the lines."

"Hmmm," I said to myself, "That is a very odd answer." I proceeded to locate and fix my eyes on one line of text and then the next one directly below it. I even placed my left and right forefingers on each line. Then I tracked my eyes across the page carefully between those two lines. And I said to myself, "There's nothing there!" At one level I knew that "reading between the lines" was an expression, not to be taken literally. But I didn't know what else to do except what Mrs. Silver told me to do.

I learned a lesson that day in Mrs. Silver's classroom. I learned not to ask Mrs. Silver questions because she wasn't going to help me get any answers.

Instruction in reading comprehension is about helping students get the answers to questions like the one I had that day in fifth grade. Indeed, the very heart of comprehension instruction is helping students figure out how to come up with answers to those tough questions that are not apparently "in the text." What I needed that day in class was Mrs. Silver to show me how to combine my prior knowledge with information in the text to get the answer to her tough question. She needed to tell me that not all the information necessary to answer questions comes directly from the text. She needed to show me how to use the information I already had in my head and combine that information with what was in the text. That was the only way I was going to come up with a plausible answer.

Apparently, though, Mrs. Silver did not know how to show me those things. She did the best she could do, which was to tell me to "read between the lines." I doubt very much that Mrs. Silver had any better idea about what that meant than I did. Mrs. Silver didn't know how to teach me or other students how to comprehend.

The focus of this chapter is on helping teachers, like Mrs. Silver, improve how they teach comprehension to their students. In general, helping practicing teachers improve their teaching is known as professional development. This chapter addresses what we know and do not know about professional development in reading comprehension.

In this chapter, professional development is defined as activities designed to help teachers improve their instruction (Little, 1992). Throughout the chapter, the terms *professional development* and *staff development* are used interchangeably.

To provide a context for understanding the professional development of teachers in reading comprehension, the chapter presents a review of the literature on professional development in general. This review is not intended to be exhaustive, and it does not include research and work with preservice teachers—those who are just learning to teach. The chapter does provide a framework for understanding older and newer models of professional development for practicing teachers. This work will then be used as a lens to examine the few studies that have specifically looked at helping teachers teach comprehension to their students.

RESEARCH ON PROFESSIONAL DEVELOPMENT

The goal of professional development is to assist teachers in becoming better at what they do. But what makes teachers better teachers? In a study by the National Center for Research on Teacher Education (NCRTE, 1991) researchers found that many teachers ranked *experience* as the single most valued asset of a teacher. Teachers believed that they become better teachers through experience. This view supports the "craft" notion of teaching (Sprinthall, Reiman, & Thies-Sprinthall, 1996) in which teachers view their field as a craft to be learned by experience. Interestingly, researchers in the NCRTE study could find no significant differences in the knowledge, attitudes, and classroom practices between the beginning and more experienced teachers they studied. Thus, the NCRTE researchers could find no evidence that experience differentiated more effective from less effective teachers, even though teachers believed it did.

Another significant finding of the NCRTE study is that teachers reported that they did *not* view staff development as an important source of professional growth. This finding is consistent with a body of research on the more traditional forms of staff development. The most common form consists of "one-shot workshops," otherwise known in some regions of the United States as the "sit and git." Experts or seasoned presenters in a given area most often conduct these workshops, even though, as the NCRTE studies found, teachers do not necessarily value "learning from experts" as something that can assist them in becoming better teachers.

Thus, teachers appear to value experience over other forms of professional development, including learning from experts, to help them become better at their work. Research on professional development over the last 20 years has confirmed that teachers find much of the staff development they receive to be ineffective. Researchers concur with teachers in this belief. Fullan (1991) concluded, "Nothing has promised so much and has been so frustratingly wasteful as the thousands of workshops and conferences that led to no significant change in practice when teachers returned to their classrooms" (p. 315).

The next section identifies some of the reasons why, in many cases, professional development has been ineffective. Even though our interest in this chapter is reading comprehension, it is helpful to know what researchers have found about the process of staff development in general, regardless of the particular content that is addressed.

WHY SO MUCH OF PROFESSIONAL DEVELOPMENT HAS BEEN INEFFECTIVE

Little and her colleagues conducted a lengthy study of the policy and practice of professional development received by teachers in 30 school districts (Little et al., 1987). The researchers looked at professional development in all subject areas and in both elementary and secondary schools. Across the schools and grades, researchers identified the most common form of professional development as the "service delivery model." Little described the model as "workshop-style offerings in which appealing materials and a fast-paced round of individual or group exercises secure favorable satisfaction ratings by participants" (Little, 1992, p. 175).

Researchers have cited several deficiencies in the service delivery model. Little and her colleagues criticized the homogenized and simplified content of gatherings favoring interesting presentations over deep coverage. Other researchers have criticized the *fragmented* and *piecemeal* nature of most workshops (Fenstermacher & Berliner, 1986). Too many teachers attend workshops on multiple, and often unrelated, topics, and they rarely receive the kind of extended, focused training they need.

Sparks (1995) was particularly critical of the satisfaction ratings used to evaluate workshops. These ratings are commonly used as the only tool for evaluating a workshop's effectiveness. This evaluation system places an added burden on the presenter to make the workshop an easy and positive experience, sometimes forsaking complex concepts and deep understanding of subject matter content.

What happens once teachers leave the workshop? To what extent is the new information integrated into teachers' understandings and instructional practice? Satisfaction ratings do not allow us to look at the extent to which teachers *apply* new learning in their classroom practice. Rarely have workshops been evaluated on the extent to which they have influenced teachers' instructional practice, and, through that, student achievement. Thus, the evaluation system set up by the service delivery model promotes a superficial evaluation that does not attend to the most important outcome—student learning.

A third major criticism of the service delivery model made by Little and her colleagues is that teachers do not have an opportunity to examine their own classroom practice or to receive help in fitting new ideas into their existing and established practices. Yet, this may be the most important kind of assistance teachers need to change their practice. After all, practicing teachers have developed relatively entrenched beliefs about what works and what does not. When a new strategy or practice is presented to teachers, teachers do not automatically accept the usefulness of the strategy. And even if they do, they often do not know where or how to place the practice within the existing structure of their day. Further, teachers work under the assumption that they are already teaching their state's curriculum. A new teaching strategy or instructional practice is often viewed as an add-on to that existing curriculum. Thus, teachers must be shown *how* new instructional practices fit into their existing practice and classroom routines.

A fourth criticism of the service delivery model is that it places teachers in a relatively passive role. Researchers consistently note that the service delivery model does not allow teachers an opportunity to actively participate in shaping the form or content of what they are expected to learn. Such passivity can lead to the kind of resistance to change documented by researchers (Fullan, 1991; Guskey, 1995; Hargreaves, 1995).

Little and her colleagues (1987) cite another problem with the professional development process in general, although it is not clear whether this problem is a cause or an effect of poor professional development. These researchers note the very small amount of financial support that goes into most professional development. The 30 districts studied by Little and her colleagues allocated about $900 per year per teacher, which is slightly less than 1% of the cost of supporting the average classroom. Further, much more of that sum is invested in the leaders—staff administrators and curriculum specialists who put on the workshops—than in the learners—the teachers participating in the workshops.

What is unclear is why so little money is invested in professional development by school districts. Is the poor quality of most professional development a cause of little money being invested? Or is the little money invested in professional development a cause of the generally poor quality of professional development? Regardless, the research conducted over the last 15 years indicates that much more financial investment in professional development is needed if we expect to make a difference in student achievement.

More Effective Professional Development

Over the last 15 years, different models for professional development have been developed and tested. The body of research resulting from the evaluation of these different models provides a good framework for guidelines to determine what constitutes effective professional development. Hawley and Valli (1999) identified several useful research-based guidelines for effective professional development. Once again, these guidelines apply to professional development in general rather than specifically to professional development in reading.

Guideline 1: Focus on Students and Student Performance

A student-centered focus, rather than a teacher-centered focus, is critical to effective professional development. In other words, the focus of staff development should be on improving student learning through an understanding of what students need to know and be able to do (Darling-Hammond & McLaughlin, 1999; Sykes, 1999).

Researchers point out that often students are not the focus of the learning. Sometimes teachers are presented with new teaching strategies and techniques that are learned for their own sake. For example, the focus of a workshop may be on "shared reading" and how to conduct it, without any information given about *how* this teaching strategy assists students in learning how to comprehend text. Another workshop may focus on "comprehension strategy activities," in which teachers are provided with handouts, page after page of activities to complete with their students. However, teachers never learn how the strategies relate to the comprehension process or to their students' comprehension of text.

Effective professional development, then, needs to focus squarely on learners. Teachers can analyze standards and curriculum frameworks, research-based knowledge about student learning, or other frameworks for understanding learning. One such framework for reading comprehension is that outlined by the National Reading Panel (NRP, 2000) whereby teachers can learn about the important relationships between fluency, vocabulary, and comprehension.

Guideline 2: Teachers Need to Be Involved

Teachers' active involvement in the learning process has been shown time and again to be critical to effective professional development. Engagement by teachers increases their motivation and commitment to learn (Hodges, 1996). Hawley and Valli (1999) point to the crucial role of principals in leading teachers to be involved in ways that help them develop a need and desire to learn. They note the importance of developing a learning community within the school building. Such a community appears to be necessary for successful school reform.

This is not to say that teachers should determine everything. For example, Borko and Putnam (1995) noted that teachers often do not see themselves as needing more content knowledge or knowledge about instructional practices. Many elementary teachers like Mrs. Silver might not identify their specific need for help in teaching reading comprehension. But the point is that teachers need to feel involved at some level. The formation of study groups, joint planning, grade team analyses of informal assessments, and peer coaching are a few ways to directly involve teachers in their own learning.

Guideline 3: Professional Development Must Be School Based

Several researchers have noted the importance of making professional development job-embedded and integral to the school community. This does not mean that teachers cannot go outside the school building to be involved in professional development. It does mean that learning about teaching must come out of and feed back into teachers' daily lives in classrooms (Smylie, 1995). Further, it means that teachers need to see learning about teaching as a part of their daily work, rather than something done outside the school day (Little, 1992; Smylie, 1995). This can be accomplished through coaching and mentoring models of professional development, with master teachers working with and collaborating with other teachers. It can also involve teachers observing each other in classrooms.

Guideline 4: Teachers Need to Solve Problems Collaboratively

A common observation made about traditional schools and classrooms is that teachers are isolated and view teaching as an individual and often lonely activity. Research has shown that teaming, study groups, and other forms of collaboration among teachers reduce the isolation that teachers feel and foster community and professional respect (Guskey, 1995; Little, 1992).

Guideline 5: Professional Development Must Be Ongoing and Supported

This guideline is perhaps the single most important one for assisting teachers in changing their instructional practice. Teachers need ongoing support and assistance, including specific and timely follow-up in their classrooms and schools. Hodges (1996) noted that "significant change in educational practice does not occur quickly, but is the result of a staff development program designed with a 3–5 year time frame" (pp. 239–240). Joyce and Showers (1995) describe a program in which teachers acquire theoretical knowledge, conduct microteaching with their peers, and practice teaching small groups of students in their classrooms. These researchers argued that teachers require many repetitions of a teaching strategy before they can effectively incorporate it into their teaching repertoire. Change will not happen unless there is specific follow-up in their classrooms.

Guideline 6: Teachers Need Theoretical Understanding

Without a theoretical understanding about learning and instruction, teachers are unlikely to retain or use what they learn in professional development (Little, 1993; Joyce & Showers, 1995). Teachers often cite a lack of understanding as one reason that they do not put theory into practice. The problem arises at two levels. Teachers may not understand the theory. Alternately, or perhaps in addition, they may not understand how the theory is applied to practice. In either case, if teachers learn instructional strategies apart from their theoretical underpinnings, they are unlikely to retain them or to use them effectively or reliably.

Guideline 7: Professional Development Must Be Part of a Comprehensive Change Process

Effective professional development that leads to change in teachers' instructional practice is a difficult process. Unless staff development is imbedded in a clear system of reform that supports change and eliminates barriers to success, it is unlikely to be effective (Guskey, 1995). District-level support is essential in a number of areas—central office support and follow-through; avoidance of Band-aids to fix problems; adequate time to learn, plan, and implement new practices; and sufficient resources (Hawley & Valli, 1999). Because change is so difficult, it is unlikely to be effective if sufficient support is not in place.

These, then, are some research-based guidelines on which to develop a staff development model that is likely to affect teachers' instructional practices. The professional development is continuous and ongoing; teachers are involved in their own learning; they are supported in their classrooms by peers, mentors, and coaches; they work collaboratively to solve problems of practice; and they have a theoretical understanding of issues germane to student learning and instruction.

PROFESSIONAL DEVELOPMENT IN COMPREHENSION INSTRUCTION

So far, several problems with the traditional service delivery model of staff development have been identified, as well as a set of research-based guidelines for more effective staff development. This next section addresses what we know about staff development, specifically in regard to teaching reading comprehension. When teachers are taught methods for teaching comprehension, do their students' comprehension abilities improve? At this point we return to my teacher, Mrs. Silver, and what she knew and did not know about how to help me comprehend my text.

Unfortunately, there has not been a great deal of research on effective staff development in comprehension instruction. Two problems occur in the existing research. First, many studies have not looked specifically at comprehension instruction. Instead, these studies addressed a range of reading subtopics, such as grouping, cooperative learning, and the like. Other studies on professional development in comprehension failed to examine student achievement. These studies examined the effect of staff development on teachers, but not on students. Sykes (1999) noted, "There must be greater attention to the core relationship between what teachers

learn and what students learn. . . . Student learning is the ultimate justifica-
tion for teacher learning and so should be brought more powerfully into
the planning and evaluation of teacher professional development" (p. 175).

The National Reading Panel (NRP, 2000) found a few studies that
provide a beginning look at how professional development might be developed to help teachers teach reading comprehension. The studies considered
what happened as a result of teaching teachers how to teach *comprehension strategies* to their students. The NRP defined comprehension strategies
as cognitive procedures that readers use when the comprehension process
breaks down. Comprehension strategies are procedures—like predicting,
asking questions, or drawing inferences—that help readers restore meaning
as they are reading. Many studies have shown that students can be taught
to use comprehension strategies, and that when they do, their comprehension improves (Dole, Brown, & Trathen, 1996; Palincsar & Brown, 1984).

However, in most of the studies reporting that students can be effectively taught to use comprehension strategies, the *researchers* did the teaching. Thus there was no need for professional development in comprehension strategies because teachers did not need to learn how to teach them.
But the question soon arose: Can *teachers* be taught to teach students to
use comprehension strategies? In the mid-1980s and early 1990s, several
researchers devised a professional development program to teach teachers
to teach comprehension strategies to their students. In one set of studies,
Duffy, Roehler, and their colleagues (Duffy et al., 1986) taught 22 teachers
to teach their students to (1) view reading as a problem-solving task and (2)
think strategically about solving comprehension problems (NRP, 2000).
Researchers described this method as "direct explanation." They believed
that the method provided students with the reasoning and thinking processes they needed to use to read strategically.

The professional development that teachers received was not ideal
from the standpoint of what we now know about effective staff development. Teachers in the study attended an initial training session plus follow-
up sessions of about 10 hours during the academic year. During these
follow-up sessions, teachers were presented with information and they designed lessons according to the model they learned. They were also observed four times during their year and discussed the lessons with observ-
ers. Thus, there were several elements of effective staff development
included in the model—theory, practice, feedback, and coaching (Joyce &
Showers, 1995).

The effectiveness of the training in strategy instruction was mixed. Researchers found greater understanding in terms of strategy awareness and
importance on the part of experimental students, as compared with control
students who received regular classroom instruction. Teachers were able to

effectively communicate to their students what strategies were and why they were important.

Yet results on standardized comprehension tests showed no differences between the experimental group of students who were taught to use strategies and the control group of students who were not. It is unclear whether the teachers were not provided with sufficient staff development to carry out the instruction, or whether strategy instruction itself does not result in improved comprehension. Based on the success of other research in which the instruction was provided by researchers, it seems that the staff development provided by Duffy, Roehler, and their colleagues (1986) at the time was not sufficient to cause teachers to change their instruction dramatically enough to make a difference in student achievement.

Duffy, Roehler, and their colleagues completed another study on reading strategies training for teachers (Duffy et al., 1987). In this study teachers were taught to reanalyze the skills they taught from their basals and reframe them in terms of strategies. For example, instead of students being asked to simply carry out a skill like "finding the main idea," they were asked to *think about how they would go about finding the main idea.* Teachers used direct explanation to show students the thinking process they (the teachers) used to determine how they would figure out the main idea of a paragraph or text.

How were teachers taught in this study? They spent 12 hours in training that consisted of one-on-one coaching, collaborative sharing among teachers, lesson observation and feedback, and videotaped model lessons. Note that these staff development activities are closer to the job-embedded learning that researchers say is critical to the success of staff development.

In this study, there was evidence of the training's positive effects on reading achievement. Students in the treatment group outperformed students in the control group on the word skills subtest of a standardized measure, but not on the comprehension subtest. However, the students in the treatment group again outperformed students in the control group on a delayed reading posttest.

The NRP also reported two other studies using Pressley and colleagues' transactional strategy instruction (Anderson, 1992; Brown, Pressley, Van Meter, & Schuder, 1996). Transactional strategy instruction has a goal similar to that of Duffy, Roehler, and colleagues—students thinking and reasoning strategically with text. In transactional strategy instruction, though, the teacher and students collaboratively discuss the reasoning associated with the use of different strategies. Further, transactional strategy instruction was designed to be interactive and not so much like a direct instruction model in which teachers do most of the talking. In one study, Pressley and his colleagues (Brown et al., 1996) used teachers who were already experts in transactional strategy instruction to evaluate the effectiveness of transactional strategy instruction. This study is not reviewed here because it did not involve any professional development.

In another study, however, Anderson (1992) worked with nine teachers of adolescent students who were severely reading disabled. She trained the nine teachers in transactional strategy instruction. The training included three intermittent 3–hour sessions over a 3–month period. In addition, teachers participated as co-researchers on the project, and a trained peer coach was available to work with each teacher. At the end of the staff development program, a higher percentage of students of the trained teachers made significant gains on the Stanford Diagnostic Reading Test than students in the comparison group whose teachers had no training.

This investigation is one of the few concrete studies in which the staff development of the teachers appeared to be effective in improving students' reading comprehension. Several important aspects of Anderson's (1992) study were consistent with research-based guidelines for effective staff development. First, Anderson appeared to be able to actively involve teachers in the learning process. In addition, the learning was job embedded and involved ongoing assistance and support from a coach. These factors are likely to have assisted teachers in their efforts to learn transactional strategy instruction.

What can we conclude from the limited research on staff development in reading comprehension? First, we can conclude that such development is difficult. There is a much larger body of research on strategy instruction in which researchers or other trained experts have done the teaching (see for example, Brown et al., 1996; Dole et al., 1996) than in which regular classroom teachers have done the teaching. Duffy and Roehler (1989) have discussed why this is so. They argued that direct explanation of thinking and strategic processing is difficult to teach to teachers. In part, this is because teachers come into staff development with their own well-established sets of beliefs and behaviors related to comprehension instruction, and these beliefs and behaviors are difficult to change. Moreover, teachers are not often aware of their own strategic processing of text because, for many adult readers, this processing has become automatic. Most adult readers do not think about how they strategically process text; they just do it. Therefore, it is difficult to make teachers cognitively aware of what they do so they can communicate that awareness to their students.

Second, we can conclude that staff development in comprehension should include job-embedded learning. What all the successful studies have in common is some kind of assistance for teachers in their classrooms. It appears that unless staff development involves the classroom at some level, it is unlikely to have a significant impact on student learning.

FUTURE RESEARCH NEEDS

If we expect research to be more helpful in delineating a program of effective professional development in comprehension, we need to address a host of issues related to the content of programs, the instructional delivery systems, and teacher beliefs and practices. The RAND Reading Panel proposed several central questions:

• *What content and sequencing of content lead to effective professional development programs?* If teachers are to improve their teaching of reading comprehension, what do they have to know and how should that knowledge be sequenced? Notice that the point is to identify what *teachers* need to know that will help them teach their students. For example, strategy instruction is but one way to improve reading comprehension. How else can comprehension be improved? Certainly, there are other ways. For example, instruction to teachers on different text structures (Armbruster, Anderson & Ostertag, 1987) and instruction about teaching techniques such as Questioning the Author (Beck, McKeown, Worthy, Sandora, & Kucan, 1996) and Text Talk (Beck, & McKeown, 2001) are likely to be helpful. Instruction about activating and building students' prior knowledge and vocabulary is also likely to be helpful (Pearson & Fielding, 1991). Although the research on comprehension reviewed by the NRP reflected only work on comprehension strategy instruction, we know that there are other effective ways to improve students' comprehension. Unfortunately, too many teachers are now under the impression that the only way to improve students' comprehension is through strategy instruction. We need to have more detailed knowledge of the many other instructional methods and procedures and the conditions under which they ought to be used.

• *How do various types of professional development influence the acquisition of knowledge and skills that lead teachers to effective instructional practices?* We have discussed many factors related to the delivery of ineffective and effective professional development. But, currently, these factors are many and reflect a conglomeration of activities about which we know far too little. For example, what knowledge and skills do teachers learn from graduate courses versus observations of other teachers versus observation of a master teacher? Different types of professional development should lead to different kinds of learning. Yet, in general, we know very little about what teachers learn from different kinds of professional development.

• *What are the critical components of professional development that lead to effective instruction and sustained change in teachers' practice?* Of the many guidelines identified for effective professional development, which are critically important to teachers' knowledge and skills such that if they are absent, appropriate learning will not take place? Which guidelines are necessary but insufficient in and of themselves? In addition, we know very little about how to sustain change in teachers' instructional practice over time. Some research indicates that teachers often fall back on old beliefs and behaviors once a school concludes an innovation. How to sustain change in instructional practice over time is a huge, unanswered question in the research on teaching in general.

• *How do teachers' existing beliefs and instructional practices influence how teachers use new information about teaching reading when new information conflicts with what they already know and do?* This is a critically important question; the literature is full of anecdotal data on how difficult it is to change teachers' attitudes and beliefs about instructional practice. What is the best course of action for professional development in working with teachers who have beliefs and behaviors that directly conflict with current research? Which types of staff development are most helpful in changing teachers' thinking and instructional practice?

• *What are various ways to support teachers so that they are willing to spend the time and cognitive effort and energy necessary to improve their comprehension instruction?* Sykes (1999) remarked that "curricular change, like all other important changes in education, ultimately relies on teacher *understanding, skill* and *will*" (p. 152) [italics mine]. To become high-quality teachers, many teachers will need to learn a new set of teaching strategies and instructional routines. However, changing one's teaching can be as difficult as a religious conversion. What would make teachers willing to participate in such an endeavor? This is a question almost no one has addressed, yet it must be addressed if we expect significant changes in instructional practices in reading comprehension.

INSTRUCTIONAL RECOMMENDATIONS

How would a school district go about helping teachers like Mrs. Silver, my fifth-grade teacher? How would a district structure professional development to help teachers know how to help students comprehend better? Based on the research we do have about professional development in reading comprehension, we suggest that a district be sure to do the following:

1. Design the staff development program in comprehension to be a long-term effort—several years' worth of support and assistance for teachers.
2. Actively involve teachers in their own learning through such activities as study groups, examinations and discussions of current stan-

dards, observations of other teachers' classrooms, and choice in the kinds of activities in which they participate.

3. Provide teachers with a theoretical understanding of reading comprehension so that they have foundational knowledge on which to build their own understandings about comprehension instruction.

4. Focus study on what students need to know and learn in order to be successful comprehenders.

5. Ensure that all teachers have opportunities to see and practice new instructional strategies and practices in comprehension in their classrooms and receive feedback on their work.

CONCLUSION

Regardless of how successful researchers are in understanding how, when, and where to teach comprehension, if educators fail to teach teachers to use and apply this knowledge effectively in their classrooms, the understandings we have gained are for naught. Although I was eventually able to learn how to comprehend effectively without Mrs. Silver's help, many students do not and will not learn without direct assistance and support from their teachers. Moving teachers to a point where they can successfully help *all* students to comprehend is a critically important goal of reading instruction. It is my hope that future research on professional development in comprehension instruction will help make teaching and learning how to comprehend easier and more successful than in the past.

REFERENCES

Anderson, V. (1992). A teacher development project in transactional strategy instruction for teachers of severely reading-disabled adolescents. *Teaching and Teacher Education*, 8, 391–403.

Armbruster, B., Anderson, T., & Ostertag, J. (1987). Does text structure/summarization instruction facilitate learning from expository text? *Reading Research Quarterly*, 22, 331–347.

Beck, I. L., & McKeown, M. G. (2001). Text Talk: Capturing the benefits of read aloud experiences for young children. *Reading Teacher*, 55, 10–20.

Beck, I. L., McKeown, M. G., Worthy, J., Sandora, C. A., & Kucan, L. (1996). Questioning the Author: A year-long classroom implementation to engage students with text. *Elementary School Journal*, 96, 385–414.

Borko, H., & Putnam, R. T. (1995). Expanding a teacher's knowledge base: A cognitive psychological perspective on professional development. In T. R. Guskey & M. Huberman (Eds.), *Professional development in education: New paradigms and practices* (pp. 35–65). New York: Teachers College Press.

Brown, R., Pressley, M., Van Meter, P., & Schuder, T. (1996). A quasi-experimental validation of transactional strategies instruction with low-achieving second-graders. *Journal of Educational Psychology, 88,* 18–37.

Darling-Hammond, L., & McLaughlin, M. W. (1999). Investing in teaching as a learning profession: Policy problems and prospects. In L. Darling-Hammond, & G. Sykes (Eds.), *Teaching as a learning profession* (pp. 376–411). San Francisco: Jossey-Bass.

Dole, J. A., Brown, K. J., & Trathen, W. (1996). The effects of strategy instruction on the comprehension performance of at-risk students. *Reading Research Quarterly, 31,* 62–88.

Duffy, G. G., & Roehler, L. R. (1989). Why strategy instruction is so difficult and what we need to do about it. In C. McCormick, G. Miller, & M. Pressley (Eds.), *Cognitive strategy research: From basic research to educational applications* (pp. 133–154). New York: Springer-Verlag.

Duffy, G. G., Roehler, L. R., Meloth, M. S., Vavrus, L. G., Book, C., Putnam, J., & Wesselman, R. (1986). The relationship between explicit verbal explanations during reading skill instruction and student awareness and achievement: A study of reading teacher effects. *Reading Research Quarterly, 21,* 237–252.

Duffy, G. G., Roehler, L. R., Sivan, E., Rackliffe, G., Book, C., Meloth, M. S., Vavrus, L. G., Wesselman, R., Putnam, J., & Bassari, D. (1987). Effects of explaining the reasoning associated with using reading strategies. *Reading Research Quarterly, 23,* 347–368.

Fenstermacher, G. D., & Berliner, D. C. (1986). Determining the value of staff development. *Elementary School Journal, 85,* 281–314.

Fullan, M. G. (1991). *The new meaning of educational change.* New York: Teachers College Press.

Guskey, T. R. (1995). Professional development in education: In search of an optimal mix. In T. R. Guskey & M. Huberman (Eds.), *Professional development in education: New paradigms and practices* (pp. 114–131). New York: Teachers College Press.

Hargreaves, A. (1995). Development and desire: A postmodern perspective. In T. R. Guskey & M. Huberman (Eds.), *Professional development in education: New paradigms and practices* (pp. 9–34). New York: Teachers College Press.

Hawley, W. D., & Valli, L. (1999). The essentials of effective professional development: A new consensus. In L. Darling-Hammond & G. Sykes (Eds.), *Teaching as a learning profession* (pp. 127–150). San Francisco: Jossey-Bass.

Hodges, H. L. B. (1996). Using research to inform practice in urban schools: Ten key strategies to success. *Educational Policy, 10,* 223–252.

Joyce, B., & Showers, B. (1995). *Student achievement though staff development.* White Plains, NY: Longman.

Little, J. W. (1992). Teacher development and educational policy. In M. Fullan & A. Hargreaves (Eds.), *Teacher development and educational change* (pp. 170–193). Washington, DC: Falmer Press.

Little, J. W. (1993). Teachers' professional development in a climate of educational reform. *Educational Evaluation and Policy Analysis, 15,* 129–151.

Little, J. W., Gerritz, W. H., Stern, D. S., Guthrie, J. W., Kirst, M. W., & Marsh, D. D. (1987). *Staff development in California: Public and personal investment, program patterns, and policy choices.* San Francisco: Far West Laboratory for Educational Research and Development.

National Center for Research on Teacher Education (1991). *Final Report: National Center for Research on Teacher Education.* East Lansing, MI: Michigan State University.

National Reading Panel (2000). *Teaching children to read: An evidence-based assessment of the scientific research literature on reading and its implications for reading instruction.* Washington DC: National Institutes of Health.

Palincsar, A. S., & Brown, A. (1984). Reciprocal teaching of comprehension-fostering and comprehension-monitoring activities. *Cognition and Instruction, 1,* 117–175.

Pearson, P. D., & Fielding, L. (1991). Comprehension instruction. In R. Barr, M. M. L. Kamil, P. Mosenthal, & P. D. Pearson (Eds.), *Handbook of reading research* (Vol. II, pp.815–860). New York: Longman

Smylie, M. A. (1995). Teacher learning in the workplace: Implications for school reform. In T. R. Guskey & M. Huberman (Eds.), *Professional development in education: New paradigms and practices.* New York: Teachers College Press.

Sparks, D. (1995). A paradigm shift in staff development. *ERIC Review, 3,* 24.

Sprinthall, N. A., Reiman, A. J., & Thies-Sprinthall, L. (1996). Teacher professional development. In J. Sikula, T. J. Buttery, & E. Guyton (Eds.), *Handbook of research on teacher education* (2nd ed., pp. 666–703). New York: Macmillan.

Sykes, G. (1999). Teacher and student learning. In L. Darling-Hammond & G. Sykes (Eds.), *Teaching as a learning profession: Handbook of policy and practice* (pp. 151–180). San Francisco: Jossey-Bass.

11

Assessment of Reading Comprehension

Researchers and Practitioners Helping Themselves and Each Other

CATHERINE E. SNOW

Two principles are widely accepted as core truths of educational reform:

1. Instruction based on a well-articulated alignment of standards, curriculum, and accountability-focused assessment can improve student performance.
2. Regular in-classroom assessment of skills helps teachers adapt and individualize teaching so as so improve outcomes.

These two principles create a substantial challenge in the domain of reading comprehension, since it is very difficult to design assessments of comprehension that meet both these goals—good alignment with high standards for comprehension achievement and provision of information to teachers that is helpful in making instructional decisions—as well as the other standard criteria of validity, reliability, and feasibility. In this chapter we briefly review the current state of comprehension assessments, sketch what an ideal comprehension assessment system would look like, then discuss what teachers can do to improve the practice and the science of reading comprehension assessment.

CHALLENGES IN DEVELOPING SATISFACTORY COMPREHENSION ASSESSMENTS

Everyone would agree that teachers need reliable and valid assessments tied closely to their curricula so that they can see which students are learning as expected and which need extra help. In addition, schools, districts, and states are increasingly calling for reliable and valid assessments that reflect progress toward reading benchmarks. Creating assessments that have these features is quite difficult, however, and the difficulty will be exacerbated as the demand for new tests increases with the provisions of federal legislation No Child Left Behind. The challenges that such assessments will have to address include the following:

1. Adequate representation of the complexity of the target domain. Psychometricians refer to the concept of *construct validity* in describing tests that do a good job of reflecting what they are meant to be about. Construct validity is hard to achieve in comprehension tests, because the target domain is itself complex; in fact, different researchers and practitioners probably would not agree completely even on how to define the full scope of "real comprehension." Under these circumstances, selecting or devising comprehension measures is extremely difficult.

2. Recurrent reliance on unduly simple measures. Widely used comprehension assessments consist of a few multiple-choice questions to be answered about each of several paragraphs or brief passages. The questions can often be answered without reference to the passage, or by simply finding key words in the passage and identifying matches with one of the multiple-choice responses. Test items of this type do not come close to replicating what goes on when real comprehension occurs, nor to reflecting the full array of skills and capacities we would agree fall under the rubric of comprehension. Unfortunately, their ease of administration and scoring means that these measures continue to be used widely (Pearson & Hamm, 2002). (See Table 11.1 for examples of items from a 2001 state accountability assessment that display these unfortunate characteristics.) Of course, tests such as the National Assessment of Educational Progress (NAEP) (and some of the more challenging state accountability tests) represent the construct of comprehension much more richly—including items that test use of information, integration of information, and analysis. But the NAEP can include items that take considerable time to complete, because it uses matrix sampling (the items of the test are distributed over several children). Thus, does not provide instructional information or produce an interpretable score for any individual child.

3. Need to distinguish breakdowns of comprehension processes (inferencing, integrating new with existent knowledge) from lack of vocabulary,

TABLE 11.1. Items administered as Part of the Third-Grade Texas Academic Achievement Survey (TAAS) in 2001

Machines probably sort crayons into boxes so the crayons can be . . .
- Melted down again
- Sent to stores and sold
- Wrapped in paper
- Kept in warming tanks

In this story, the word *labels* means . . .
- Ribbons
- Wires
- Tubes
- Wrappers

What happens to broken crayons in factories?
- They are thrown away.
- They are put in boxes.
- They are made into candles.
- They are melted down again.

Wax is stored in big warming tanks so it will . . .
- Smell good
- Stay soft
- Grow stronger
- Cost more

The reader can tell that workers in crayon factories are probably . . .
- Quiet
- Busy
- Friendly
- Angry

Which of these is a FACT in the story?
- Each box of crayons has 16 colors.
- Crayons are easier to use than paints are.
- Pictures made with crayons are beautiful.
- Crayons with bubbles are melted down again.

Note. These questions are meant to assess students' understanding of a six-paragraph expository passage, but, in fact, prior knowledge and good guessing are sufficient to answer most of these items successfully.

of domain-specific knowledge, of word reading ability, or of other reader capacities involved in comprehension. It is not helpful to know that a student has failed a test—we need to know why the failure occurred if we are to address improvement with targeted instructional or curricular enhancements.

4. Need to reflect both the developmental nature of reading comprehension and its sensitivity to instruction. Ideally, teachers would have comprehension assessments that both placed students on a developmental con-

tinuum and helped identify strengths and weaknesses in ways that suggest the next focus for instruction. Furthermore, these assessments should also be helpful in letting teachers know whether the instruction was successful.

5. Need to avoid the tendency to narrow the curriculum. Comprehension assessments that do not focus on the more interesting outcomes of reading—comprehension for engagement, for aesthetic response, for purposes of critiquing an argument or disagreeing with a position—can lead to neglect of such activities in the classroom, under pressure of ensuring that all students pass the test. And, of course, assessments that privilege certain genres or certain types of topics inevitably lead to emphasis on those genres and topics in the classroom.

6. Need to address issues of reliability and validity. Ironically, the kinds of assessments that teachers find most informative, such as the Academic Reading Inventory or informal talk-aloud protocols while reading, are the hardest to make reliable across administrators and testing sessions, whereas those that are the most standardized are, conversely, the least informative. Researchers attend to issues of reliability and validity for their own purposes in test development, and such issues are considered seriously (though not always resolved fully) in the more challenging state assessments (e.g., the Massachusetts Comprehensive Assessment System). Yet, researchers have not typically worked with teachers to enhance the utility and the psychometric properties of the tests most likely to be used in classrooms.

Most currently used comprehension assessments, including the NAEP and the challenging state tests, reflect the purpose for which they were originally developed—to sort children on a single dimension. But precisely because (as is made clear in the preceding chapters of this book) comprehension is a complex achievement that reflects success across an array of domains, no good test of comprehension can be unidimensional. Successfully comprehending a text reflects having done an adequate job with all the many challenges involved: having read the words accurately and fluently, possessing and accessing the background and vocabulary knowledge required for the text, using textual clues to understand relations across elements of the text as well as the writer's perspective, and making the appropriate inferences. Failing at any one of these several tasks disrupts comprehension. Of course, however, the implications for the teacher are quite different if the failure is one of word reading, of vocabulary knowledge, of discourse knowledge, or of inferencing ability.

Teachers and researchers alike need assessment procedures that can evaluate a wider range of learner capacities than are typically measured—in fact, the full range of capacities that excellent teachers are striving to develop in their students:

- To modify old or build new knowledge structures.
- To use information acquired while reading in the interest of problem solving.
- To evaluate texts according to particular criteria.
- To acquire new vocabulary items from reading.
- To become absorbed in reading.
- To develop affective or aesthetic responses to text.
- To enter into a dialogue with the author of the text.

Assessments that reflect the first three of these capacities are increasingly common, even on widely used accountability assessments. Nonetheless, assessments that reflect the entire list have are not part of standard assessment practices. Knowledge, application, and engagement are defined in *Reading for Understanding* (RAND Reading Study Group, 2002) as the crucial consequences of reading with comprehension; a clear implication is that good comprehension assessments will reflect all these three of these outcomes. Although some current comprehension assessments operationalize comprehension as a multifaceted task, others still do not. Until the multiple consequences are universally attended to in assessment, we can hardly expect them to receive the attention they deserve in instruction.

WHAT WOULD A GOOD COMPREHENSION ASSESSMENT SYSTEM LOOK LIKE?

Moving ahead in ensuring comprehension success, through both better research and better practice, requires that every teacher receive information from an adequate system of instrumentation for assessing reading comprehension. We cannot even estimate the seriousness of the problem of reading comprehension in the United States, nor ascertain the nature of the decline in comprehension outcomes that is the source of much worry, without a system that reflects the same underlying construct across the school years. Furthermore, assessing the effect of changes in instruction depends on having valid, reliable, and sensitive assessments.

We are clearly not talking about a single test here. To address the multiple needs of teachers who want to know how to adjust instruction to the diverse students in their classrooms, of researchers who want to characterize comprehension levels, subcategorize poor comprehenders, and evaluate instructional and curricular innovations, and of policy makers who want to track progress and compare demographic groups, we will need a comprehension assessment *system*, a coordinated set of instruments that range from formal to informal, criterion- to norm-referenced, and holistic to analytic.

Clearly, a system of reading assessment must reflect the full array of important reading comprehension consequences. In addition, a research program to establish expectable levels of performance for children of different ages/grades on this full array of consequences is necessary. Such a program is prerequisite to developing criteria for performance at different age/grade levels, and to pursuing questions about reader differences associated with instructional histories, social class, language, and/or culture in reading comprehension outcomes.

In addition to those ensuring information about the full array of desired consequences, assessments designed to reflect the reader's cognitive, motivational, and linguistic resources and processes as they approach a reading activity are also necessary. For instance, when an outcomes assessment identifies children who are performing below par, process assessments may be helpful in indicating why their reading comprehension is poor. Furthermore, diagnostic assessments are crucial in dissecting the effects of particular instructional or intervention practices.

Ideally, we would move ultimately toward assessment systems that can also reflect the dynamic nature of comprehension, for example, by assessing increments of knowledge about vocabulary and particular target knowledge domains that result from interaction with particular texts. The development of an assessment system for reading comprehension has a very high priority in national efforts to improve reading outcomes. Such a system should be based on contemporary approaches to test development and evaluation. Of course, developing a comprehensive, reliable, and valid assessment system is a long-term project that will require the focused attention of many researchers and psychometricians. In the meantime, teachers who are doing a good job of tracking their own students' progress in reading comprehension can contribute enormously by systematizing and sharing their techniques. Such an effort is crucial to helping more teachers know more about the children in their classrooms and the effectiveness of their own practice.

A comprehensive assessment program reflecting the thinking about reading comprehension presented in *Reading for Understanding* (RAND Reading Study Group, 2002) would have to satisfy many requirements that have not been addressed by any assessment instruments, while also satisfying the standard psychometric criteria. A list of requirements for such a system would, at a minimum, include:

• Capacity to reflect authentic outcomes. Although any particular assessment may not reflect the full array of consequences, the inclusion of a wider array than currently tested is crucial. For example, students' beliefs about reading and about themselves as readers may constitute supports or obstacles to their optimal development as comprehenders; teachers could benefit enormously from having ways to elicit and assess such beliefs.

• Congruence between assessments and the processes involved in comprehension. Assessments must be available that target particular operations involved in comprehension, in the interest of revealing inter- and intra-individual differences that might inform our understanding of the comprehension process and of outcome differences. The dimensionality of the instruments in relation to theory should be clearly apparent.

• Developmental sensitivity. Any assessment system must be sensitive across the full developmental range of interest and reflect developmentally central phenomena related to comprehension. Assessments of young children's reading tend to focus on word reading rather than comprehension, and assessments of listening comprehension and oral language production, both of which are highly related to reading comprehension, are rare and tend not to be included in reading assessment systems despite their clear relevance. The available listening comprehension assessments for young children do not reflect children's rich oral language processing capacities, because they reflect neither the full complexity of their sentence processing nor the domain of discourse skills.

• Capacity to provide for the identification of individual children as poor comprehenders. An effective assessment system should be able to identify individual children as poor comprehenders, not only by assessing prerequisite skills such as fluency in word identification and decoding, but also by reflecting cognitive deficits and gaps in relevant knowledge (background, domain specific, etc.) that may adversely affect reading and comprehension, even in children who have adequate word-level skills. It is also critically important that such a system provide for early identification of children who are apt to encounter difficulties in reading comprehension because of limited resources to carry out one or another operation involved in comprehension.

• Capacity to identify subtypes of poor comprehenders. Reading comprehension is complexly determined. It therefore follows that comprehension difficulties may come about because of deficiencies in one or another of the components of comprehension specified in the model. Thus, an effective assessment system should have the means for identifying subtypes of poor comprehenders, defined by differences in the components and desired outcomes of comprehension, and both intra- and interindividual differences in acquiring the knowledge and skills necessary for becoming a good comprehender.

• Instructional sensitivity. A major purpose of assessments is to inform instruction and to reflect the effect of instruction or intervention. Thus, an effective assessment system should not only provide important information about a child's relative standing in appropriate normative populations (school, state, and/or national norms groups), but it should also provide important information about a child's relative strengths and weaknesses for purposes of educational planning.

• Openness to intra-individual differences. Understanding the performance of an individual often requires attending to differences in performance across activities with varying purposes, and with a variety of texts and text types.

• Utility for instructional decision making. Assessments can inform instructional practice if they are designed to identify domains that instruction may target, rather than providing summary scores useful only for comparison with other learners' scores. Another aspect of utility for instructional decision making is transparency of the information provided by the test to nontechnically trained teachers.

• Adaptability with respect to individual, social, linguistic, and cultural variation. Good tests of reading comprehension, of listening comprehension, and of oral language production will target authentic outcomes and reflect key component processes. If performance on a test reflects differences due to individual, social, linguistic, or cultural variation that are not directly related to reading comprehension performance, then the test may well mislead policy makers and teachers.

• A basis in measurement theory and psychometrics that addresses reliability within scales and over time, as well as multiple components of validity at the item level, concurrently with other measures, and predictively relative to longer-term development of reading proficiency. Studies of the dimensionality of the instruments in relationship to the theory motivating their construction are particularly important. Test construction and evaluation of instruments are important areas of investigation and highly relevant to the proposed research agenda.

As noted earlier, no single assessment would meet all these criteria. Instead, we would need an integrated system of assessments, some of which may be particularly appropriate for particular groups (e.g., emergent or beginning readers, older struggling readers, second-language readers, readers with a particular interest in dinosaurs). Furthermore, the various assessments included in the system would address different purposes—for example, a portmanteau assessment for accountability or screening purposes, diagnostic assessments for guiding intervention, curriculum-linked assessments for guiding instruction, and so on.

The sorts of questions asked by researchers while developing a comprehensive assessment system for reading comprehension would, no doubt, include the following:

- What is the effect of various response formats on performance?
- How does performance vary across text types?
- How do students use information from pictures, figures, and graphic representations?
- What is the effect of various kinds of formats and accommodations on the test performance of learners of English as a second language?
- How does performance vary across a variety of discourse types and genres, including hypertext?
- What is the effect on performance of specifying different purposes for reading?
- How different are the skills needed to do well on tests of reading in different domains or subject matter?
- How can capacities beyond the traditional rubric of comprehension, such as scanning, intertextuality, domain-specific strategies, consulting illustrations, and so on be assessed?
- What are the reliability, validity, and dimensionality of different assessment instruments and approaches?

Some, though not all, of these issues should be of concern to the practitioner as well. Certainly, it is important to think about whether the average good reader does as well with comprehending textbooks as novels, or with print as with electronic presentations of information, even if only through informal assessments. We can only hope that researchers will grapple with and make progress on these issues over the next several years.

PRESSING ISSUES IN COMPREHENSION ASSESSMENT RELEVANT TO INSTRUCTION

The RAND Reading Study Group (2002) identified a number of key questions and issues that an assessment research agenda should address. Almost all of these issues were directly relevant to the improvement of tools for teachers:

- How can we measure strategic, self-regulated reading, including the students' use of strategies such as questioning, comprehension monitoring, and organizing knowledge gained from text?
- To what extent are performance-based assessments of reading sensitive to students' competencies in such areas as vocabulary, cognitive strategies, writing ability, oral language (syntax), reading fluency, domain content knowledge of the texts, and dispositions such as motivation and self-efficacy for reading?

- How do we design valid and reliable measures of self-regulated strategic reading that teachers can administer in the classroom to inform their instructional decisions?
- What informal assessments should teachers use to identify children who may need additional or modified instruction within the classroom to prevent referral to special education services?
- How do we construct informal assessments that enable teachers to determine how students who are low in reading comprehension can be helped? For example, how can teachers identify children who need to be taught specific reading strategies or supported in domain knowledge acquisition or motivational development?
- What reading comprehension assessment that can be administered efficiently by all teachers in a school can be used across grades to document student growth and guide teacher decisions about the appropriate texts, tasks, contexts, and learning activities for students?
- What measures of motivation and engagement in reading are available that can be linked to reading competencies, related to growth over time, and used to guide classroom learning activities?
- What measures of reading fluency can be used at the level of the individual student, the classroom, and the school, and can be related to reading comprehension and reading motivation?
- Which measures of reading comprehension are sensitive to specific forms of reading instruction and intervention for all readers?

WHAT TEACHERS CAN DO
ABOUT COMPREHENSION ASSESSMENT

It may well seem that comprehension assessment is beyond the power of the practitioner, who usually has not received training to develop good tests and who does not have the power to influence district or state testing policies. We would hazard, though, that many of the best, richest, and most informative comprehension assessments currently in use are those that have been developed by thoughtful practitioners for their own purposes. Their work can inform the directions that researchers take as they try to develop assessment instruments. Here are some suggestions for teachers—most easily implemented in the context of teacher learning groups within schools—to improve their own assessment practice, and perhaps even to further the larger research agenda on comprehension assessment.

- Build an analysis of comprehension into school-level professional development efforts. Teacher learning groups can use their time together to approach questions like "What does reading comprehension really mean to us? How would we like to have our students responding to text?" These questions address the nature of the *comprehension construct*, which is prerequisite to thinking about how to assess comprehension. Then the next set of questions to be addressed deals with the operationalization of the construct—for example, "What evidence can we see, in students' answers to questions, in classroom discussion, in written responses, that they were in fact responding in ways that truly reflect what we mean by comprehension?" Systematic analysis of student responses in the teacher learning groups can help to inform and refine both the construct and the proposed methods for operationalizing it.

• Build a mindful evaluation of comprehension assessments into teacher-learning activities. Productive activities for teacher learning groups or other forms of professional development sessions include sharing information about how each member of the team is "seeing" comprehension in student responses, observing across classrooms to see what others are doing to evaluate comprehension in the classroom, and analyzing the state and district tests to see how comprehension is operationalized there and whether that operationalization makes sense.

• Review standardized assessments. A comparison across various tests that all purport to reflect comprehension can reveal how others conceptualize comprehension, and may well provide hints about ways to assess comprehension, as well as those that should be avoided.

• Consider the full array of information you might like to have about your students. Even those teachers who do not have the advantage of collaborative professional development can become more reflective about their assessment practices. Of course, whether a student can read a paragraph without errors and answer a few questions about it constitutes one sort of valuable information. But students' beliefs about reading and about themselves as readers also influence their development, as do their particular interests and motivations to read; teachers may benefit enormously from having ways to elicit and assess information about these dimensions of their students as readers.

• Consider assessing not just outcomes, but also the several skills and processes involved in comprehension. Knowing about a student's word-reading accuracy and speed, about attention span, about gaps in vocabulary or background knowledge, about familiarity with various sorts of narrative and expository texts, and so on, can help teachers understand why comprehension of particular texts is hard or easy and why various approaches to instruction are ineffective. There are many features that contribute to poor comprehension in individual children, and it is silly to be reteaching components that children know well while ignoring those with which they are struggling.

• Work with colleagues teaching at other grade levels in thinking about how to define and to assess comprehension. Working across grade levels will benefit teachers at any grade, because every class is likely to include students comprehending at levels prescribed for previous as well as later grades. A developmental view of comprehension makes clear that knowing about listening comprehension is key in understanding reading comprehension and that some seemingly sophisticated comprehension outcomes may be found in the reactions of poor word readers if they are given sufficiently simple texts. Furthermore, it is critically important to ensure that kindergarten and first-grade teachers are involved in thinking about comprehension and its assessment; the early identification of children who are apt to encounter difficulties in reading comprehension because of limited resources to carry out one or another operation involved in comprehension greatly improves the chances for educational interventions to work.

• Focus on how the assessments link to the instruction activities and foci. Major purposes for assessments are to inform instruction and to reflect the effect of instruction or intervention. Thus, an effective assessment system should not only provide important information about a child's relative standing in appropriate normative populations (school, state, and/or national norms and groups), but it should also provide information about a child's relative strengths and weaknesses for purposes of educational planning. Instruction may be working very well, but in ways that the assessments being used do not pick up. Alternately, failures of instructional efficacy may be being masked by assessments that are too easy or too limited.

• Think about intra-individual differences before despairing of any particular student. We know that students who fare poorly in comprehending some texts or taking certain kinds of tests may do very well under other circumstances—when reading about a topic of particular interest or responding in a different format. Understanding the performance of an individual often requires attending to differences in performance across activities with varying purposes, and with a variety of texts and text types.

• Think about the appropriateness of the assessments being used from the perspective of individual, social, linguistic, and cultural variation. Good tests of reading comprehension, of listening comprehension, and of oral language production target authentic outcomes and reflect key component processes. If students do not understand the purposes for which they are reading (or if they reject those purposes), or if they do not understand the goals behind the tests they are taking or the questions they are being asked, they may well perform in ways that give little information about their real abilities. Just as "alignment" means that teachers need to understand their districts' and states' standards and accountability systems, it also means that students should have a chance to understand their teachers' purposes and assessment procedures.

• Attend to the psychometric properties of the tests being used in your district and state. Tests vary widely in quality and in appropriateness for the purposes for which they are being used. Some states have done a great job of developing state-wide accountability tests that are challenging, multifaceted, and well designed. In other cases, states and districts have made serious errors in selecting tests—tests with poor items, tests for which the scoring systems are error-ridden, tests that do not connect adequately to curriculum or standards, and so on. In addition, it is easy to misrepresent the meaning of test scores or changes in test scores. Teachers need to grapple with the difficult task of coming to understand the tests their students are taking, and the meaning of scores on those tests, in order to protect their students and themselves. It would be a serious mistake to adjust one's instruction so as to get better scores on a poor test that does not adequately reflect the full complexity of reading comprehension.

Ideally, teachers would have the opportunity to engage in all these various sorts of reflection and self-analysis and to make the products of their reflection public. The untapped wisdom of excellent practitioners is a wasted resource in most schools, but teachers need to take some of the responsibility for getting their own good ideas and successful practices communicated to their colleagues and available for public evaluation. Studying student work collaboratively is a powerful method for professional development, as is sharing recommendations and practices for assessment and evaluation. Ideally, practitioners would work with researchers to generate an inventory of the assessment techniques that have been developed for use in classrooms, with evaluations of their strengths and weaknesses. If such an inventory were undertaken, researchers could start on their task of developing a comprehensive assessment system with a substantial head start from practice-based techniques and knowledge.

CONCLUSION

This chapter makes the argument that we need assessment strategies and instruments that robustly reflect the dynamic, developmental nature of comprehension and that represent adequately the interactions among the dimensions of reader, activity, text, and context. Such strategies and instruments are crucial to stimulating instruction that reflects a deeper, richer, more multifaceted conceptualization of the construct.

We have argued that many of the currently available comprehension assessments are based on an inadequately articulated theory of comprehension and thus cannot provide adequate data about how serious the problem of comprehension achievement in the United States is. These considerations, as well as the thinking about the nature of reading comprehension discussed in this book create a demand for new kinds of assessment strategies and instruments that more robustly reflect the dynamic, developmental nature of comprehension, represent adequately the interactions among the dimensions of reader, activity, text, and context, and satisfy criteria set forth in psychometric theory.

The approach to assessment proposed here differs from current approaches to reading assessment in that it would both grow out of and contribute to the development of an appropriately rich and elaborated theory of reading comprehension. Assessment procedures generated by this approach are thus also more likely to be influenced and changed by theoretically grounded reading research. This approach places high value on the utility of assessment for instruction and on the need to mine the wisdom of excellent teacher-developed classroom assessment practices. Of course, comprehensive assessment systems can place high demands on the time of students and teachers; thus, we have an obligation to develop assessments that are embedded in and supportive of instruction, rather than limited to serving the needs of researchers or of program accountability at the local, state, or federal level.

Both researchers and practitioners have their own obligations if assessment is to improve. Researchers need to engage in efforts that will build toward an integrated system of assessments, some of which may be particularly appropriate for particular groups (e.g., emergent or beginning readers, older struggling readers, second-language readers, readers with particular interests). Furthermore, they need to develop assessments to address different purposes (e.g., a portmanteau assessment for accountability or screening purposes, diagnostic assessments for guiding intervention, curriculum-linked assessments for guiding instruction, and so on).

Practitioners, meanwhile, could give researchers a thrust in the right direction if they focused their own thinking on comprehension and comprehension assessment to generate practice-infused definitions and operationalizations of the construct, and guidelines for the kinds of assessment that are truly helpful in practice. The assessment techniques they use and value in their classrooms, those they would be willing to make public and subject to collegial scrutiny, should be inventoried and categorized as a first step to ensuring that researchers neither reinvent the wheel nor ignore the pressing needs of practice.

REFERENCES

Pearson, D., & Hamm, D. (2002, October 17–18). *Comprehension assessment: How it managed to weather the theoretical storms of the 20th century.* Paper presented at OERI/CIERA conference "Assessment of Reading Comprehension: Directions for the Future," Ypsilanti, MI.

RAND Reading Study Group. (2002). *Reading for understanding: Toward an R&D program in reading comprehension.* Santa Monica, CA and Washington, DC: RAND Corporation.

12

A Research Program
for Improving
Reading Comprehension

A Glimpse of Studies Whose Findings
Will Aid the Classroom Teacher
in the Future

ANNE POLSELLI SWEET

BACKGROUND

The chapters in this book are written for practitioners. They augment
*Reading for Understanding: The Report of the RAND Reading Study
Group*, which was written for the Department of Education's Office of Educational Research and Improvement (OERI)[1] to inform the development
of a research agenda for reading. This initiative came about in 1999, when
Kent McGuire, then assistant secretary for OERI, launched an agenda-
setting effort for federal education research, focused on mathematics and
reading education and managed by the RAND Corporation. Two study
groups were formed, each charged with identifying the most pressing needs
in its particular area.

---

[1] No official support or endorsement by the U.S. Department of Education is intended or
should be inferred.

In the case of reading, the RAND Reading Study Group (RRSG) was formed. The RRSG was composed of 14 experts[2] representing a range of disciplinary and methodological perspectives in the field of reading. This group functioned as an expert panel for little more than 2 years (2000–2002) to establish a convergent perspective on what is known about reading, what the most urgent tasks in developing an integrated research base are, and what needs to be done to improve reading outcomes. The study group formulated an initial draft of a report in the summer of 2000, which was used to solicit commentary and guidance to the committee in devising its final report. That report was published early in 2002 as a book entitled *Reading for Understanding: Toward an R&D Program in Reading Comprehension*. The RRSG report served its primary purpose by providing the impetus for OERI to create a whole new Program of Research on Reading Comprehension (PRRC), under the leadership of successor OERI assistant secretary, Grover J. Whitehurst. The U.S. Department of Education's research agency, formerly OERI, is now called the Institute of Education Sciences (IES), having been reauthorized by the U.S. Congress during November 2002.

NEW RESEARCH HORIZONS

Although we know a good deal about best practices in reading, particularly early reading (Snow, Burns, & Griffin, 1998), there is much more we need to learn, especially about reading comprehension and reading comprehension instruction (National Reading Panel, 2000; RAND Reading Study Group, 2002). While using the best of currently known evidence-based practices, we must look to future research to fill in the gaps in our knowledge base. For example, we need to learn more about comprehension strategies across the full range of age and grade levels and across a range of variation, such as reader differences, text types, and instructional contexts.

To address these research needs, the U.S. Department of Education (OERI) initiated a new research initiative, the Program of Research on Reading Comprehension (PRRC), which is designed to advance the science of reading comprehension. This program is a direct outgrowth of the RRSG's report. The major objective of the PRRC is to expand scientific knowledge of how students develop proficient levels of reading comprehen-

---

[2] Members of the Rand Reading Study Group (RRSG) were Catherine Snow, study group Chair, Donna Alvermann, Janice Dole, Jack Fletcher, Georgia Earnest Garcia, Irene Gaskins, Art Graesser, John Guthrie, Michael Kamil, William Nagy, Annemarie Sullivan Palincsar, Dorothy Strickland, Frank Vellutino, and Joanna Williams. Anne P. Sweet was the RAND reading study director.

sion, how it can be taught most optimally, and how it can be assessed in ways that reflect, as well as advance, our current understanding of reading comprehension and its development. Toward this end, the program is designed to obtain converging empirical evidence on the development and assessment of comprehension that coheres with scientifically supported theories of the processes involved in reading comprehension. It is also designed to provide a scientific foundation for approaches to comprehension instruction that allow students to achieve proficient levels of comprehension across a range of texts and subjects. Thus, the studies are to be scientifically sound and the research findings are to be useful to practitioners and policy makers in making decisions that will change instructional practice and promote academic achievement.

This program is benefiting from a significant investment of research dollars. Funds available for IES's reading comprehension research grant program are expected to rise substantially in upcoming years, far beyond the total funds awarded under the program ($6 million over 3 years) during the first cycle in 2002. Six research grants were awarded under the PRRC 2002. A description of the research conducted in each of these projects follows, along with a preview of how impending findings may help to inform educational practice.

PRRC 2002 RESEARCH PROJECTS ON READING COMPREHENSION

Study 1

Bridget Dalton (CAST, Inc.), Annemarie Sullivan Palincsar, and Shirley Maugnusson (University of Michigan) are the researchers conducting the study entitled *Reading to Learn: Investigating General and Domain-Specific Supports in a Technology-Rich Environment with Diverse Readers Learning from Informational Text*. This research project consists of one descriptive and two experimental studies. Together, these studies are designed to (1) compare the cognitive activity and learning of upper elementary students as they read and learn from digital narrative and informational (science) texts, as well as a new genre, multimedia informational (science) websites; (2) compare the processes and outcomes of engaging in comprehension instruction with informational text in the service of promoting subject matter learning versus engaging in comprehension instruction with informational text that features domain-general strategy instruction; and (3) investigate the outcomes of providing cognitive supports to enhance students' abilities to learn from multimedia, web-based texts.

This research will be conducted with 32 urban fourth graders using a computer-based learning environment with features such as text-to-speech decoding with synchronized highlighting of text, and an embedded system of scaffolded cognitive prompts, hints, and modeling. This learning tool is CAST's *Thinking Reader,* which supports readers with diverse characteristics (decoding ability, vocabulary knowledge, cognitive engagement) in a variety of ways. Each of the instructional studies also engages students in interactions with other students, supported by the guidance of adult teachers. Results will be used to enhance our understanding of young children's comprehension of informational text, and to inform teachers' practices, the design of texts and technology, and the design of websites. IES will expend $1,499,281 to support this project over a 3–year grant award period.

Implications for Teachers

The future results of this research will hold promise for advancing our understanding of comprehension challenges and learning supports, particularly with respect to struggling readers. Further, the findings of this research will be used to inform the design of reading curricula that advance not only students capacity to learn from text, but also their learning from informational text in domain-specific ways. These findings also promise to support teachers in advancing students' comprehension of text in all subject matter areas. Finally, newly acquired understandings of the challenges that students face in the complex text and multimedia environment of the web can be used to improve the design of websites to make them more effective learning tools. In sum, the future findings of this research hold potential for helping classroom teachers by enhancing our understanding of young children's informational text, informing teachers' instructional practices, and, informing the design of texts and technology, as well as the design of websites.

Study 2

Scott Baker (Eugene Research Institute), Lana Edwards (Lehigh University), and David Chard (University of Oregon) are the researchers conducting the study entitled *Story Read-Aloud Intervention for First Graders.* The goal of this project is to add to our understandings about the relationships between children's knowledge and use of comprehension strategies, their understandings of story-specific and strategy-related vocabulary, and the use of instructional discourse to foster complex thinking about text. A series of design experiments will be conducted in year 1, leading to a feasible story read-aloud intervention for use with groups of first graders. At the same time, validity studies of an assessment framework for screening and monitoring students' progress will be conducted. In year 2, the read-aloud intervention will be evaluated experimentally, involving 400 students from diverse urban and suburban communities. In year 3, hypotheses related to the role of potential mediating variables in the improvement of students' comprehension of specific texts, their use of text structure knowledge, and their complexity of interactions during read aloud instruction, will be tested.

The following outcomes are anticipated: (1) an empirically validated read-aloud instructional approach for developing first graders' vocabulary and strategic thinking about texts; (2) curriculum materials jointly developed with first-grade teachers that promote improved listening and reading comprehension; (3) a validated assessment framework for predicting which first-grade students are at risk for experiencing difficulties in comprehension; and (4) an understanding of the instructional variables that must be considered in order to enhance comprehension and vocabulary for a wide range of learners. IES will expend $1,019,249 to support this project over a 3-year grant award period.

Implications for Teachers

The findings of this research are expected to assist classroom teachers' instructional practices in a variety of ways, most prominently by featuring an approach to read-alouds that anchors children's understanding of stories in narrative text structure and strategic vocabulary instruction, using dialogic interactions between teacher and students. Interactions of this sort can facilitate comprehension and word learning for children. The Read-Aloud project also promises to advance practice by informing us about the features of read-aloud instruction that are most critical to promote change in children's responses to text understanding and vocabulary knowledge. The researchers expect that critical instructional features, such as explicit discussion of text structure in dialogic interactions, will help children focus more on the story elements and less on their background knowledge and pictures of read-aloud instruction.

Study 3

Ian Wilkinson, Anna Soter (Ohio State University), and Karen Murphy (Pennsylvania State University) are the researchers conducting the study entitled *Group Discussions as a Mechanism for Promoting High-Level Comprehension of Text*. The purpose of this project is to identify converging evidence on the use of group discussions to promote high-level comprehension of text and to advance understanding of how teachers can implement discussions and assess their effects in ways that are sensitive to instructional goals. The objectives of the project are to (1) develop a conceptual framework to help teachers understand different approaches to conducting group discussions of text; (2) examine evidence of the effects of different approaches to conducting group discussions, including estimation of the magnitude of effects and analysis of indicators of quality discussions; and (3) implement a professional development program for teachers to facilitate quality discussions, and develop tools for assessing individual students' cognitive and affective processes during discussions as well as their high-level responses to texts.

Three studies are being conducted: Study 1 is a synthesis of existing research on group discussions designed to promote high-level comprehension of text. In study 2, discussion approaches on a common set of discourse features known to characterize "quality" discussions will be evaluated. In study 3, the conceptual framework and model of discussion that promotes high-level comprehension of text, derived from studies 1 and 2, will be merged to examine teachers' implementations of this model with 12 fourth-grade and 12 sixth-grade language arts and other content area classrooms. In addition, tools for assessing the impact of discussion on students' high-level comprehension of text will be examined. IES will expend $786,372 to support this project over a 3–year grant award period.

Implications for Teachers

The findings of this research project are expected to benefit a variety of educators. The conceptual framework developed herein is aimed at helping both experienced and novice teachers to select an approach that is suited to their needs, to their students, to the subject areas they teach, and to the classroom community in which they work. It is anticipated that the outcomes of this project will be useful to classroom teachers searching for an instructional approach that will increase students' abilities to think reflectively and to critically analyze the texts they read. Moreover, they are expected to enable teacher-educators to provide preservice teachers with an in-depth understanding of group discussions.

Study 4

Thomas Landauer and Simmon Dennis (University of Colorado) are the researchers conducting the study entitled *Research on and with Novel Educational Technologies for Comprehension*. This research project consists of a series of laboratory experiments and field trials that will be embedded in the ongoing Colorado Literacy Project Initiative that is supported by the Inter-Agency Educational Research Initiative—a partnership between the U.S. Department of Education's IES, the National Science Foundation, and the National Institute of Child Health and Human Development. The objective of this research project is to create, perfect, and evaluate several novel computer-based tutorials and assessment tools. More exactly, the studies are designed to evaluate novel computer-managed activities that engage, assess, and exemplify precise use of words in connected discourse.

The laboratory research will analyze the cognitive processes measured and affected and guide the design of new interventions. Randomized field trials will evaluate effects on and assessment of word knowledge, comprehension, writing, and reading to learn. The new automated assessment instruments will also make possible otherwise impractical research on the precursors and concomitants of comprehension competency. Latent Semantic Analysis, a machine learning method that simulates human understanding of words and text, will be employed in the study of these new technologies. Sixteen schools will participate in year 1, and the number of participating schools is expected to double in year 2, and double again in year 3. Subjects will total at least 700 students who are in grades 6, 7, and 8. IES will expend $799,884 to support this project over a 3-year grant award period.

Implications for Teachers

The central focus of this research project is the reciprocal relation between vocabulary and its use in reading comprehension, knowledge expression, and knowledge acquisition by reading. The line of research pursued in this project is aimed at creating a vocabulary learning environment that can contribute importantly to improvements in literacy attainment. This research project holds promise for helping prospective and classroom teachers in their literacy education and improving vocabulary and its use in comprehension, composition, and learning. The primary means of accomplishing this goal is through the project's development of new computer tools that can offer a significant addition to traditional methods, both for learning and for relevant assessment.

Study 5

Danielle McNamara, Arthur Graesser, and Max Louwerse (University of Memphis) are the researchers conducting the study entitled *Coh-metrix: Automated Cohesion and Coherence Scores to Predict Text Readability and Facilitate Comprehension.* The long-term goal of this project is to improve reading comprehension in classrooms by providing tools to improve textbook writing and to ensure that textbooks are more appropriately matched to the intended students. More specifically, the primary objective is to develop an automated cohesion metric tool (Coh-metrix) that computes properties of text cohesion and that computes a cohesion score that integrates text cohesiveness with the reader's world knowledge and aptitude. The term *cohesion*, as used here, refers to properties of the text with reference to the intended readers' sociocultural knowledge, and *coherence* refers to the interaction between the text and reader characteristics. A corollary objective is to develop an automated tool that identifies specific cohesion gaps in text (Coh-GIT). A second goal is to further our understanding of the complex interactions between the text, reader, tasks, and levels of comprehension, and thereby calibrate the aforementioned tools.

Toward this end, six experiments will be conducted to investigate the effects of text cohesion for young readers (210 students in grades 3–5) and young adult readers (300 college students) and how these effects depend on text genre, prior knowledge, and word-based reading skills. A third goal, to fine-tune and validate the coherence measurements, will be achieved by (1) using existing data and new data to calibrate and test the metrics; (2) examining and comparing cohesion metrics and readability scores across a set of K–14 basal readers and instructional texts; and (3) empirically verifying the validity of Coh-GIT by identifying cohesion gaps in texts and comparing them to eye-tracking patterns. IES will expend $1,425,200 to support this project over a 3–year grant award period.

Implications for Teachers

The overarching goal of this research project is to improve reading comprehension in classrooms by providing a means to improve textbook writing and more appropriately match textbooks to the intended students. Thus, the products yielded by this research are expected to benefit classroom teachers and others in very practical ways. The tools that are specified for development will allow readers, writers, editors, and educators to more accurately estimate the appropriateness of a text for their audience and pinpoint specific problems with text. Moreover, these tools will assist textbook publishers and education assessment firms (test builders) to develop commercial products for use in schools that more aptly reflect the instructional needs of students, thereby facilitating teachers' teaching.

Study 6

Charles Perfetti, Eric Reichle, Isabel Beck, and Margaret McKeown (University of Pittsburgh, Learning Research and Development Center) are the researchers conducting the study entitled *Word Learning and Comprehension: New Laboratory Approaches and Classroom Studies*. This research project consists of a series of closely connected laboratory experiments using Event-Related Potentials (measures of word components related to word meaning) and eye-tracking methods that provide unique information on the learning of new words and on the consequences of this learning.

Perfetti, the principal investigator, maintains that these methods converge to allow fine-grain, temporally sensitive measures of cognitive word processing and comprehension. These experiments will also test the theoretical distinction between word familiarity and word knowledge, using a statistical tool for measuring word and text meaning (latent semantic analysis). Expected results include finding out what influences how well word meanings can be learned from context and how texts with unknown but familiar words may differ from texts with truly unfamiliar words.

The laboratory studies are complemented by a classroom study that will provide new information on the value of direct instruction in young children's learning of vocabulary. More specifically, it seeks to determine the effect of increased instruction on the outcomes of the instruction embedded in Text Talk (Beck & McKeown, 2001). Text Talk is an approach that involves reading aloud and discussing some 25 trade books over the course of a school year, whereby specific vocabulary instruction is rendered for several words that appear in each story. Thus, the project seeks to bridge laboratory and classroom research, setting a context for increasing mutual influence between them. Twenty-four adult subjects will be used in the laboratory studies, and 75 children in kindergarten and first grade (six intact classrooms, three at each level) will serve as subjects in the classroom study. IES will expend $498,903 to support this project over a 3–year grant award period.

Implications for Teachers

The impending research findings of this project are expected to strengthen the research foundations for word learning and thereby benefit classroom teachers' reading instruction for students. Follow-up activities that augment Text Talk will be developed (and tested) that provide children with more encounters with a word in meaning-relevant ways. This additional instruction will provide systematic word engagement tasks that require children to attend to word meaning, thus assisting teachers in instructing their students in concrete ways.

CONCLUSION

The U.S. Department of Education is committed to supporting reading comprehension research that is scientifically sound and aimed at being useful to practitioners and policy makers in making decisions about instructional practice that promote academic achievement. This program of research is designed to answer both fundamental and applied questions about reading comprehension in a way that is translatable into practice, so as to have a very real impact on what is happening in the classroom. Recipients of the PRRC 2002 grants are well poised to begin the long-term work needed to meet this challenge. In subsequent years of this program, one of the greatest challenges that the U.S. Department of Education's Institute for Education Sciences faces is to garner a good number of applicants (researchers and research collaborators in schools and classrooms) who propose to conduct the kind of comprehension research that will advance the field in significant ways. We hope that you are ready and willing to help us meet this challenge.

REFERENCES AND RESOURCES

Baker, S., Gersten, R., & Grossen, B. (2002). Remedial interventions for students with reading comprehension problems. In M. R. Shinn, G. Stoner, & H. M. Walker (Eds.), *Interventions for academic and behavior problems II: Prevention and remedial approaches* (pp. 731–754). Bethesda, MD: National Association of School Psychologists.

Beck, I. L., & McKeown, M. G. (2001). Text Talk: Capturing the benefits of reading aloud for young children. *Reading Teacher, 55*(1), 10–19.

Beck, I. L., McKeown, M. G., & Kucan, L. (2002). *Bringing words to life: Robust vocabulary instruction.* New York: Guilford Press.

Chard, D. J., Vaugn, S., & Tyler, B. (in press). A synthesis of research on effective interventions for building reading fluency with elementary students with learning disabilities. *Journal of Learning Disabilities.*

Dalton, B., Pisha, B., Eagleton, M., Coyne, P., & Deysher, S. (2002). Engaging the text: Reciprocal teaching and questioning strategies in a scaffolded computer learning environment. Final report submitted to the U. S. Office of Special Education. Washington, DC: U. S. Office of Special Education.

Dennis, S., Bruza, P., & McArthur, R. (2002) Web searching: A process-oriented experimental study of three interactive search paradigms. *Journal of the American Society for Information Science and Technology, 53*(2), 120–133.

Gersten, R., Baker, S., & Edwards, L (1999). *Teaching expressive writing to students with learning disabilities: A meta-analysis.* New York: National Center for Learning Disabilities.

Gersten, R., Fuchs, L. S., Williams, J. P., & Baker, S. (in press). Teaching reading comprehension strategies to students with learning disabilities: A review of research. *Review of Educational Research.*

Graesser, A. C., Person, N., & Hu, X. (2002). Improving comprehension through discourse processes. *New Directions in Teaching and Learning, 89,* 33–44.

Graesser, A. C., Weimer-Hastings, P., & Wiemer-Hastings, K. (2001). Constructing inferences and relations during text comprehension. In T. Sanders, J. Schilperoord, & W. Spooren (Eds.), *Text representation: Linguistic and psycholinguistic aspects* (pp. 249–271). Amsterdam and Philadelphia: John Benjamins.

Kintsch, W. (1998). *Comprehension: A paradigm for cognition.* New York: Cambridge University Press.

Landauer, T. K., & Psotka, J. (2002). Simulating text understanding for education applications with Latent Semantic Analysis: Introduction to LSA. *Interactive Learning Environments, 8*(1), 1–14.

Louwerse, M. M., & Graesser, A. C. (in press). Coherence in discourse. In P. Strazny (Ed.), *Encyclopedia of Linguistics.* Chicago: Fitzroy Dearborn.

McNamara, D. S. (2000). Reading both high and low coherence text: Effects of text sequence and prior knowledge. *Canadian Journal of Experimental Psychology, 55,* 51–62.

McNamara, D. S., Kintsch, E., Songer, N. B., & Kintsch, W. (1996). Are good texts always better? Text coherence, background knowledge, and levels of understanding in learning from text. *Cognition and Instruction, 14,* 1–43.

Murphy, P. K., & Alexander, P. A. (in press). Learning from text: The integral roles of knowledge and beliefs. In J. W. Guthrie (Ed.), *The encyclopedia of education* (2nd ed.). New York: Macmillan.

National Reading Panel (NRP). (2000). *Teaching children to read: An evidence-based assessment of the scientific research literature on reading and its implications for reading instruction.* Washington, DC: National Institute of Child Health and Human Development.

Palincsar, A. S., & Herrenkohl, L. (2002). Designing collaborative learning contexts. *Theory into Practice, 41*(1), 26–32.

Palincsar, A. S., & Maugnusson, S. J. (2001). The interplay of first-hand and text-based investigation to model and support the development of scientific knowledge and reasoning. In S. Carver & D. Klahr (Eds.), *Cognition and instruction: Twenty five years of progress* (pp. 151–194). Mahawah, NJ: Erlbaum.

Perfetti, C. A., & Hart, L. A. (2001). The lexical bases of comprehension skill. In D. Gorfien (Ed.), *On the consequences of meaning selection* (pp. 67–86). Washington, DC: American Psychological Association.

Pressley, M. (2000). What should comprehension instruction be the instruction of? In M. Kamil, P. Mosenthal, P. D. Pearson, & R. Barr (Eds.), *Handbook of reading research* (Vol. III, pp. 545–562). Mahwah, NJ: Erlbaum

RAND Reading Study Group (RRSG). (2002). *Reading for Understanding: Toward an R&D Program in Reading Comprehension.* Santa Monica, CA, and Washington, DC: RAND Corporation.

Reichle, E. D., & Rayner, K. (2002). Cognitive processing and models of reading. In G. K. Hung & K. J. Ciuffreda (Eds.), *Models of the visual system* (pp. 565–604). New York: Kluwer Academic.

Snow, C. E., Burns, M. S., & Griffin, P. (Eds.). (1998). *Preventing reading difficulties in young children.* Washington, DC: National Research Council, National Academy Press.

Soter, A. O. (1999). *The new literacy theories and young adult literature.* New York: Teachers College Press.

Sweet, A. P., & Snow, C. (2002). Reconceptualizing reading comprehension. In C. C. Block, L. Gambrell, & G. M. Pressley (Eds.), *Improving comprehension in-*

struction: Rethinking research, theory, & classroom practice (pp. 17–53). San Francisco: Jossey-Bass.

Taylor, B. M., Pearson, P. D., Clark, K. F., & Walpole, S. (1999). Effective schools/accomplished teachers. *Reading Teacher, 53*(2), 156–159.

Torgesen, J., Rashotte, C., & Alexander, A. (in press). The prevention and remediation of reading fluency problems. In M. Wolf (Ed.), *Dyslexia, fluency, and the brain.* Timonium, MD: York Press.

Turner, J. C., & Meyer, D. K. (2000). Studying and understanding the instructional contexts of classrooms: Using our past to forge our future. *Educational Psychologist, 35*(2), 69–85.

Whitehurst, G. R., & Lonigan, C. J. (2001). Emergent literacy: Development from prereaders to readers. In S. B. Neuman & D. K. Dickinson (Eds.), *Handbook of early literacy research* (pp. 11–29). New York: Guilford Press.

Wilkinson, I. A. G., & Townsend, M. A. R. (2000). From Rata to Rimu: Grouping for instruction in "best practice" New Zealand classrooms. *Reading Teacher, 53*, 460–471.

Index

Acquisition of reading. *see* Reading acquisition
Activity of reading
   see also Constructing meaning; Purpose in
     reading
   in defining comprehension, 2–4, 3*f*, 90–91
   description, 7–9
   instructional recommendations, 163
   taking responsibility for, 161–162
   variables, 159–160
Adolescent literacy
   history of, 13–14
   motivation, 21–23
   struggling readers, 18–20
   teaching, 14–15, 15–18
Aesthetic reading, 16
Alphabetic knowledge
   see also Word recognition
   description, 54–55
   orthographic awareness and, 57–58
   phonics instruction and, 70–71
   phonological awareness and, 56–57
ANOW strategy, 162
Assessment
   description, 204–205
   developing, 193–196, 194*t*
   instructional recommendations, 200–201
   role of teacher in, 201–204
   system of, 196–200
Attention, 65, 146, 163
Autobiographical knowledge, 64
Automaticity, 90
   see also Fluency

Background knowledge
   see also Knowledge; World knowledge
   coherence relations and, 84–87
   description, 89, 156–157
   electronic text and, 170–171

   English-language learners and, 32–33, 45, 46
   incorporated into CORI, 116–117
   instructional recommendations, 163
   motivation and, 21
   prediction and, 101
   struggling readers and, 20, 161
Beliefs of readers, 148–150
Benchmark School, 142–143
   see also Activity of reading; Reader; Text
Bilingual education, 44–45, 46
   see also English-language learners; Teaching
     comprehension
Bilingual status, strategies unique to, 37–38
   see also English-language learners

Chronology, 93–94
   see also Coherence relations
Clarifying, 100–103, 153–156
Classroom environment, 19–20
   see also Sociocultural context
   adolescents and, 23–27
   bilingualism and, 44–45
   challenges, 141–143
   comparisons of, 24–25
   effects of, 9–10
   struggling readers and, 19–20
Code mixing, 17, 37–38
   see also English-language learners
Code switching, 17, 38
   see also English-language learners
Cognate relationships, 17, 36, 47
Cognitive Academic Language Learning
     Approach, 43–44
   see also English-language learners; Teaching
     comprehension
Cognitive strategies
   description, 66, 144–148
   incorporated into CORI, 116–117